PROCESS

PROCESS

THE WRITING LIVES OF GREAT AUTHORS

SARAH STODOLA

amazonpublishing

Published by Amazon Publishing, New York

www.apub.com

Amazon, the Amazon logo, and Amazon Publishing are trademarks of Amazon.com, Inc., or its affiliates.

ISBN-13: 9781477801086
ISBN-10: 1477801081

Cover design by Rodrigo Corral Design

Library of Congress Control Number: 2014913443

Printed in the United States of America

For Ed and Sue
and for Scott

CONTENTS

THE SOCIAL BUTTERFLY AND THE LONE WOLF

TWO TAKES ON THE DIGITAL AGE

FOREWORD

For the past few years, I have written a weekly interview column in which I discuss the writing life—tips, quirks, and tricks of the trade—with fellow authors. I have conducted more than eighty of these interviews, many with heroes of mine. My interviews are riffs on a set questionnaire I have prepared, inspired by a popular nineteenth-century parlor game called the Confession Book. In this game, a host would pass around a book that was blank, aside from the same set of questions printed on every page. Each guest would fill in his or her answers, and the responses would prompt lively dinner party discussions. The most famous variation on the Confession Book was penned by Marcel Proust (supposedly when he was only fourteen years old) and was adapted by a variety of sources, from *Vanity Fair* to *Inside the Actors Studio*. My version of the Confession Book is all about writing and the lives of writers. The idea of asking the same questions of many people allows for horizontal and vertical comparisons: What did Virginia Woolf, Margaret Atwood, and Edith Wharton eat for breakfast? How many authors wrote freehand? Over the years, dozens of writers, editors, publishers, publicists, and aspiring authors have written to tell me how helpful they find interviews with writers about writing. Read enough of them, and you start to spot trends that can be helpful to your own work. For instance, dozens of authors feel that a successful writing day will produce one thousand words, and many recommend mapping out one's plot on index cards.

Sarah Stodola has managed to do something I never thought possible: to "interview" famous writers who are long dead. Alongside renowned living authors, such as Junot Díaz, Joan Didion, and Margaret Atwood, we have James Joyce, Vladimir Nabokov, and Jack Kerouac. She has sifted through reams of text to pull out the writing processes of an all-star cast of authors whose habits, methods, and oddities not only tell us much about them personally, but also offer sheaves of wisdom for modern writers to harvest.

Inventing interesting things to write about, and new ways to convey them, is exhausting. It is also rewarding, which is why we do it and why so many people from other walks of life dream of writing a book of their own.

Readers tend to overlook the intricacies involved in bringing a work to completion, and they see writers as a cult of pseudo-magicians, capable of conjuring worlds out of thought, spinning characters from thin air, and surely having a great time while doing so. In truth, a career as a writer is enjoyable, but also lonely. Tell that to a construction worker, a nurse, a truck driver, and you will likely be mocked. But conceiving of interesting ideas and conveying them in words is intellectually, if not physically, arduous. There are few Graham Greenes out there who polish off a few dozen lines in a few hours, then spend the majority of their day polishing off gin and tonics at Jamaican resorts. The writing life can be a slog, with twelve-hour days in self-imposed isolation, endless rewrites, hundreds of pages discarded by ornery editors, and a life's work dismissed at the stroke of an overly clever critic's pen. Writers tend to live within their own minds, rarely working with others, socializing with their comrades largely to gripe about the publishing industry, not to collaborate in the midst of a project.

It is refreshing, then, to learn that so many great writers share certain characteristics with their less-renowned colleagues (myself included), that the experience of being a professional writer has remained largely similar, whether in nineteenth-century Ireland, twentieth-century New York, or, in my case, twenty-first-century Slovenia. Habits, often bizarre, tend to propel writers forward, and it is reassuringly rare to find a writer who seems or self-describes as "normal." Some have proverbial magic hats that they must wear while writing, from Virginia Woolf's preference for purple pens to Junot Díaz's odd choice of listening to movie sound tracks while typing away (including that of *Conan the Barbarian*). Learning these wonderful details turns famous names into three-dimensional characters—some Dickensian caricatures—the sort that one might say sound like pure fiction. We tend to deify authors, thinking of them as disembodied names who produce the works we crave and admire, failing to realize the long hours, aching fingers, and racked brains that these very human, warts-and-all people suffer in order to complete the books that we take for granted (often grumbling about having to pay ten dollars for them, if we pay for them at all).

Process combines author biography with lively details about writing habits, a sort of group biography through the lens of professional technique. This presents readers (many of whom will be aspiring writers) with a combination of demystification and mystification. The methods of famous writers are revealed (demystified), but the cultish details of how those writers work, in order to produce the masterpieces we so admire, demonstrate both the huge effort required and the bizarre, pseudo-mystical behavior that functions like oil in the cogs of their minds: Some authors must write in sealed rooms fitted with blackout blinds, while drinking massive quantities of iced tea prepared in a restaurant-grade brewer (I'm looking at you, Michael Connelly). Without these exotic conditions, one writer just cannot produce, whereas another (that would be Arthur Phillips) works best in a busy café, with a steady flow of pastries and beverages and the hum of the crowd flitting around him, while his beagles lounge at his feet. Fewer authors have an entirely flexible regimen, bereft of neurosis, than wear magic hats, listen exclusively to movie sound tracks, or write only on yellow legal pads between one and five in the morning.

This book will appeal both to writers and to lovers of literature. Just like watching cooking shows is as much a pleasure for enthusiastic eaters as it is for amateur cooks, so this book is written in such a way that one can glean lessons to apply to one's own writing process, or simply paint a deeper picture of the authors one admires, regardless of whether one also wishes to write. The biographical aspect of this book deals less with personal relationships and more with professional involvement, the idiosyncrasies that keep writers sane when their days are spent lost in imaginary palaces, planets, and personalities. This is all presented in lovely, easy-reading prose that demonstrates fine writing just as it writes *about* fine writers.

Writers who look to this book as a manual for how they might make their own work approach that of their literary heroes will find that, and there are consistencies, the writing process is largely unique, individual, and can sound very weird indeed. Some use the Internet actively, others turn to e-mail as a refreshing break before the hard work, and some cannot function if the temptation of e-mail and the Internet is within reach and lock themselves away from the media overload that is twenty-first-century life. Some writers blaze through first drafts and then edit, whereas others polish every phrase as they go, lucky to craft a few paragraphs on any given day. Readers of *Process* will be entertained, informed, and encouraged, and will ultimately learn that each writer must hit upon the right working process to maximize efficiency and production. There is no one way to write, just as the joys and rewards are myriad for those who complete a good book, writers and readers alike.

Noah Charney, PhD
Ljubljana, Slovenia
July 2014

INTRODUCTION

For most writers, including those represented in this book, the definitive moment comes much earlier. But for me, the decision to become a writer arrived during my senior year of college. The decision was not a calculated one, in which I realized that a choice needed to be made, laid out my options and weighed them and selected one. Instead, the decision simply appeared. One day I was open to anything as a career, the next I wanted to write.

The earliest version of what might be called my writing process unfolded that year on my twin bed—the largest that would fit in the smallest room of the off-campus house I shared with two roommates. I'd been assigned that room when I drew the shortest straw. I remember my senior year as a long stretch of time spent on that twin bed, salvaged from my grandparents' house. Those stretches were of course interrupted at intervals by classes and parties and watching TV. But early and earnest efforts at serious writing took place there, in secret, most often at night. I had not yet found what worked for me with regard to a process, and I retain none of my output from that time.

Today I know that I write with far more acuity in the mornings, while the tendency to write slouched on a bed or sofa even though the desk is right there remains. As I worked on this book, I was forever comparing my own habits with those of the writers I was researching. Almost everyone writes better in the morning, I discovered—a point in my favor. Far fewer of them write on the couch, ever—a point against me. The score keeping was foolish but irresistible. My habits are not as quirky as many writers; I don't write on 120-foot-long scrolls like Kerouac, or in the bathtub like Nabokov, or in a room painted black like David Foster Wallace. But not all great writers are so peculiar. Hemingway's writing days were straightforward, even if the rest of his life was not. Richard Price showed me his writing desk, and it was just a desk, albeit a real nice midcentury modern one.

Of the elements that make up my own process, one ritual has proven crucial. Some writers never read the work of others while writing their own, but I have always done so, as have Zadie Smith, Ernest Hemingway, Philip Roth, and Virginia Woolf—another point for me. Reading of and about great authors has helped me think better about my own work and has often sparked that elusive idea to drive me forward. Were I not this way, writing this book would have been impossible. Yet as I consider my writing process as the author of a book about the writing process, I realize that over the course of the project this line of thinking has had a tendency to send me reeling. To engage in the activity of which you are peeling back the layers is to also engage in a meta-project that inevitably pokes at insecurities and questions things previously thought certain. You're never quite sure if you're writing about someone else, or if in writing about someone else you're unmasking something about yourself. But maybe that's the whole point.

When I learn that Nabokov's novels came to him all at once, the plot complete, or that Toni Morrison has only a small spark of an idea in her head when she gets started, I inevitably think of how I've gotten started on my own ideas. I then realize that I don't remember coming up with the idea for *Process*. I only remember running it already formed past my boyfriend and, seeing his enthusiasm, moving forward with the project. I was with my mother, waiting to be seated for an alfresco lunch at the Fontainebleau in Miami Beach—an extravagance for us—when the e-mail came in announcing that my agent wanted the project, and I remember being glad that this would forever be the setting for that moment. As we ordered cocktails to celebrate, the book was already morphing from a nebulous concept into a tangible object, even though it would be many months still before the deal was done and I got down to work. During that time, I didn't think a lot about what the book-writing process would look like, or how I would approach it. I only thought, as most first-time authors must, of the part that would come after, when I would be a published author.

When I started, I did so with a deliberate schedule: three weeks per chapter and I'd finish on time. Loosely defined, the first week entailed research, the second writing, the third revisions. I worked at a taco shack on the beach on Saturday mornings that summer, which proved invaluable in getting me out of my own head for a few hours. On a daily basis, optimistic midmorning hours ceded to panicky late-afternoon scrambles. I took frequent walks from my apartment to the Mid-Manhattan or main branch of the New York Public Library. I got bogged down by research, feared the opening paragraph above all, undertook to *just get the writing down* and worry about the organization of the thing later. I felt acutely that each finished page did nothing to get me closer to the end. That changed once I reached the halfway point and each page became part of a countdown.

I worked on *Process* in many corners of the world, but most commonly at my tiny desk in my tiny apartment, or on the couch next to it. And also at the restaurant Maialino near where I live, a tough reservation at night but in the mornings a calm and blissful place free of access to the Internet, where the green and sun flood in through the windows from Gramercy Park, and where one morning I took a break to see on my Instagram feed that Gary Shteyngart had at that moment posted a shot of his breakfast from a couple of tables over. I surveyed the room and spotted him, then worked on *Process* as if buoyed by having made a new and important best friend.

All the while, the unstructured nature of the daily workload presented unique stresses involving not so much self-doubt as a doubt in my self-confidence. *Should I be feeling as though I can and am doing this?* The work bears down on you—its presence makes clear thinking harder. Holidays are invariably working holidays when you're in the thick of it, and you're no longer comfortable with the concept of relaxation. But most of the time I was writing the book, I was happy to be doing so. To paraphrase Salman Rushdie, writing can be a grueling, unforgiving business, but even at its worst it's better than having a regular job.

Writers looking to this book for guidance on how to go about their craft will not find a definitive blueprint. Instead, they will find what I did: validation of one's own neuroses and several templates with which to put those neuroses to work. They will find that they likely need to put more effort into a project than they previously understood to be necessary. Happily, they will realize that some of the problems that continually plague their writing days can be managed. Even Margaret Atwood struggles with Internet binges, after all. Atwood loves the Internet, but she nonetheless keeps two computers in her study, one of which has no hookup, so she can get her work done on it. (For me, the solution was the Internet-blocking program Freedom.)

But *Process* will also interest those who love literature without wishing to create it themselves, in the same way that seeing the way a car motor works can be fascinating for mere drivers. One of the great surprises of writing this book was that looking under the hood did nothing to diminish the awe that my favorite books inspire in me. If anything, I grew more fascinated.

I chose to include authors partially on the basis of their impact on subsequent generations of writers. These are writers whom aspiring writers want to write like. They are writers whom successful writers name as early influences. The earliest writers represented came into their own in the early decades of the twentieth century, as the typewriter was becoming ubiquitous and changing writing processes forever, just like the word processor would toward the end of the century. The most recent authors included are still cementing their reputations. All of them help to provide a thread from one generation to the next and in that way guarantee their greatness.

Great writers, we are led to believe, come uniquely equipped to deliver perfect sentences onto the page. Those sentences, in the right hands, collect themselves into paragraphs, chapters, and novels that by their very nature do physical things to us: quicken our heartbeats, send shivers down our spines, keep us awake turning one more page long after we should have been asleep. They send us shaking our heads at the sheer effortlessness of what we're reading. They show us genius having emerged fully formed onto the page.

But the great writers represented in this book made it in via their many talents, only one of which is an ability to put the right words on the right page at the right time. Genius, I have concluded, is the presence of not one ability but several that work together in tandem. Genius is far more tedious, far less romantic, far more rote, far less effortless, than we imagine it. The great writers in this book do not by and large put the right words on the right page in the right order on the first try. But in the place of perfection, they possess the quality of perseverance and a willingness to recognize their own shortcomings. F. Scott Fitzgerald, a writer known to write with otherworldly facility, in fact rewrote his first novel, *This Side of Paradise*, three times completely before having it accepted for publication. Zadie Smith rewrote the entire last section of *NW* after finding early readers consistently unimpressed by it. Junot Díaz spent ten years laboring over *The Brief Wondrous Life of Oscar Wao*, at one point becoming so hopeless that he made a list of alternate careers he might pursue once it was clear he could no longer be a writer. And then he kept going.

These anecdotes serve a dual purpose when one is writing a book about the writing process, becoming both subject and fuel. They were the gems with which I was looking to pepper the book. They inspired me to write a better sentence. They provided comfort on those occasions I found myself disappointed to discover upon rereading my own drafts that they hadn't come out perfect the first time. The thing I learned in writing this book is that they never do.

NINE-TO-FIVERS

1

FRANZ KAFKA

On a Sunday morning in 1912, Franz Kafka woke up but did not get out of bed. He was lovesick, hoping for a letter that would not come from the woman he loved, Felice Bauer. The previous few nights of writing had gone poorly. He was in the doghouse with his best friend, the fellow writer Max Brod, whose engagement party he'd missed the day before. In this state, maybe staring at the ceiling, or at the light seeping through the window, a single image came to him, lucid and grotesque, of a man transformed into a terrible insect.[1] It was the seminal moment—producing the seminal image—of Kafka's most famous work, *The Metamorphosis*, and it's no coincidence that in its pages, Gregor Samsa would make the discovery of his transformation from human to bug as he awoke in bed on a gloomy morning.

A similar disquieting image plucked from Kafka's imagination would emerge as the central component in many of Kafka's stories, often morose, always autobiographical in their subtext. Some have become famous: a man being arrested for what he does not know (*The Trial*), or a brutal machine used to torture a prisoner ("In the

Penal Colony"). Each story grew out of one such image, expanded upon it, elucidated it, and used the image to show how incomprehensible existence can be. Unlike the moment of origin for *The Metamorphosis*, these images likely came to him late at night, while he agonized over life alone in his room, having sabotaged his chances at conventional happiness in an effort to sacrifice all for literature.

Despite his fanatical commitment to writing, for many years Kafka kept his literary aspirations secret. Not even his eventual literary confidant and alter ego, Max Brod, would learn of them until five years into their friendship. The two met while still teenagers at Prague's Charles University and bonded over their interest in literature. Both went on to secure conventional careers and keep their writing pursuits going on the side. But Brod projected his literary ambitions from the start. Kafka, on the other hand, timidly presented a story to Brod as his first-ever reader at a point when Brod not only had established himself as part of the local literati, but had already published respected work.[2]

Kafka famously studied law and soon after entered into employment with the Prague Workers' Accident Insurance Institute, where he would end up working for ten years, until sickness enabled a leave of absence and eventually a pension. Miserable as it apparently made him, Kafka seems to have taken his job seriously, and not only that, he was good at it. A diligent and valued employee, he was rewarded with several promotions and increasing responsibility through the years.[3] What he saw as the existentially crushing weight of employment within the bureaucracy of a large company hampered the pure writing life that Kafka felt he was meant for. And yet it was the very experience of navigating and existing within that faceless establishment that inspired much of what has come to be known as "Kafkaesque" in his writing: the insubordination of the individual to the larger machine, the overwhelming and confusion-inducing bureaucracy, the incomprehensible structure imposed from some nebulous above. He didn't see it that way, but his full-time employment inspired some of Kafka's greatest writing, including *The Trial* and *The Metamorphosis*.

The unwelcome demands put on him by his family, especially his father, took their toll as well, but as with his career, they provided abundant material for his writing. His family was not one prone to accommodating the creative pursuits of its offspring. Instead, children—and especially Kafka, as the only male to survive into adulthood—were expected to carry on the family business and strive to increase the family wealth. These expectations came to a head when the family decided to open an asbestos factory outside Prague and looked to Kafka to oversee its daily operations. That he mostly failed at this endeavor, neglecting the factory altogether when it began to eat into his writing time, gave his father one more reason to be disappointed by him. Overbearing father figures run through his fiction, and a forty-five-page letter that Kafka wrote to his father in 1918 has become a well-regarded piece of literature in its own right. In it, Kafka explains, "My overmastering sense of nothingness . . . stems largely from your influence."[4] For Kafka, nothing good came of father figures, a sentiment reflected in his stories.

As was common at the time, the unmarried Kafka remained living with his parents into his thirties. His three sisters likewise stayed on until their marriages. For a time, there were seven adults living in their one apartment.[5] Kafka's room was for years a glorified corridor between his parents' room and the living room. He couldn't bear to write while other activity was under way in the apartment, and thus waited until all the many family members who lived under that one roof had retired to their beds before he brought out his notebooks, kept safely hidden in a compartment in his desk.

In late 1913, when Kafka was thirty years old, his family moved to a larger apartment, providing him with a level of privacy that had previously been denied to him. It helped his writing.

Solitude was a compulsory feature of Kafka's writing process. "Being alone has a power over me that never fails," he once wrote in his diary. "My interior dissolves (for the time being only superficially) and is ready to release what lies deeper."[6] The better Kafka's writing was going, the more isolated a person he became.[7] Late night was the only time of day he could achieve his solitude, and as he courted Felice Bauer, he made it clear that this unusual daily existence would continue should they be married.[8] When World War I broke out, Kafka's brother-in-law went off to fight, and his sister moved back in with their parents. Kafka switched places with her, moving into her apartment, the first time in his life he had a space of his own.[9] Later on, he'd secure his own "writing apartment," another move that proved productive for him.

Kafka could be a stickler for routine. When he woke in the morning, he spent a long spell in the bathroom getting ready for the day. He was meticulous in his grooming, always worried about how others perceived him. He always arrived at the office at 8:15 a.m. on the dot, always ate a plain roll while he walked there.[10] He returned from the office around 2:30 p.m., at which time, if he could get away with it, he took naps lasting up to four hours, in order to have energy for writing into the late night.[11] "Now, in the evening," he wrote in his diary one night, "out of boredom, washed my hands in the bathroom three times in succession."[12] Maybe Kafka was indeed bored. Or maybe he had obsessive-compulsive tendencies. He became a vegetarian and adopted an eating technique called fletcherizing, which involved chewing each bite for several minutes before swallowing.[13]

Despite his affinity for formal structure in his life and his knack for creating a routine and sticking to it, in the act of writing itself a different Kafka emerged, incapable of conjuring his work on command or being meticulous in its organization. As one biographer, Joachim Unseld, put it, "The mere attempt to write in a calculated manner or to structure his texts logically or analyze them rationally would have destabilized his 'inspiration.'"[14] Although Kafka stuck to a careful routine in life, the hours spent writing were unpredictable. To try to control his writing was to destroy its ability to take shape. He could only work by writing impulsively.

Unsurprisingly, his longer works were composed in no particular order. He wrote the beginning and end of *The Trial* first, but was unable to impose any conventional structure on it beyond that, and other works took shape in a similar manner. Kafka had no problem coming up with ideas to spark a work, but it was a continual struggle for him to see those ideas through as comprehensive stories.[15] It was in fact Max Brod who was largely responsible for editing some of the work into a readable configuration after Kafka's death.

What Brod had to deal with was mostly contained in the copious diaries Kafka left behind. Kafka's diaries were the central artery of his writing life, and taken as a whole, they provide a map of his thought process as a writer. He recorded not only his concerns, his fears, his glum hopes, and the minutiae of his everyday life, but he also used his diaries to write what would turn out to be great literature. A story from his day would be recorded, then retold several times, edited repeatedly, tweaked in the hopes of approaching perfection, page after page written in his tight handwriting, in retrospect the very visual embodiment of bottled-up anxiety. It's clear from this approach to writing that Kafka was hardly able to separate the writing of literature from life itself. In addition, this method gave future researchers a play-by-play of his writing and editing process. He clung to his diaries when nothing else seemed to be going well. "I won't give up the diary again," he wrote in one in 1910. "I must hold on here, it is the only place I can."[16]

When he began working on *The Trial*, for example, he copied down the dash that in his diary always indicated the beginning of a new literary effort, then wrote the original first sentence:

Someone must have slandered Josef K., for one morning, without having done anything wrong, he was captured.

The next day, realizing one word didn't sit right, he wrote the sentence over again, changing "captured" to "arrested," and *The Trial* had its opening.[17]

Kafka wrote "The Judgment" in his diary during a single frenzied night, from 10 p.m. until 6 a.m.[18] With this achievement, Kafka felt he'd made a breakthrough in his writing and redoubled his efforts to work on it every night. He also figured it was time for a novel. Kafka made the strange decision to base his first novelistic effort in America, without ever having been there. In the place of firsthand experience, he embarked on a determined program of research. The Kafkas had relatives in America, and he scoured their letters for details.[19] He paid careful attention to newspaper accounts from the New World, attended any lecture on the subject, and read any literature on it he could get his hands on. His ears perked up when coworkers talked about new technologies from America.[20]

But Kafka also had impressive firsthand powers of observation, and many scenes and scenarios from his life made their way successfully into his fiction, sometimes hardly altered from the way he observed them. When his sister Ottla, usually his most staunch defender within the family (and one of his few early readers), sided with their parents over his failure to help out at the asbestos factory, it took him only a few weeks to put this sense of sibling betrayal directly into *The Metamorphosis*.[21] *The Trial* was an appropriation of a trial Kafka himself had been subjected to in a Berlin hotel room, when Felice Bauer, her friend Grete Bloch, and her sister Erna sat in a row facing Kafka, demanding answers about the cold feet he was exhibiting toward his fiancée. The verdict? The engagement was off.[22]

Among his literary influences, none loomed larger than Goethe, whom Kafka discovered during secondary school. Throughout his life, references to the great German writer peppered his diaries, and in 1912, on one of their trips together, Brod and Kafka visited Goethe's former house in Weimar, now open to tourists, to pay homage. Kafka likely took his interest in the psychological elements in literature at least partially from Goethe, although their approaches to it contrasted markedly.

Kafka didn't own a lot of books, but on the shelves of his room could be found, along with Goethe, the German writers Heinrich von Kleist and Friedrich Hebbel, the Austrian dramatist Franz Grillparzer, and the Swedish author August Strindberg, as well as Flaubert and Dostoyevsky.[23] Another great influence is one that at first glance appears at odds with the dystopian antilogic of Kafka's work: Charles Dickens. Kafka named *David Copperfield* as the single most important literary model during the writing of his story "The Stoker." What he took from Dickens most notably was the focus on, as he described it, "menial labor, the sweetheart at the country house, the dirty houses."[24]

Kafka enjoyed only three major creative bursts in his life, phases that bear uncanny similarities, suggesting a man who in his utter inconsistency as a writer nonetheless was a completely consistent character. All three lasted for five months. All three were followed by a lengthy dry spell. "I haven't written anything for a year," he noted of one such spell in April 1914, in a letter to Grete Bloch, Felice Bauer's good friend and a sometimes object of fascination for Kafka.[25] During the more common and longer unproductive phases, when he might write no fiction at all, or throw out what he did write, Kafka wrote letters obsessively—Bauer received more than five hundred such compositions over the course of their relationship.[26] All three bursts also followed turmoil in his personal life, especially with regard to Bauer. It was a cruel cycle for Kafka: When the writing wasn't coming, he began looking to more conventional satisfactions like marriage to fill the gap. When those pursuits inevitably soured, he returned to writing with renewed intensity, which could not last.

The inconsistency in Kafka's writing routine can also be partially blamed on his infinite powers of self-criticism. The man was a perfectionist in most areas of his life: His morning hygiene routine was rigid; in photos, he always appears fastidiously groomed. His work at the office was never left unfinished. But in his writing, the perfection he sought was, in his eyes, rarely achieved. For every written page he ultimately approved of, there were ten or more that he considered kindling for the fireplace.[27] Or he might write three pages, then decide that a single sentence from them was the only one he'd been looking for.[28] In a fit of stating the obvious, he wrote in his diary near the end of 1910, "That I have put aside and crossed out so much, indeed almost everything I wrote this year, that hinders me a great deal in writing."[29] Kafka burned an estimated 90 percent of everything he ever wrote.[30] "Today burned many old, disgusting papers," he wrote in his diary in 1912.[31]

Kafka's perfectionism contributed to his trouble writing novels—of the three he began, none was ever completed, although all were published posthumously. Sustaining an idea through hundreds of pages proved too heavy a burden for a mind that second-guessed every move. Kafka often halted work on a novel when a short-story idea came to him. This resulted in some of his greatest literature—*The Metamorphosis* interrupted his first novel (with a working title "The Man Who Disappeared," but eventually published as *Amerika*) and "In the Penal Colony" stopped *The Trial*—but it also invariably ruined the flow of his novels.[32]

Kafka rarely felt ready to put his work out into the world. In almost every instance that Kafka managed to publish during his lifetime, he owed it to Brod, for whom networking and self-promotion came naturally, and who believed wholeheartedly in Kafka's genius, as opposed to Kafka himself, who felt comfortable with neither networking nor his own abilities, and eventually came to the conclusion that seeking out publication at all was detrimental to his ultimate goal of finding truth through writing. Brod provided Kafka with a firsthand template of how to conduct a successful writing career, but it was a template that Kafka's temperament would not allow him to emulate.

Brod convinced publishers and editors to print Kafka's work, but he also played a more immediate role in the development of Kafka the writer. The two friends spent many evenings together taking walks and discussing literature or whiling away some hours at fellow Prague writer Oskar Baum's apartment (where Kafka met Bauer for the first time one evening when she had stopped for a night in Prague during her travels). Brod and Kafka often took trips together when they could get time off from their full-time office jobs. They took one such holiday to Riva on Italy's Lake Garda in the summer of 1909, at which time Kafka had failed to write anything for a span of many months. Brod planted the idea in Kafka that they should both keep a travel diary in order to compare notes and interpretations at the end of the trip, thinking this might reignite Kafka's pen. The scheme worked: With the structure and time constraints of the small project, Kafka was able to find the parameters he needed to get words on the page.[33] Were it not for Max Brod, most of Kafka's work never would have been read by the public. He overrode Kafka's wishes to have his work burned after his death.

Kafka's posthumous success only underscores the gloom that permeated his life. The total of three engagements Kafka entered into (twice with Bauer, the other with Julie Wohryzek, a poor hotel chambermaid) disintegrated, generally speaking, because of Kafka's inability to envision any kind of what we today call work-life balance. His asceticism was meant to foster his writing, but it also made him a largely unhappy person, which hampered his efforts. Near the end of his life, he wrote in his diary of the severity that led him to become a "physical wreck": "I did not want to be distracted, did not want to be distracted by the pleasures life has to give a useful and healthy man." By this point, well into the tuberculosis that would kill him a month shy of his forty-first birthday, he understood the possible folly of his approach, adding, "As if illness and despair were not just as much of a distraction!"[34] It's entirely possible that had he let a little more life into his days, he would have written far more prolifically over the course of them.

A DAY IN THE WRITER'S LIFE . . .

For the better part of his adult life, Franz Kafka rose every morning well before seven, quickly getting his exacting morning hygiene routine under way. He'd then walk with his long strides to work while eating a plain roll and arrive at 8:15 a.m. Returning to the apartment around 2:30 p.m., Kafka took a long nap, then rose again for dinner, followed by a walk or an evening with Max Brod at the home of another Prague writer, Oskar Baum. Afterward, he'd return home and sit in his room, listening for signs that the household was settling in for a night of sleep. During this waiting period, Kafka often wandered to his window and looked out over the city's Vltava River, contemplating his gloom. Finally, he'd bring out his notebooks. He might write in his diary, or another letter to Felice Bauer—or on rare occasions when things were going well, he'd write great fiction.

2

TONI MORRISON

One day in elementary school, a little black girl stood in front of Toni Morrison and announced with relaxed candor that she wished she had blue eyes. Her strange lack of pride, along with the swirl of unexamined self-loathing Morrison saw as implicit in her wish, hit Morrison in a permanent way. For the first time she can remember, Morrison became aware that perceptions of beauty can be informed by forces that have nothing to do with beauty, that the little girl found blue eyes beautiful not because of their inherent attractiveness but because of something else they represented. As a young adult, she found herself continually trying to tease out the exact reasons for the little girl's wish. Morrison continued to revisit that memory for decades and must have known that in some way it was formative to her worldview. Finally, she wrote a book about it. *The Bluest Eye* became her first novel. Toni Morrison was thirty-nine years old. Some seeds are sown long before anyone understands what they'll eventually grow into.

The Bluest Eye took Morrison five years to write. At the beginning of those five years, she put the story on paper almost by accident. While living in Washington, DC, and teaching at Howard University, she joined a writing group just for fun and because the food was good. Because she wasn't allowed to keep attending unless she finally wrote something, Morrison thought back to the little black girl who wanted blue eyes and started working on a story. She finished it and put it away. As it happened, it wasn't long after that she divorced her husband and moved with her two young sons to Syracuse, New York, for a new job. She had few friends there and didn't expect to stay long, so she figured, why go through the effort to make any? Writing became the thing that kept her company. She brought the blue-eyes story back out and began turning it into a novel.

The Bluest Eye was her first serious effort at writing, and yet Morrison had been learning how to write, unbeknownst even to herself, since childhood. Growing up, storytelling was a way of life in her family. Her parents told ghost stories every night, and then prodded her to recite them the following night. And throughout her childhood, she heard and reheard the folklore of her ancestors—her novel *Tar Baby* was based on one such story she knew well. She always loved books, and as her mind grew more sophisticated, Morrison discovered writers like Faulkner, Tolstoy, Woolf, Dostoyevsky, and Jane Austen.[35]

But when she grew up, Morrison channeled her love of stories and literature not by writing, but by majoring in English in college, earning a master's in English literature (with a thesis on Virginia Woolf and William Faulkner) and becoming an English professor. After her divorce, she became an editor, first of textbooks in Syracuse, then of literature at Random House's headquarters in New York City, where she was responsible for publishing Angela Davis and Henry Dumas, among other important African American writers.

When she eventually did begin writing, James Baldwin was one important influence. "He could say something in a phrase that clarified all sorts of conflicting feelings," she says.[36] But Morrison was especially beholden to African novelists like Chinua Achebe, Camara Laye, Bessie Head, Léopold Sédar Senghor, and Aimé Césaire, all black writers who didn't write about black culture and characters as reflected through the eyes of white men, as she felt so many black American authors did. "These African writers took their blackness as central," she says, and the notion of black centrality became a core perspective of her own writing as well.[37]

Despite her love of literature, Morrison doesn't read much literary fiction when she's writing her own work. "If I read fiction, I want to be in the author's head, and I have to be in mine," she says.[38] Instead, she generally reads detective novels, which don't interfere with her sense of her own work while she's entrenched in it.[39]

There were of course other, greater interferences to keep at bay. Writing around single motherhood and a full-time job came with obvious challenges, but also a silver lining: There was no time to waste, and Morrison thus had no choice but to keep herself in line. "There was an urgency—that's all I remember," she says. "Not having the leisure to whine."[40] She also had to choose her priorities. "It's not a bad thing to please a husband or a lover, but I couldn't do that. It took up time and thought."[41] The priorities rose effortlessly to the surface: being a good mother and being a good writer. She happily sacrificed everything else. It helps that Morrison doesn't seem too interested in having a social life. "I don't do any of the so-called fun things in life," she says without regret.[42] Ultimately, she found the choice to write was where the real fun started, anyway. "The writing was the real freedom, because nobody told me what to do there," she says.[43]

Early on, when working on a book, she got in the habit of rising at 4 a.m. to write uninterrupted until her children woke up, and after that, she headed to work. When she quit her editing job thirteen years after the publication of her first novel, Morrison was surprised to find that the early-morning routine still suited her. "Eventually I realized that I was clearer-headed, more confident and generally more intelligent in the morning," she says. The cup of coffee in the moments before light began tiptoeing up from the horizon became a reliable beacon. "For me this ritual comprises my preparation to enter a space that I can only call nonsecular . . . For me, light is the signal in the transition. It's not being *in* the light, it's being there *before it arrives*. It enables me, in some sense."[44]

In the new light, she sits down and gets to work, writing on yellow legal pads with, if possible, a Dixon Ticonderoga No. 2 soft pencil (a pen will do in a pinch). These days, she often writes through the morning. After lunch, she admits she's prone to taking a nap.[45] And she has copped to enjoying Court TV (now TruTV) and soap operas in the afternoons.[46] Writing after work or in the evenings, she claims, never came easily. "I am not very bright or very witty or very inventive after the sun goes down," she says.[47] Still, if "something is urgently there," she goes out of her way to put everything else aside in order to see the writing through.[48] She's made periodic references to writing in the evenings, even once explaining her tendency to not socialize as a way of keeping her nights free for it.[49]

If she could find the time, Morrison could seemingly write anywhere. She'd write as her two young sons frolicked around her. She'd write on weekends or mornings or weeknights. She's always thinking about writing while doing other things, washing the dishes or when she was putting her sons to bed, so that when she does find herself in front of a piece of paper, she's ready to put something on it.[50] For Morrison, the prospect of sitting down to write doesn't come laced with the dread that cripples so many writers. Quite the opposite, in fact: "Writing has always been a solace," she says. It's "where I spend the liveliest, most confident part of my day."[51] When she's writing, she feels "almost . . . magnificent."[52]

If she hits a streak when the writing isn't coming, she considers it not writer's block, but another crucial part of the writing process. She turned the idea for *Beloved* around in her mind for three years before getting started on it.[53] "It's a sustained thing I have to play with. I always start out with an idea, even a boring idea, that becomes a question I don't have any answers to," she says.[54] The process always starts with a question like this, a void in the canon of literature that Toni Morrison wants to see filled. The question might lead her to explore friendships between females, which she found unaddressed in fiction (*Sula*), or peel the layers back on what she felt was the overly optimistic "black is beautiful" mantra (*The Bluest Eye*), or peel other layers back on the shallow general happiness of the 1950s (*Home*). If something hasn't been done before that Morrison herself wants to see, she envisions the book to satisfy her own interest.

And she loves this brainstorming part of the process. "I am profoundly excited by thinking up or having the idea in the first place," she says.[55] But she might not write at all during these times. If the idea hasn't coalesced for her, she doesn't force it. "I might write each day for three months, then not write at all for the next three months," she says. "I always thought I should have a routine of some kind, but I've discovered I can never force it."[56] It's the perspective, perhaps, of someone who came to writing at a mature age, already familiar with the challenges and frustrations of adult life, and able to enjoy writing as an antidote to that. However she has arrived at this outlook, it's one that has seldom been shaken.

Once Morrison starts a novel, if she gets stuck, it's because she's lacking a certain impression, a certain image that has to come to her before she can go on. These images often come from the haphazard notes she takes down as ideas come to her. While writing *Sula*, one sentence became the seminal impression: "It was too cool for ice cream." This phrase triggered exactly the kind of day she was looking for as a setting: not cold, but not warm enough for certain activities, either—a very particular kind of outdoor day. During the writing of *Song of Solomon*, she was having trouble encapsulating the aura of the small town she was writing about. Then she found in her notes a reference to a woman walking through the street with nothing in her possession, not even house keys. "That was just what I wanted to say because the place where one can do that, just get up and walk out the door and go," was exactly the town she was envisioning.[57]

Visual imagery looms large in Morrison's fiction. She uses it to establish her stories, and she lets it course through them. She has said, in fact, that she takes more influence from painters in her work than she does from other writers.[58] Sometimes the image is a structural one (she calls it a "controlling image") that doesn't factor in the story itself. She saw *Sula* "as a cracked mirror, fragments and pieces we have to see independently and put together," she explained.[59] For *Song of Solomon*, the image was of a train. This was the first time she'd made a man the central character in a work. Instead of being centered on domesticity, as were her previous novels, "this was going to move out. So, I had this feeling about a train . . . sort of revving up, then moving out as he does . . . [T]hat image controlled the structure for me, although that is not something I articulate or even make reference to."[60]

Single, powerful images often come to her and drive the story forward. In *Song of Solomon*, she used an Edvard Munch painting "almost literally" to help her describe a scene she was having trouble with, of a man on the run from responsibility and from himself.[61] In 2008, she was in a phase of thinking generally about the project that would become *Home* when she was struck seemingly from nowhere with the image of horses fighting. A phrase came along with the image: "They stood up like men." She followed through on that image and ultimately used it to formulate the outline of her character, a boy struggling with being a man and being vulnerable in the 1950s.[62]

Along with those images, Morrison uses color to convey moods and settings. She knew from the outset that she wanted the opening of *Song of Solomon* to be red, white, and blue, and she deliberately wrote the novel in what she called "painterly language."[63] She approached color far differently in *Beloved*, overtly rendering it nearly devoid of pigment, but using it for maximum impact when it does appear, as in the room that Baby Suggs uses to "talk-think":

> There wasn't any [color] except for two orange squares in a quilt that made the absence shout. The walls of the room were slate-colored, the floor earth-brown, the wooden dresser the color of itself, curtains white, and the dominating feature, the quilt over an iron cot, was made up of scraps of blue serge, black, brown and gray wool—the full range of the dark and the muted that thrift and modesty allowed. In that sober field, two patches of orange looked wild—like life in the raw.

Morrison doesn't know where a story will ultimately go when she starts it, but she usually figures it out early on. "When I really know what it is about, then I can write that end scene," she says. "I wrote the end of *Beloved* about a quarter of the way in. I wrote the end of *Jazz* very early and the end of *Song of Solomon* very early on."[64] Conversely, knowing the end doesn't mean that she's figured out the middle. The end is the "what happened." Morrison's novels are concerned with the "*how* it happened." The narrator in *The Bluest Eye* sums it up as well as Morrison ever has:

There is really nothing more to say—except why. But since why is difficult to handle, one must take refuge in how.

"It is like a detective story in a sense," she says. "You know who
is dead and you want to find out who did it."[65] The book itself is
Morrison's way of explaining how that ending could unfold, and
it's why she always knows the ends of her novels before the beginnings. The beginnings, in fact, often come late in the game, and
she struggles with them. She took four months to rewrite the first
four pages of *Sula*, for example—"a whole summer of nights."[66]

The characters themselves are part of the why and how. They
come after that initial idea. "Once you have an idea," she says,
"then you try to find a character who can manifest the idea for
you."[67] Once they are imagined, she keeps tight control over them.
"They are very carefully imagined," she says. "I feel as though I
know all there is to know about them, even things I don't write—
like how they part their hair."[68]

Morrison loves getting the words down on the page and
seeing a project develop. In terms of her self-worth, struggling
through the work is "more important to me than publishing it,"
she says.[69] That word "struggle" is apt: Even though Morrison is
the rare writer who takes joy in the creation of her work, she is
not a fast writer. She once spoke to the *New York Times Magazine*
of working on her novel *Paradise*. At the time, it was going particularly well. "I'm having the best time ever. I wrote 13 pages in
three days. I've never done that in my life," she said.[70] Before she
quit her full-time editing job, she might write six pages in a single
session, but not very often.[71]

With a completed handwritten draft, Morrison then types the
manuscript on her computer, and the revision process is under
way. Part of revising for Morrison involves going away from the

work and coming back to it with a fresh eye. As a cautionary tale, she told an interviewer of the time she spent a summer writing fifty pages that she felt were "really first-rate." Because of other obligations, she wasn't able to return to the pages for revision until the following winter. "When I read them each page of the fifty was terrible. It was really ill-conceived. I knew that I could do it over, but I just couldn't get over the fact that I thought it was so good at the time."[72]

Revision, then, is crucial for Morrison. "That's the best part," she says.[73] She might revise a manuscript six, seven, or even more times, and she's been known to go so far as rewriting the entire novel, as was the case for *The Bluest Eye*. When she did so, she added two little girls into the equation and told some of the story from the point of view of one of them. This required a restructuring of the novel, which she accepted in stride.[74] She has described the experience of that rewrite as "thrilling."[75] The entire process typically takes her anywhere from three to five years. At some point, thrilling though it may be, the revision has to stop. "There's a line between revision and fretting, just working it to death," she says.[76]

Perhaps no great writer is better positioned to sympathize with the suggestions and efforts of her editors than Morrison, who never intended to become a writer when she accepted a job as an editor at Random House in her early thirties. The job not only imbued her with sympathy for that particular craft, but also a respect that made her a better writer in her own right. "The good ones make all the difference," she says. She goes on to add, "There are editors so rare and so important that they are worth searching for, and you always know when you have one." For Morrison, one editor in particular has proven critical in the development of the final product. She calls Robert Gottlieb, who edited all but two of her novels, "superlative."[77] He helps her to step back from her writing emotionally. She had written a scene in *Sula* that she believed was gorgeous, the characters' pain perfectly rendered. When she showed it to Gottlieb, he said it didn't work, because the pain was clearly hers, not her characters'. She ultimately agreed.[78]

Morrison borrows from historical events for her fiction, and she does her research to ensure an authentic story. *Beloved* is based on a mother and child who lived in Cincinnati during slavery in the 1850s. Morrison discovered the story while researching a coffee table book on the African American experience in American history.[79] For her novel *Home*, set in the 1920s in a small southern town that disappears, Morrison scoured census records to find just such a place and then set her story there.[80] For her first novel, *The Bluest Eye*, she borrowed from even closer to home. In that novel, the girl, named Pauline, cleans the immaculate house of a wealthy white family, just as Morrison did around that age.[81] But that's as far as she'll take the borrowing. Appropriating people from her own life for her novels falls beyond the pale for Morrison. "If [my characters are] based on somebody else, in a funny way it's an infringement of a copyright," she says.[82] At the same time, historical authenticity proves less crucial to her than the authenticity of *feeling*. "I wanted to translate the historical into the personal," she says of the writing of *Beloved*.

Once she has done that, once a novel is complete, "a kind of melancholy" sets in. She experienced it the first time after completing *The Bluest Eye*, and it didn't lift until she came up with the idea for her second book, *Sula*.[83] Morrison eventually came to terms with that melancholy and understood that she needed that mood and time between books in order to come up with her next idea. Because Morrison only works on one book at a time—she never envisions a next novel until a current one is complete—there's no way around the melancholy period. This time, she understands, is the quiet before the next creative storm.

A DAY IN THE WRITER'S LIFE . . .

In many ways, a day in the life of Toni Morrison has been the life of harried single moms everywhere. This mom, though, is also a Nobel Prize winner. For most of her writing life, Morrison would rise well before the sun, as early as 4 a.m., and put on a pot of coffee, and as the light went gray and then bright, she'd sit down to write until her children woke up. She'd get them ready for school, then head off to work herself. At night, provided there was nothing else that took priority, she might revisit her writing. Morrison happily cut socializing from her daily life, narrowing her focus to two key elements: her kids and her writing. She doesn't force the writing if it's not coming, but even in those dry moments, she's always thinking about her next words.

PRODUCTIVE
PROCRASTINATORS

3

DAVID FOSTER WALLACE

She'd rather be a character in a book than a real person. So said a college girlfriend to David Foster Wallace once, maybe expressing a long-held sentiment, maybe offering the kind of throwaway remark spoken late at night when exhaustion has turned thoughts inside out. Or perhaps she only felt bored, and wouldn't it be nice to experience the novelty of a more noteworthy life for a while? Whatever the impulse behind it, it struck Wallace and stuck with him. He found himself thinking about just what she'd meant: What's the difference between a character in a book and a real person, and how does language dictate one or both?[84] He thought about the concept so much that a story grew up around it. Wallace spent a good chunk of his senior year at Amherst College feverishly turning it into his first novel, *The Broom of the System*, in which the plot becomes secondary to the twenty-four-year-old protagonist's doubt in her own reality and belief that word choices are controlling her life. Wallace himself was twenty-four years old when the novel came out. His own concerns about reality were already firmly entrenched.

Broom was the first of what would turn out to be only three novels, the third one left unfinished when Wallace died by his own hand in 2008 at the age of forty-six. Each explores a simple yet overarching theme that for Wallace was one of life's most complicated puzzles. Given the young Wallace's tendencies toward over-indulgence—with drinking, pot smoking, and women, to scratch the surface—it's no surprise that as he made his way to Arizona for an MFA program after *Broom*, his thoughts turned to that very modern, very American concept of excess. He became obsessed with the idea of *too much*—too much drug intake, too much entertainment at our fingertips, too much expectation for our talents.

Wallace began to articulate this obsession through several writing projects that eventually merged into one. In his midtwenties, Wallace started a story about a video so entertaining that viewers watch it until they die. Soon after, he started a separate one about a tennis prodigy and the peculiar neuroses of his very modern family (Wallace himself was a competitive tennis player in high school). Several years later, after a failed attempt to quit writing altogether and earn a PhD in philosophy at Harvard, Wallace went into treatment for alcohol addiction. At the tail end of it, he moved into a halfway house outside Boston. He took copious notes while there about the people he met for whom excess had nearly become a death sentence. In particular, an outsized character known as "Big Craig" became the basis for a story about a man named Don Gately.[85] It occurred to Wallace then that the three stories belonged together, and his dizzying second novel, *Infinite Jest*, began to take shape. After half a decade of incubation, he wrote it in three years.

As Wallace matured—he was thirty-three when *Infinite Jest* came out in 1996—he began to formulate a calmer life, staying in at night and avoiding substances, teaching at various universities to keep himself grounded. It was around this time he began to notice that in the midst of all that excess, humans maintain a crystalline capacity for boredom. Boredom as a concept for Wallace was interesting to think about precisely because it was so tedious to experience, and because it thrived amid the availability of more entertainment than the human race had ever known. Wallace chose the IRS as his vehicle for exploring the phenomenon—a massive bureaucracy the very mention of which makes grown adults suppress a sigh. He set out to learn everything he could about it, taking accounting classes, reading IRS manuals cover to cover, and compiling hundreds of pages of notes.[86] Wallace must have spent time observing his own boredom as well, and armed with a unique grasp of this imprecise concept, he began to ponder its redeeming qualities. The results made their way into *The Pale King* in passages like the following:

> It turns out that bliss—a second-by-second joy + gratitude at the gift of being alive, conscious—lies on the other side of crushing, crushing boredom. Pay close attention to the most tedious thing you can find (tax returns, televised golf), and, in waves, a boredom like you've never known will wash over you and just about kill you. Ride these out, and it's like stepping from black and white into color. Like water after days in the desert. Constant bliss in every atom.

The frailty of reality, the pitfalls of excess, the maddening persistence of boredom—one after another, Wallace took these notions to weird extremes, distorted them in ways one wouldn't expect to provide clarity, but did. It was the concept of reality, in particular, that led to Wallace's most famous stylistic quirk: extensive endnotes that tailed much of his work, especially *Infinite Jest*. "Reality is fractured right now, at least the reality that I live in," he said to explain why he started using them. "The difficulty about writing . . . about that reality is that text is very linear, it's very unified. You—*I*, anyway, am constantly on the lookout for ways to fracture the text that aren't totally disorienting."[87]

Looming existential concepts consumed the adult Wallace. But life started out less fraught. Raised in Champaign, Illinois, in a big-hearted household, his parents encouraged literary and intellectual tendencies. Wallace showed early intelligence and wit, but also a typical kid's interest in things like Evel Knievel and the Chicago Bears. After a successful but undistinguished high school career, he arrived at Amherst and quickly became recognized as a phenomenal intellect, preternaturally adept at navigating both literary and mathematical realms, and suddenly ambitious in his academic pursuits. He didn't take up writing fiction until his sophomore year, though, and only then as an exercise while convalescing from the first of the four mental breakdowns he would suffer by the age of twenty-six.[88]

Wallace found his first major go at fiction a breeze; he seemed to come with the fully realized ability to write. By 1995, though, as the publication of *Infinite Jest* was nearing, his easy enthusiasm had ceded to something darker. "I have a lot of dread and terror and inadequacy-shit, now, when I'm trying to write. I didn't used to," he wrote to Don DeLillo that year.[89] In 1998, reminiscing about the journey of a writer in his essay "The Nature of Fun," he wrote, "In the beginning, when you first start out trying to write fiction, the whole endeavor's about fun. You don't expect anybody else to read it." But success in writing changes the writer, he believed. "Things start to get complicated and confusing, not to mention scary." To come out on the other side, he wrote, one can "sustain the fun of writing only by confronting the very same unfun parts of yourself you'd first used writing to avoid."[90]

By the time he was working on *The Pale King*, the insecurity had set in more or less permanently. He did not, in the end, come out on the other side. Which isn't to say that he could no longer write. Wallace wrote things that weren't *The Pale King*, but when it came to the next great novel that he viewed as his most important project, he felt enduringly stuck. (And yet we have a 547-page unfinished novel called *The Pale King*.) Most writers start out not knowing how to write and gradually gain a sense of competence, if things go well. Wallace came out of the gate knowing what to do, but slowly lost his ease around words. The struggle produced an anxiety that soaked his writing days. "If past experience holds true," Wallace said of his future writing in 1997, "I will probably write an hour a day and spend eight hours a day biting my knuckle and worrying about not writing."[91] The angst spread well beyond his writing. "He had anxiety about *everything*," says Juliana Harms, who was engaged to Wallace in the late nineties.

When Wallace did get down to writing, he wrote first drafts in his small, slanted handwriting in notebooks or, during at least one phase in the 1990s, on legal pads.[92] Part of a draft of *The Pale King* was written in a notebook with a character from the animated TV series *Rugrats* on the cover, another in one featuring a photo of kittens.[93] These drafts came after the running observational notes he kept, often in steno pads filled with text that could be serious or veer toward screwball, and also with a fair number of doodles dotting the pages. Wallace once called himself a "five draft man," writing three drafts by hand, then typing out two further drafts, all destined to have copious notes in the margins, words crossed out, and the occasional smiley-face sticker placed near a passage he felt he'd done well with. Wallace happily declared himself to be the fastest and most adroit "two-finger typist" he'd ever heard of, not that he necessarily faced stiff competition in that realm.[94] Of course, his claims of such exacting processes have to be understood as a goal more than a reality. Wallace didn't necessarily stick to his own rules.

If Wallace was writing well, the words tumbled out of him in bursts that could last for a string of hours or a couple of days. While writing *The Broom of the System*, he claimed at one point to have written twenty-four pages of it in three hours.[95] He once showed up on a Monday after disappearing over the weekend to tell his girlfriend that he'd written a thirty-page short story called "Little Expressionless Animals" "straight through."[96] His old room-mate, Mark Costello, claimed Wallace could at certain times write twenty-five thousand words in *one day*.[97]

Wallace didn't need a particular writing space when things were clicking. He felt he could write anywhere—in a coffee shop or his apartment or at the library. When his then fiancée Juliana Harms accompanied him to a gathering of MacArthur "geniuses" in 1999, he stayed in the hotel room much of the time to write. When they took a trip to Jamaica, he wrote in the hotel bathroom.[98]

And yet he was dedicated to the strange writing spaces he set up for himself at home. Starting in college, he laid towels out around his writing spot, by-products of the several showers he was known to take every day. When he lived in Syracuse for a short time while working on *Infinite Jest*, he chose an apartment so small that when he wrote, he moved everything off the desk and onto the bed, and when it was time to sleep, did the reverse.[99] When he moved back to Illinois for a teaching job and bought his first house, he chose a writing room and painted it completely black, then filled it with old lamps.[100] He stacked books on the floor and constantly pinned drafts or other printed materials to the walls.[101] He sipped mineral water with a lime wedge throughout the writing day there and looked on the room as his inner sanctum. When he moved to California to teach at Pomona College, the lamps came along, too, settling into the garage of his new house there. His wife, Karen Green, took charge of the paint this time, covering the walls in red, along with some random things that had made the move out west with him, including a poster of Gustav Klimt's *The Kiss*.[102]

Prolific phases could make Wallace euphoric. The writing came with such a thrilling force, it hardly required organization or a schedule. "Routines and disciplines go out the window simply because I don't need them," he said of these phases.[103] They also made him superstitious. He'd sometimes make sure to use the same pen as the previous day when things were humming along, calling it his "orgasm pen."[104]

But being on a roll may have caused Wallace to become careless. Maybe things were going so well he forgot to see the need for his edifying daily jog, or a reasonable bedtime. "As the healthy activities diminished," says Harms, "that is when he started working later, sleeping later, and watching more television."[105] And then the writing began to suffer.

When writer's block descended, it lingered like sludge. "It was an agonizing pull for him to really try to come back from that," says Harms.[106] Wallace sought out plenty of tricks to combat it, none of them reliably successful. He set up those previously unnecessary schedules. He asked other writers about their routines. Before he quit both for good, he smoked pot or drank in an effort to kick-start his mind. He twice went to the elite Yaddo artists' retreat in upstate New York in order to get into the right frame of mind. The first visit was successful, the next a dismal failure. Another writers' retreat in Marfa, Texas, also got him nowhere. Harms calls these techniques, cumulatively, his "antiprocess." "David, especially with his addiction issues, and his very, very, very busy mind, he craved a sense of routine, but he also fought against it," she says.

And as always, he found himself chronically distracted. He was obsessive about television and could sit for hours on end watching it. On the other hand, Wallace wrote—and maybe even convinced himself—that watching television could be valuable research. The tube's "kind of window on nervous American self-perception is just invaluable in terms of writing fiction," he once observed in an essay in which he delved seriously into the connection between the contemporary novelist and the tube.[107] In the same essay, he dissected not only why television is such an appealing time-suck, but also how it can distort reality for the fiction writer in dangerous ways.

Another of his go-to distractions from writing involved, of all things, writing. Wallace typed old-fashioned letters to any number of people, many of them writers: Mary Karr, whom he dated; Jonathan Franzen, with whom he became friends via these letters; and Don DeLillo, whom he'd never met but who allowed him to pick his brain about the writing life. In one letter to DeLillo, he wrote of his problem "taking half-hours off to write letters like this and still calling it Writing Time."[108] Perhaps no great writer has ever been so effusive about his writer's block. Wallace wrote and wrote about his inability to write. "My thoughts now have the urgent but impeded quality of speechlessness in dreams," Wallace wrote in a letter to Franzen.[109] In these letters, he'd marvel at the ability of other writers to stick to their routines, to simply get down to work when they told themselves to.

Surprisingly, Wallace didn't have a problem with the Internet. In a 1998 interview he claimed never to have been on it before, although that would seem an exaggeration.[110] Indeed, he participated in an online interview in 1996. His reasons for staying away may have been manifold. "One, I think his comfort was in handwriting," says Harms. "But two, I also think he had enough wisdom to know that the Internet might do *to* him as opposed to *for* him."[111] Considering his ingenious ability to encapsulate the pitfalls that come with access to unlimited stimuli, the Internet preoccupied Wallace far less than one would expect.

Wallace did remain preoccupied by teaching, which he began while earning his MFA at the University of Arizona and never let go of. He yearned to no longer be financially required to teach. But when the money from *Infinite Jest* starting coming in while he was at Illinois State University—along with some grants, including the lucrative MacArthur—he continued with it. He may have found himself ultimately unable to let go of the structure that teaching brought to his life. He may have felt tied to the health coverage, or he may have sensed that quitting would mean facing writing head on, all day every day. Whatever the reason, long after money ceased to be an issue, Wallace held on to teaching positions, moving to California to take one at Pomona College in 2002, where he remained until his death.

Once Wallace had fought through the distractions and the anxiety to produce work, he entered the critical next phase of letting others read it. He was often dissatisfied with what he wrote. "For me, 50% of the stuff I do is bad," Wallace once said. "The trick is to know what's bad and not let other people see it."[112] This admission speaks to his anxieties and insecurities, but also to the fact that Wallace needed an editor to keep his unwieldy thought process in check. He generally accepted this fact, if sometimes grudgingly, and took suggested edits very seriously. The novelist Steven Moore gave Wallace feedback on parts of an early version of *Infinite Jest*, and he described the manuscript as "a mess—a patchwork of different fonts and point sizes, with numerous handwritten corrections/additions on most pages, and paginated in a nesting pattern (e.g., p. 22 is followed by 22A–J before resuming with p. 23, which is followed by 23A–D, etc)."[113] That novel eventually became several hundred pages shorter than the submitted manuscript under the guidance of its editor, Michael Pietsch. The process involved an extensive back-and-forth, with Wallace obsessing over each comma, over the concepts behind every sentence.

The process was similar with his shorter pieces. "You didn't really edit David. Instead you played tennis with him using language as the ball," recalls Colin Harrison, who edited Wallace's essay "A Supposedly Fun Thing I'll Never Do Again" (published as "Shipping Out") for *Harper's*. Harrison went on to say, "David liked the push and push-back of this, the here's-what-I-think, what-do-you-think rallies that sometimes went on for many minutes. It was exhausting and exhilarating, with points won, points lost."[114]

Throughout his life, Wallace was an enthusiastic reader, and he used reading as a thought exercise for his writing—the heavily annotated books in his personal library stand as testament to this. In the college years, the postmodernists captivated him, and for a time, he modeled himself as something of an heir apparent to them. Thomas Pynchon in particular struck a thunderbolt. Wallace's college roommate, Mark Costello, remembers when Wallace discovered the writer: "For Dave, that was like Bob Dylan finding Woody Guthrie."[115] The first short story to get Wallace really excited about the possibilities in that realm was Donald Barthelme's "The Balloon," about a balloon that expands over Manhattan.[116] He also took to Don DeLillo early on.

Over time, though, his influences changed, along with his goals for his fiction. Wallace reread Pynchon's *Vineland* in 1991 while bedridden by torn ankle ligaments, and he discovered the author who had most captivated him early on no longer impressed him.[117] The maturing of Wallace's writing coincided with his newfound appreciation of writers ranging from Hart Crane to Edith Wharton. He developed a passionate respect for the work of Cynthia Ozick, which baffled many observers, who couldn't see the connection between his early postmodern high jinks and her severe fiction.[118] And Wallace took influence from the work of certain nonfiction writers as well, including Frank Conroy, Joan Didion, and Pauline Kael.[119] Throughout his life he continued to love and revere DeLillo, whose work was his favorite to reread.[120]

Eventually, he settled into a preference for literature that resembled what Wallace himself was trying to accomplish with fiction. He said in 1999, "Most of the modern writing I like the best is both sophisticated and colloquial—that is, high-level and complicated but at the same time intimate, sort of like a smart person is sitting right there talking to you—and I think I do little more than try to achieve this same high-low blend."[121]

Influences ran beyond literature as well. Wallace told Charlie Rose in 1997 that David Lynch's film *Blue Velvet* "came at a time for me when I really needed to see it, and it helped me a lot in my own work." What hit him was the way that most everything in Lynch's worlds was banal, but it took only one little tweak of reality to create the strangest, most unsettling worlds.

A DAY IN THE WRITER'S LIFE . . .

David Foster Wallace's writing days were, in his own words, a ricocheting contest "between periods of terrible sloth and paralysis and periods of high energy and production."[122] Wallace *meant* to write every day, and he strove to attain a reliable schedule for himself. When his plans were working, he woke in the morning, got a cup of coffee, and retreated to the room he'd set up for writing, the most famous of them painted black and full of antique lamps. Later, he'd go on a run, watch some TV, and get to bed at a decent hour. But when the writing was going well, he often grew complacent with his routine. Then he'd watch too much TV, stay up too late, sleep through the morning, and watch the writing suffer for it.

RICHARD PRICE

He's been known to say he hates writing. He takes projects for the money. He would have given up the whole racket long ago if it hadn't come so easily to him. He speaks not in the high-handed verbiage of the literati but in the gritty, rhythmic vernacular that lingers from his Bronx upbringing. At first glance, you wouldn't classify Richard Price as a writer's writer, one who's in it for the pure love of literature. You also wouldn't necessarily peg him as a writer for whom the written word commands a humble respect. In spite of appearances, Price is exactly that, taking the big money one day only so he might focus on the pure art of fiction the next.

Price was published early on, with a first novel, *The Wanderers*, under his belt at the age of twenty-four. Three more novels came quickly, all before age thirty-two, and for a time, Price lived every aspiring writer's dream, an authorship happily devoid of unpublished struggle or years spent toiling in obscurity. And like countless others who broke into publishing with a youthful, navel-gazing debut, Price drew almost exclusively on personal experience in his early work, especially from the place he grew up: the Parkside

Houses in the Bronx, a "blue-collar, racially mixed, punch-on-the-nose-at-worst housing project."[123] Built in 1951, the houses consisted of the monolithic, repetitive redbrick buildings that are a dead giveaway of a Robert Moses–era development. Outside his window, the subway rumbled back and forth twenty-five yards away, day and night.

Price's home environment was far removed from a classic literary environment: no rarefied book collections, no erudite dinner parties, no uncles at the *New Yorker*. But from this setting sprang a very particular kind of writing, its style and subject matter together invoking the rough edges of the author's personal history. In those projects at age eleven Price wrote his first story, "a line-by-line plagiarization of a House of Mystery comic," he says. By age twelve, he was known as the writer of his school—"I was the Shakespeare of Olinville Junior High."[124]

Despite being a self-proclaimed "major screwup," Price gained entrance to the elite Bronx High School of Science, did well enough there to get into Cornell, and, after that, embarked on graduate studies at Stanford and an MFA at Columbia. Although he chose a practical course of study—industrial and labor relations—he pursued writing, experimenting with the popular styles of the day. But it wasn't quite clicking. "Nothing that I had ever written came from within me," he said of that time; "it was all 'Twilight Zone,' Mad Magazine, Greenwich Francisco 1957, Paris 1923. I was writing around myself."[125]

Though he hadn't yet thought to use it as a literary device, Price's childhood environment remained a vital part of his identity. He emphasized his "Bronxness" at Cornell, a defense mechanism meant to preserve his roots in the high-culture sea of the Ivy League, and began to feel a blooming nostalgia for the neighborhood he'd grown up in. During this formative time he read two books that, with a thundering smack, showed him the way to the writer he'd become. With Hubert Selby Jr.'s *Last Exit to Brooklyn*, Price felt a kinship with the people and places in a novel for the first time, and realized with a shock "that my own life and world were valid grounds for literature."[126] On the heels of this discovery came *The Essential Lenny Bruce*. "Here I found The Voice, The Pace. That shruggy, tongue-clucking delivery, that 'what can ya do' tone just slicing through the fabric of the culture."[127] He read these two books over and over. "These writers are important not because they are the greatest writers I've ever read, but because I read them at the exact formative time in my life to get me to the next place . . . It's strictly about being young and who makes you want to write," he says.[128]

Price has always read widely and voraciously, and continues to do so today; "I read so much I can't tell you what I read on Wednesday," he has said.[129] In his workspace, he likes to have books around him; in addition to those arranged on shelves, he keeps a small stack of antique books on urban topics on his desk—one on police brutality, another on prostitution—there for conceptual inspiration more than anything. But he discovered his major influences when he was young, and, like *Last Exit*, they tended to deal with the underbelly of the urban milieu. Of earlier African American literature, especially Richard Wright and James Baldwin, he explained, "I responded . . . because it was grounded in social realism," naming Wright's *Native Son* as a particular influence.[130] Price also took direction in tone and attitude from the Beats. He is famed for his social realism, but thanks to Lenny Bruce and the Beats, he makes a point of injecting his prose with a little more brash wit than the typical author in that genre.

His early influences weren't always strictly literary. Henry Miller's *Tropic of Cancer* made the writer's life seem like a goal in itself. Price latched on to Miller's description of his own existence: "I have the most enviable life, I don't have a pot to piss in but

I'm fucking everything that moves. I don't have to answer to any-body."[131] Martin Scorsese's *Mean Streets* made Price "yearn to do on paper what [he] just saw," and the 1950s scat singer Lord Buckley "just electrified urban talk for me," he says.[132]

By his early twenties, he'd read his foundational books and had an overwhelming compulsion to crystallize his own history in writ-ing. "Every night for the better part of a year, I would sit down with a record player, an old stack of 45's, some vodka, and work myself into a sensory memory trance that eventually became 'The Wander-ers,'" he says.[133] After this, he never again felt motivated to write on those literary subjects that became the most prevalent of his genera-tion—suburban domestic dramas, the spiritual and cultural strug-gles of middle-class immigrants, the latent rebellion of white-collar professional ennui. Instead, he gave brilliant literary treatment to a less-polished, less-entitled element of American experience.

Price reads less while in the midst of writing a book, and he steers clear of anything that might be too closely related to his own work, or too good, which is "like trying to sing while somebody else is sing-ing another song in the background," he says. He once made the casual mistake of reading *Sophie's Choice* while writing *The Breaks*. The book's singular hellishness threw him off track completely.[134]

Luckily, the *Sophie's Choice* incident proved only a minor hic-cup in his writing process. As Price entered his thirties, there would be major glitches. He began to find that his well of personal experi-ence had run dry: "My first four novels were sort of autobiographi-cal, and I was so fucking bored. I mean, what am I going to write about next? What I had for breakfast?"[135] Whether he realized it, he needed to get outside of himself, and when an opportunity pre-sented itself he jumped. More than eight years passed before he published another novel.

When producers came knocking, Price allowed himself to be wooed by the financial promise of the film industry. Once there, he wrote screenplays about things that had nothing to do with him or his own life, simply because the people paying his bills were telling him to. The change of course was what he needed to pull himself out of his rut. Unlike the exhausting string of eminent authors before him who tried their hand in Hollywood and failed (Fitzgerald and Nabokov among them), Price had a knack for the screenplay. He got an Oscar nomination for *The Color of Money* in his midthirties and was generally flying high.

He was also, "like every other idiot in the 1980s," developing a cocaine habit, and eventually found himself unable to write at all without it.[136] He now claims to have never written anything good while under its influence. "And here comes another day's worth of deluded flop-sweat trying to pass for art," he wrote of his routine at that time. Eventually, he quit "through self-disgust."[137]

Despite his success over ten years in Hollywood, Price didn't have the passion for screenwriting that he did for novels. "Some of the movies turned out good, but none of them were me," he has said. "I was not an artist on any of them. I was a craftsman on all of them."[138] Still, he acknowledged that the screenwriting ultimately helped him become a better novelist. He'd exhausted himself as a topic, and through screenwriting he learned how to mine other subjects for material. "Not everything has to be about my internal angst," he remembers realizing.[139] He began to look outward. "You can take your talent and go off and learn something, and then you can write about it as well as if not better than the stuff you know from personal experience. So I got kind of hooked on going out. Going out. Going out."[140]

The "going out" became perhaps the key ingredient in his writing process moving forward. For the first novels he wrote in his post-Hollywood era, *Clockers* and *Freedomland*, the going out meant shadowing cops and drug dealers in Jersey City. The routine became addictive; even after years of it, he'd bow to the temptation to take on just one more day out in the field, because that might be the day some experience would unfold and blow his mind, perhaps become a catalyst for his next novel. The going out was the fun part: the adrenaline rush of going out on a bust with the cops, of convincing a four-hundred-pound drug dealer you're not one yourself. He could hardly stop.

For Price's 2008 novel, *Lush Life*, the going out meant heading down to New York City's Lower East Side, where the novel takes place, and talking to whoever would give him the time of day. He knew he wanted a story that incorporated the myriad worlds coexisting in the legendary neighborhood: hipster, immigrant, yuppie; housing projects and lingering ethnic enclaves; the major and minor players in crime and punishment. He spent three years observing the neighborhood, hanging out in Schiller's Liquor Bar, which would become the model for the main character's workplace and the image on the book's cover; in the nearby projects, where a good chunk of the action takes place; and with the remaining Orthodox Jews, the Chinese immigrants, the cops—always looking for those quirks that give a place its texture.[141] He found himself particularly rapt by the jarring juxtapositions of gentrification, such as two side-by-side tenements he discovered that from the outside had nearly identical weathered brick facades. Behind one, though, was a yuppie couple's carefully redesigned apartment; behind the other, a boardinghouse for Chinese immigrants, who slept on narrow boards, several to a small, dank room—two worlds separated by nothing more than a century-old wall and, at the same time, by an enormous, less tangible chasm. These were precisely the anecdotes he'd been looking for.

Price reached a point where he had an ever-growing repertoire of such anecdotes at the ready, but still no story in which to deposit them. He needed an anchor around which he could organize the numerous elements. The novel finally coalesced around two real-life murders of bar-hopping white kids on the Lower East Side—both standard-issue muggings that got out of hand. "The [murder] investigation can legitimately enter all the worlds down there to come to a conclusion. It gave me access," he said.[142] Price had his point of entry.

Inevitably, it comes time to write. Price can get creative when it comes to evading writing, like a child trying to elude bedtime. Six months after a publisher bought *Clockers*, he had yet to write a word of it. "I was simply afraid," he says. He talked about it a lot, relayed anecdotes, got worked up, but there was nothing on the page. Ultimately, his editor took him to lunch, praised the ideas behind the book, then said, "Let me just ask you . . . What's the first sentence?" Price needed that jolt.[143]

He got down to writing, knowing the trick now was to turn everything he'd observed into something unique. The challenge, he says, is "making art and not in just compiling notes or compiling observations. You're meeting interesting people, then you have to take all that ocean of interaction and carve an allegory, carve a truth that is not a journalistic truth, but sometimes you can nudge it into a greater truth."[144] Although Price takes notes during his research phase—sketches of something he observed, a perfect line he heard someone say—he tends to find them less helpful than he'd been expecting. He partially blames his less-than-thorough note-taking skills, but he also realizes that he's not writing journalism. "I constantly have to remind myself: You can make stuff up," he says. "You're not gonna get in trouble by making stuff up."[145]

And he makes it up as he goes along, for the most part. "Usually, I don't have any plot in mind whatsoever, I just know that I'm interested in *this*, there's something *here* that I want to get into," he says. "The actual story can almost be like an afterthought."[146]

For Price, writing is inextricably linked to dialogue, his brand of which happens to be arguably the best of contemporary times.

Price, it turns out, takes his cues from the madmen—he talks to himself. "Basically I do improv with myself—that's how I get my dialogue. Sometimes I'll do it quietly, other times I'll be mouthing it. And I used to have a loft on Great Jones and Broadway . . . and I rigged myself up this office, and my daughter was four years old, five years old, and you know how they have playdates? Well, I was in my office—I think I was writing *Clockers*—so I'm sitting there going, 'Fuck you, motherfucker, I'll fuck you up, I'm-a fuck your ass shut.' And I look up and there's my daughter with her little playdate, this other five-year-old girl . . . The next day, I got an office in the Flatiron Building."[147]

The dialogue is the easy part. Getting the prose to read like something other than deliberate prose presents a higher challenge. "With dialogue it's pretty much all there, the first shot at it. I have a much more difficult time with the King's English, you know, descriptive paragraphs. I torture them to death to get them to work."[148] The quest for perfect prose can keep Price frozen in his office for hours.

That office is an ever-evolving concept. Like his writing routine, it has not remained a constant. He's kept an office at home and has also secured one deliberately outside of and separate from it. The truth, at least over much of his career, is that he has maintained both, and he'd try working alternately in one if the other is failing. "I have offices all over the place and I avoid work everywhere," he has said.[149] He had a home office in his NoHo loft, as well as in his town house in the Gramercy Park neighborhood a few years later, with a big centerpiece desk graced with trinkets and mementos, plus a coffee table holding notebooks and drafts—the kind of overtly literary space he never had in his youth. But just one office located within ten paces of the distractions of home life back then wasn't enough. "It's important to me to have a place to work outside of where I live. So I have always found myself an office. I go off to work as if I had a clock to punch; at the end of the day I come home as if I had just gotten off the commuter train."[150] The concept of the workspace, it would seem, became a continuous experiment in tricking himself into working.

Today, though, Price seems to have settled into a simpler arrangement. When he moved into a Harlem brownstone in 2008 with the writer Lorraine Adams, for the first time he placed "this really fancy 1948 desk" he'd bought in an open space in the house. Books line one wall of the expansive room, along with some of his favorite photography prints, but he keeps the desk itself clean, tidying it up at the end of every day so it's ready for him the next morning. Both Adams and Price, married since 2012, work from the house all day. "For the first time in my life, I feel like this place is my writers' colony. This is my Yaddo," he says.[151] Price no longer even requires a door to close between him and the rest of the world.

Not that he no longer procrastinates. Like so many authors, Price confesses that he hates writing. "The only thing worse than writing is not writing," he once told the *London Telegraph*.[152] Which could be the key to the whole thing—choosing the anxiety of writing over the small death of not doing it. Still, it takes him a while to get there. Price has admitted to spending a good part of the morning "reading the *Daily News*, answering phone calls, lining up paper clips, doing anything but working."[153] These days Price writes on a MacBook, but up until the writing of 2008's *Lush Life*, he handwrote everything. Which means that only recently has the Internet become a danger—he wastes two or three hours on it on a typical day. He can put off writing until as late as 2 p.m. on the worst days. But then, at some point, inevitably, he says, "I just somehow get whatever Word document up there, and next thing I know I'm staring at it, next thing I know I'm fiddling with it."[154]

Once it finally starts, the writing can proceed intensively for three to six hours. Price is a writer who edits as he goes. "Typically, what I'll do is write a page, reread it, edit it, write half a page more, and then I'll go back to the very first thing I wrote that morning . . . I don't know whether I'm editing, reediting, or writing something new, but it's kind of a creeping, incremental style of writing. I always sort of half-know where I'm going."[155] Some days involve more revision than others. "Sometimes all I did was fix and fiddle," he says, "and some days I just wrote great gouts of original stuff."[156]

The writing can go quickly or at a painfully slow crawl, depending on the book, and on how in sync Price finds himself with the material and especially the characters. *Ladies' Man* burst forth—he wrote the first draft in just three weeks, with a complete outline of the plot and structure already solidified in his head. *The Breaks*, on the other hand, was tortuous. It was the last of his four early novels, and he was burned out on his own life. He finished that one before taking up screenwriting full-time, but it was slow and arduous. There were two other novels that he started and discarded. The writing slowed to a crawl and finally to a full stop. Nothing was clicking. Price admits now that at the time, his only motivation to write was a fear of his star dimming. The result was empty.[157]

Once he finishes a draft, there's still a substantial round of editing to be dealt with. Price tends to overwrite. He'd written one thousand pages of *Clockers* when his editor stepped in. Over the following year and a half, they started over at page one three times, getting it down to a far more manageable six hundred pages by the time it was published. When it came time to edit *Lush Life*, he and his editor spent six months trimming two hundred pages.[158]

Today, Price has settled into a more sanguine approach to writing, and he's more grounded all around than in his sudden-success youth. He's completely cleaned up—the hardest stuff he indulges in these days is a glass of wine here and there. He also doesn't do much at all outside of writing. He might drop in on the occasional party, but most of his activities stem from either writing or researching the writing. The kid who was once so smitten by his own talent has given way to a man who has found, as all thinking people must, that the more you know, the more ignorant you understand yourself to be. "The older I get, the more insecure I feel about my work, although I do think it's better," he says.[159] Richard Price, in the end, is a writer's writer after all.

A DAY IN THE WRITER'S LIFE . . .

Richard Price rises and, by 10 a.m. or so, meanders to his desk. He spends a good part of the morning procrastinating. By late morning, though, he usually admits the inevitable, that there's nothing left but to start writing. He does so in fits and starts, edits as he goes, reviews a paragraph as soon as he writes it, sometimes goes back to the very beginning. If he's writing dialogue, which is often, he might be overheard talking to himself, working the lines out to an empty room. That's on the writing days—Price can spend years on research, heading out every morning with an enthusiasm he finds difficult to keep in check. At night, Price might settle in with a glass of wine, or he might go out on the town if someone drags him. It's a far cry from his hectic youth, when writing as often as not involved booze or drugs, and the words came out almost too easily.

AUTODIDACTS

$$5$$

EDITH WHARTON

In the opening scene of Edith Wharton's famous novel *The Age of Innocence*, the young bachelor Newland Archer arrives late to the opera. It's a calculated move on his part and, rather than revealing a maverick nature, shows his tendency to fall in line with expectations: Among the nineteenth-century New York elite, arriving early to the opera is "not the thing" to do, and Newland is one to oblige. Once inside, Newland's eyes cross the expanse of the theater and come to rest on his fiancée, May Welland, perfect marriage material with her simple good looks and exacting adherence to standards of culture and propriety. Still, Newland hopes to broaden her narrow worldview, because "in matters intellectual and artistic, Newland Archer felt himself distinctly the superior of these chosen specimens of old New York gentility"—even if outwardly he adheres to their cultivated Philistinism. In the midst of this reverie, a woman—at a glance beautiful, unconventional, and exotic— walks into May's box, her cousin Ellen Olenska. The reader now understands precisely where Newland Archer's life is headed.

This plot foreshadowing was entirely deliberate, as were most things about Edith Wharton. She always knew each of her characters and their fates this well, having worked out "from the first exactly what is going to happen to every one of them."[160] She worked hard to project the outcome at the outset. "It is always a necessity to me that the note of inevitableness should be sounded at the very opening of my tale," she wrote in her autobiography.[161] Her success in this endeavor has become a defining trademark of her fiction.

When Wharton was young, it would have seemed anything but inevitable that she would become a great writer, even if the signs were there. She was born into the same New York City upper class that doomed Newland Archer. Wharton's clan lived insulated from the wider concerns of the day and avoided the kind of serious thought that might lead members to question established belief systems. She never should have picked up a book, much less a pen, save to write the occasional conscientious letter. And after a childhood of obvious but unnurtured literary inclinations, for a couple of decades she never did. Instead, she married "well" and fell into step with her set, living a life of narrow leisure with her happy-to-oblige husband. Wharton would not become a published author until her late thirties, when her innate desire to write books finally—and indeed inevitably—bubbled to the surface. She would go on to write a total of forty-four books.

Daisy Chanler, a good friend of Wharton's and also a writer, liked to joke that both Wharton and Theodore Roosevelt (another good friend) were self-made men—the joke being that while neither had to earn her or his own fortune, both had to cultivate the defiant independence that allowed them to break out of their stagnant cultural scene.[162] Despite her early creative inclinations, Wharton described a "childhood and youth of complete intellectual isolation."[163] Reflecting on her younger years, she wrote of "grow[ing] up in an atmosphere where the arts are simply nonexistent" and "every aspiration ignored, or looked at askance."[164]

Still, she had access to her father's gentlemanly library, assembled more out of convention than a genuine love of literature, and rarely used by anyone aside from the strange little girl who read any book she could get her hands on and wrote story after story on any piece of paper that came her way. The list of formative books Wharton catalogs in her autobiography goes on for two dense pages and includes historians, memoirists, poets (with French poets listed separately), French prose writers, art critics and historians, philosophers, essayists, and, listed last, novelists.[165] Among these, no single influence stands out in those early years, but the cumulative education they offered provided a clear foundation for her own writing career. In the absence of traditional schooling or literary mentors in her life, these books were her teachers, showing Wharton how to go about writing good prose.

In adulthood, specific influences gradually emerged from the varied and extensive pack (Wharton read literature in five different languages). Nathaniel Hawthorne, Honoré de Balzac, Stendhal, Leo Tolstoy, George Eliot, and, of course, Henry James gave Wharton a template to work from—all were authors able to make incisive cultural critiques via stories that swept through the gauntlet of a particular time and place's social milieu, or as she explained in her book *The Writing of Fiction*, "their viewing each character first of all as a product of particular material and social conditions."[166] But it wasn't just fiction that informed her writing. Wharton's reading of philosophers and social scientists helped hone her ability to dissect the world around her.[167] There's a straight line between Thorstein Veblen's *The Theory of the Leisure Class* and Wharton's work, for example.

It's no surprise that Wharton believed reading to be the crucial element in the development of a writer. "Technique can be cultivated," she wrote to Teddy Roosevelt's younger sister, Corinne Roosevelt Robinson, who at the time had a book of her own in the works, "and chiefly, I think, by reading only the best and rarest things, until one instinctively rejects the easy, accommodating form."[168] To the writer educated by her own will, and in isolation from either encouragement or kindred spirits, reading would have to serve as mentor, inspiration, and guide.

Wharton wrote a novel by age fifteen and had poems published in the *Atlantic Monthly* by age eighteen, but then her literary output fell off a curious and definitive cliff. That natural urge to "make up," as she called it, had been stifled by the time she reached adulthood, a life of literature not at that time considered a proper path for a woman of Wharton's standing (or any woman at all). Her husband, Teddy, shared none of her intellectual curiosity and preferred activities that taxed the mind less than literature and art.

There's little record of Wharton's first efforts in literature as an adult. Her writing then was something she tended to keep to herself, and she didn't yet keep a journal. But even in her twenties she was cultivating the kind of intellectual friendships that would fuel her writing later. She did publish a short story at the age of twenty-nine, but follow-up efforts were sporadic at best, until she cowrote a book on interior design at thirty-seven and finally published her first novel at thirty-nine.[169]

Even then, however, she had yet to attain a command of her craft. "With all my trying, I can't *write* yet," she wrote to her great friend Walter Berry during her work on that first novel, *The Valley of Decision*.[170] At first, she wrote by fits and starts, setting the work aside when social obligations or travel arose. But ultimately, one opportune event pushed her toward total command during the writing of *The House of Mirth*. As was common at the time, the novel was being serialized in *Scribner's Magazine* before publication in book form. "I had let months drift by without really tackling my subject," she recalled. And then the serialization before hers was canceled, and *The House of Mirth* was on deck. She accepted the moved-up publication date, leaving only four or five months to complete the novel. The pressure inspired a daily work routine that up to then had been erratic. "The effect on my imagination," she wrote, was magnificent and played a central role in turning her finally into a masterful writer.[171] With *The House of Mirth*, Wharton discovered not only the motivating powers of the dead-line, but also the value of a strict, regular writing schedule.

Sure as she was of the first and last pages, Wharton didn't always know *how* her characters were to arrive at their fates when she wrote the first lines. Details often escaped her until the novel took shape; she considered them unnecessary in the early stages for their lack of impact on the plot. "I never know more than the main lines of any novel that I am writing. The subsidiary incidents develop as I write," she explained.[172] It wouldn't be a happy ending for Newland Archer, she knew, but that gripping moment when he futilely declares his love for Ellen Olenska in her drawing room probably came as a surprise to Wharton as well. "These people of mine, whose ultimate destiny I know so well, walk to it by ways unrevealed to me beforehand," she wrote.[173]

This two-pronged approach—part studied control, part spontaneous creation—again finds a likeness in Wharton's own life. On the opening page of her autobiography, *A Backward Glance*, she grapples with the simultaneous need to follow habits and to break free of them. She denounces habit as a "producer of old age." Two sentences later, she admits, "Habit is necessary." Wharton built her days and years around this seemingly contradictory belief system. Mornings were always for writing, often from her bed, where she made herself famous for dropping blue pages filled with line after line of her tightly controlled handwriting, always in black ink, on the floor to be fetched and organized by the help.[174] Wharton pecked away at a typewriter soon after it was invented in the 1870s, but didn't take to the machine and never did type up her own works.[175] Her secretary, however, might retype up to ten revisions of a work.[176] She had a writing board with an inkpot fitted for use in bed. She'd have papers scattered around the comforter, plus her small dogs to keep her company, and write straight through the morning. The image of her thus situated became so iconic that in 2012, *Vogue* magazine re-created it in its pages, with the model Natalia Vodianova posing as Wharton.

Afternoons were reserved for life's pleasures, as conceived by Edith Wharton: adventure, conversation, and cultured living. She shied away from the showy social events that were her birthright, preferring instead small gatherings of people who shared her interests. In 1904, she bought her first car, at the time an instrument for leisurely adventures, and she often took friends on tours around the countryside in the afternoons. In the evenings, she loved to assemble intimate groups with whom she could enjoy a few hours of intellectual stimulation.

On a larger scale, Wharton continually fed her appetite for travel and often organized months-long trips around Europe or, once, to North Africa. But hers was a controlled sense of adventure—adventure never quite wrested control from Edith Wharton, in her life as in her work. And indeed, she stuck to her morning writing routine even when traveling. On one visit to Berlin, she threw a childish fit over the placement of the bed in her room at the Hotel Esplanade; she needed it facing the window in order to work from it, she complained, and it had been otherwise situated.[177]

Wharton always had several writing projects under way at once, a by-product of not a wandering mind, but a deliberate strategy. "I have never been able to write one novel without having another going at the same time, or at least writing 2 or 3 short stories, and I always return to my chief work stimulated by the change," she wrote.[178] Between 1907 and 1912, she worked on four novels simultaneously, though perhaps this was overdoing it, since during that time she didn't finish any of them.[179] A more successful result came when she temporarily abandoned *The Custom of the Country* as the idea for *The Reef* came to her all at once.[180]

Wharton knew that coming back to a work with a fresh mind could result in a more perceptive revision. She liked to leave a manuscript alone for a chunk of time before coming back in for the final edit. "I shd [*sic*] greatly like to revise the last 6 chapters after an interval of a fortnight," she wrote to Morton Fullerton when finishing up *The Reef*, before emphasizing that it's the kind of thing "Scribner always lets me do."[181]

Some projects were left alone so long they fermented into different works altogether. She made a habit, in fact, of recycling work that hadn't quite clicked before into seemingly fresh pieces of literature.[182] A novel she worked on in the first years of the twentieth century, called "Disintegration," would never be finished, for example, but its characters and subject would find new life in *The Mother's Recompense*, published in 1925.[183] And in 1913 and 1914 she began work on a novel titled "Literature," also never finished, but much of it finally co-opted for her 1929 novel *Hudson River Bracketed*.[184]

Wharton always kept a donnée book (a French word meaning the nascent elements of a story) in which she recorded the plot outlines, little one-liners, social critiques, and clever analogies that would someday be used in one of her books. "Mrs. Plinth's opinions were as hard to move as her drawing room furniture" was a particularly biting one that made its way into the short story "Xingu."[185] The keeping of a personal journal, on the other hand, was not something that loomed large in Wharton's writing life. She didn't have one at all, in fact, until 1918, the year she turned fifty-six.[186] The records of Wharton's daily life existed more thoroughly in her letters, which she composed every day and which served as a valuable writing exercise.

Those letters were written chiefly to her great friends, many of them fellow writers, along with a smattering of other culturally or intellectually interesting types. Wharton cultivated her friendships with the zeal of a curator putting together a fine art exhibit. She used them for the conversation she so valued, but also as sounding boards and sources of continuing education, which in turn fed her writing. The Frenchman Paul Bourget became her first writer friend, when he came to America around 1893 on assignment for the *New York Herald*.[187] Bernhard Berenson and Charles Eliot Norton also loomed large.

Walter Berry, the rare member of Wharton's original New York set who shared her love of reading, writing, and all things cultural (and whom she may have been in love with), served as her lifelong adviser and first reader. "The instinct to write had always been there," Wharton wrote; "it was [Berry] who drew it forth, shaped it and set it free."[188] Minnie Jones, Wharton's sister-in-law, enthusiastically conducted research and confirmed places and dates for Wharton over several decades. Morton Fullerton, a writer of marginal talent with whom Wharton embarked on the only known passionate love affair of her life, helped to expand the emotional range of her fiction and also for a time served as an early reader. Fullerton came and went, but Jones and Berry were constants. At times, the relationship with Berry became so crucial that Wharton read her morning's work to him every evening for critique.[189]

And then, most famously, there was Henry James, a major early influence; Wharton revered him before she became a famous writer herself. They became tentative friends at first, and later the closest of friends, but as their friendship deepened, she grew less impressed with his work—even as she became more devoted to him—and in fact proclaimed his later works unreadable.[190] Wharton resented being seen as his protégée, or as a female version of him. Still, his presence in her writing life was unmistakable. Sometimes the influence on her works is overt: For example, the name for Newland Archer's character is taken from two James characters, *The Portrait of a Lady*'s Isabel Archer and *The American*'s Christopher Newman. And it was thanks to the urgings of James, along with Walter Berry, that Wharton turned her eye to the New York scene she knew so well in the first place, when she was thinking of setting her second novel, like her first, in Italy.[191] But James's true influence came in the form of a decades-long exchange of ideas during travels and dinners and car rides. He encouraged her to use her "ironic and satiric gifts" in her writing and was a longtime early reader of her work—at first she was devastated by his critiques, but in time learned to appreciate them on a professional level.[192]

The almost two decades of Wharton's adult life when she did not call herself a novelist provided endless material for her work—life lived in the leisure of Newport and Europe; making the rounds of the New York "season." The resistance she began to feel and finally to exhibit against her privileged, provincial set would show up again and again in her characters. She worked hard to approach this and other topics with a detached sentiment. "The subjective writer lacks the power of getting far enough away from his story to view it as a whole and relate it to its setting," she observed in *The Writing of Fiction*.[193] That detachment could lead her to be callous in her borrowing from real life: A carriage accident in which a neighbor fractured her skull and died went straight into *The Fruit of the Tree*.[194] And the infamous sledding accident in *Ethan Frome* came from an actual tragedy in the winter of 1904 near her home in Lenox, Massachusetts.[195]

Wharton would strenuously deny accusations that any of her characters had come from real-life templates. "Any one gifted with the least creative faculty knows the absurdity of such a charge," she wrote.[196] Still, those characters arrived from the ether via the fashionable New York streets where real people lived. And once she betrayed herself when she said to her friend Bernhard Berenson in a restaurant while looking at a young man at the next table, "When I see such a type my first thought is how to put him into my next novel."[197]

Acknowledging a tendency to borrow from real-life characters would have offended Wharton's own reverence for privacy, a principle that in two senses of the word governed her philosophy on life. At home, she required a definitive space of her own—privacy from daily life. She abhorred layouts that were too open to enable cloistered thought. When she built her house in Lenox, the only home she ever designed from the ground up, she not only designated an entire suite for herself—including a bedroom and a sitting room containing her desk—but she had it placed on the second floor above the library, to ensure full quietude.[198] After moving to Paris, she chose her apartment in large part for its equivalent sense of privacy, its hushed tone and separate entrances to each room.[199] Every morning, she remained shut inside those rooms, emerging only after a satisfactory morning of reclusive work.

In the other sense of the word, she went to great lengths to preserve a sense of privacy from public scrutiny, going so far as to kill the publication of certain works that threatened to expose more of her personal life than she felt comfortable with.[200] Self-promotion was poison to Wharton. When she could, she burned letters she'd written to others. In her autobiography, she omitted key events in her life, including her relationship with Fullerton, and only glanced briefly over her marriage, divorce, and other events that touched on money or sex.

Her omissions were calculated, as Wharton paid very close attention to detail, in life as in writing. As one example of her meticulous consideration of the way in which words form the intended effect, Wharton biographer Hermione Lee assembled a series of edits in a crucial sentence near the end of *The House of Mirth*, when Lily Bart is about to slip away.[201] The sentence was first written as: "She settled herself into a position."

Upon first revision, it became: "She settled herself into an easier position, pressing a little."

In the next iteration, she added to the end of the sentence: "into an easier position, hollowing her arm to receive the little head, and holding her breath lest a sound should disturb the child's sleep."

Wharton subsequently made another subtle tweak—"child's sleep" becomes "sleeping child."

The line finally appeared in the novel as: "She settled herself into an easier position, hollowing her arm to pillow the round downy head, and holding her breath lest a sound should disturb the sleeping child."

In those days long before word-processing software made revising a matter of a couple of mouse clicks, Wharton engaged in fervent cutting and pasting in the literal sense. When a draft would become too marked up to remain sensible, she'd paste strips of paper over certain passages, rewriting and revising those words on fresh paper. Sometimes the original page would be cut apart as well, and new passages inserted between previously neighboring paragraphs.[202]

Creating a sense of the inevitable from page one, it turns out, required many manipulations, the stamping out of behind-the-scenes uncertainty, the pasting over of efforts that didn't work. It required that dead ends be reversed and side plots rearranged. In Wharton's life and in her work, inevitable was anything but, in the beginning.

A DAY IN THE WRITER'S LIFE . . .

For Edith Wharton, waking up did not necessarily cor-relate with getting up. Instead, she'd work right there in bed, her little dogs keeping her company, a writing board fitted with an inkpot enabling the task. She never emerged before lunchtime, after which her writing was done for the day. Even during her frequent and extended travels, mornings were for writing, and her hotel rooms had to be arranged to accommodate it. In the afternoons and through the evenings, Wharton fed her love of a few close friends, conversation, and adventure, often taking visitors around the countryside in her car, a novelty at the time. At night, Wharton might have hosted an intimate dinner, or she might have read her day's work aloud to her great friend Walter Berry, her most consistent literary confidant over the four decades of her career.

6

GEORGE ORWELL

"Down and out." These first three words in the title of George Orwell's first book also encapsulate his approach to writing. The key for Orwell was a denial of creature comforts. Wherever he might encounter luxury, he eschewed it. Whenever he might find respite from penury in his "lower-upper-middle-class" background, he turned his back on it. His penchant for asceticism seeped into his writing, permeating his string of living quarters and his routine. Ultimately, through these conditions, he developed a writing style that was inextricably linked to his environment of manufactured hardship. Orwell found his voice as an author through the down-and-out lifestyle, and his continued dedication to living austerely helped him become one of the great writers of the twentieth century.

As he tells it in his famous essay "Why I Write," Orwell knew he would be a writer by the age of five or six, the way some children "know" they will be astronauts, the difference to be found in the ultimate realization of his aspiration. By nature, he narrated his own life in his head, as if it were a story in midconstruction.

"For fifteen years or more," he wrote, "I was carrying out a literary exercise . . . [T]his was the making up of a continuous 'story' about myself, a sort of diary existing only in the mind." Orwell pushed a door open and entered a room; the words that sprang into his head at that moment? "He pushed the door open and entered a room."

His brain functioned like a writer's without any prompting, but he resisted this impulse to become one well into adulthood. As a respectable descendant of gentility, he first went into what he thought was a more appropriate career with the Indian Imperial Police in Burma. He wouldn't stick with that career path, but it gave him his first dose of the kind of adventure that would fuel his writing. When Orwell finally gave in to his writing ambitions, the method of self-narration he'd honed growing up expanded into far more sweeping plots through experiences like the one in Burma, as his characters, plot twists, and settings were invariably rooted in his own dogged experiences.

Orwell was not a writer prone to invention. He needed concrete events upon which to draw, that person entering a room whose actions he could describe. His first book, *Down and Out in Paris and London*, rose out of his time in Paris—washing dishes in a restaurant and scraping by in the bohemian Left Bank—and living among the tramps of East London. His second, *Burmese Days*, drew on his years as an officer in Burma. On it went like this: *The Clergyman's Daughter* drawing on his time as a schoolmaster, *The Road to Wigan Pier* on his time in the working-class towns and coal mines in northern England, and *Homage to Catalonia* on his service in the Spanish Civil War. He modified the approach slightly with his last and most famous two novels, in which his writing had become acutely motivated by politics, and he allowed the ideas to ferment for long periods in order to come up with the ideal construct. But even then, as we'll see, he required input from others in order to realize his novels.

Orwell's childhood prophecy only started to manifest at age

twenty-four. After resigning his post in Burma, he decided to live in London on the savings he'd accumulated during the previous five years and figure out how to be a writer—a move that may sound familiar to anyone who once arrived in a big city with a big dream. He rented a plain, cheap room on London's Portobello Road (not then the tony place it has become today) and figured that at his current rate of expenditure, his savings would last him a year. With a guileless tenacity, he got down to his self-administered apprenticeship.

At the end of that year, though, despite consistent efforts, his writing went nowhere. His one writer friend, Ruth Pitter, suggested that instead of inventing stories, he might do better following that age-old advice "write what you know." Orwell took this advice, but instead of reflecting on his accumulated experiences, he headed out into the field to gather new ones. He posed as one of the vagrants of East London, which provided him with material that proved important in that it was grippingly dramatic and dealt with the downtrodden. He'd sometimes go undercover in the slums for a few weeks at a time, and it was this experience that finally freed him of the clichés and contrivances he'd been struggling with up until then.[203] He found he could write about this experience with clarity and from a singular perspective. It brought him to the breakthrough he'd been waiting for, along with the onset of the direct, unembellished prose style that would characterize his writing going forward, like in this passage from *Down and Out*:

> It is altogether curious, your first contact with poverty. You have thought so much about poverty—it is the thing you have feared all your life, the thing you knew would happen to you sooner or later; and it, [sic] is all so utterly and prosaically different. You thought it would be quite simple; it is extraordinarily complicated. You thought it would be terrible; it is merely squalid and boring.

Such prose ultimately became synonymous with the name Orwell. Before that could happen, however, the name Orwell had to be invented. The pseudonym—he was born Eric Blair—was very likely a tool for preserving his privacy as well as a psychological ruse, part of an effort to get himself writing in a certain style; his writing as Orwell stood in contrast to the work he did as Eric Blair, allowing him to let go of sentimental propensities that had marred his early work. "One can write nothing readable unless one constantly struggles to efface one's personality," he wrote in "Why I Write." Surely the pseudonym played some role in that effacement.

Like his clear prose, the plain room became a running theme as well, garnished with the mere fundamentals of furniture, lighting, and functionality. After Portobello Road, there was his sister's house in Bramley, a rundown onetime vicarage that she and her husband could not afford to repair. Later, a faded room in a house in Hayes, where he took a position as a schoolmaster. As he prepared to move to London in 1934, a friend referred him to a flat in the respectable Bayswater neighborhood, which he declined in favor of "somewhere in the slums." He ultimately ended up in Hampstead, albeit in a dingy room overlooking the back of a row of shops.[204] After he married in 1936, he moved into a small, ramshackle house in the country with no electricity or hot water, three miles from the nearest town. There, he wrote on his typewriter in the downstairs room that also served as a sitting and dining room. His wife, to her great credit, remained convinced that with this man, she'd hit the jackpot.

Orwell may have entertained only one exception to his general rule of asceticism during his writing life; one that, ironically, was born of necessity: intermittent spells of living with his well-off parents while writing *Down and Out*. But even that comfort was alleviated by his frequent ventures into the slums in search of more material.[205]

An air of melancholy became a balm to Orwell, so much so that he could hardly do without it. "This afternoon," he wrote to a friend in 1931, "wanting to be in a gloomy frame of mind in order to get on with what I was writing, I went into Kensal Rise cemetery."[206] Establishing a dreary atmosphere became so central to Orwell's writing life that once he'd attained literary and financial success, he went to great lengths to re-create a sense of privation. After the publication of *Animal Farm*, which brought wealth and renown, he longed to escape both, telling the writer Arthur Koestler, "Everyone keeps coming at me wanting me to lecture, to write commissioned booklets, to join this and that, etc—you don't know how I pine to get free of it all and have time to think again."[207]

This was just around the time that he absconded to Jura, securing a remote house on the little-populated Scottish island, a twenty-four-hour journey from London if one is being optimistic, including a multimile walk on foot for the final stretch. Upon arrival, visitors would be greeted by a lonely white farmhouse, bereft of humanity's imprint for miles in every direction. They would also enjoy freedom from electricity and running water. With the house on Jura, Orwell achieved his goal of re-creating the poverty under which he'd worked before, finding success and then some. He rarely took a break from writing (unless he was researching), but when he got to Jura, he claimed to leave it alone completely for a stretch—"I needed 2 months of complete idleness and it has done me good," he wrote at the time.[208]

When he did start writing again, it resumed as an all-consuming activity. As in Orwell's early days, there was no schedule, no routine; there was just writing. "All the time his typewriter would go tap tap tap in the upstairs rooms," his brother-in-law recalled. "And half the night I'd hear his typewriter go tap tap tap."[209] His brother-in-law's observation later echoed those of visitors to Jura, who reported tapping at all hours as Orwell worked on *1984* in the bedroom above the kitchen, at a small desk in front of a window through which the not-so-green Scottish countryside might remind him how melancholy an existence he'd managed to achieve.[210]

During the few years that he held full-time employment, he wrote unceasingly at night. When he worked in a bookstore in London, he'd walk down to chat with the morning clerk, then return to his barren room to get started on three hours of writing, continuing until it was time for his shift. In the evenings he'd write again, unless a social obligation kept him from it.[211] Putting words on the page didn't induce anxiety for Orwell, just a general fatigue. He once claimed that writing is "a horrible, exhausting struggle," but still he wrote unceasingly.[212]

Orwell's dedication to writing superseded all else that might be considered important in life, including friendships and romances. Biographers and other Orwell experts often conclude that Orwell was simply awkward with women, but the truth is that Orwell maintained several dalliances during his youth, though he kept his love interests always at an arm's length. That changed to a certain extent when he met his future wife. But even after he married, the union seemed to work only because Eileen sacrificed her own ambitions in service of his. Eileen herself once said, "His writing comes before anybody." Even on his wedding day, he found time for it.[213]

Perhaps it goes without saying that writer's block seldom struck Orwell. But the rare occasions when it did hit coincided with the times he'd run out of life experiences to draw from. At this point, he'd inevitably dive into another extreme episode, living as a vagrant in the slums, or joining the action in the Spanish Civil War, or moving to a desolate Scottish isle, undergoing long periods of research before spewing forth a book.

When he did get started on a project, he worked quickly. Orwell wrote *Down and Out* in nine or ten months, following almost five years of research. After letting the idea incubate for years, if not decades, he was relentless in the writing of *1984*, going at it until 3:30 in the morning and then waking at 7:45 to get started again.[214]

Similarly, he had the "main outlines" of *Animal Farm* in mind for six years before writing the novel out in a few months.[215] It finally took shape after a very specific aha moment in the small village of Wallington, where he lived. There, he saw a young boy driving a carthorse along a path too small to properly accommodate it. The boy whipped the horse each time it balked at going farther, and as he watched, Orwell became struck with the impression that if animals were to become aware of their strength in relation to humans, humans would lose their power over them. To him, it was the perfect metaphor to explain the suppression of the proletariat at the hands of the rich, a concept he'd been eager to examine in his fiction. "I proceeded to analyse Marx's theory from the animals' point of view," he said. "From this point of departure, it was not difficult to elaborate the story."[216]

The crudeness of the first draft didn't concern him the way it concerns so many writers. Instead, Orwell wrote almost constantly—especially while working on his later books, when taking breaks to earn outside income was no longer a necessity—to get that first draft down on paper, then edited and revised obsessively to shape the work into its ultimate form. "The rough draft is always a ghastly mess bearing little relation to the finished result, but all the same it is the main part of job," he told his publisher in 1947.[217] That famous first line of *1984*—"It was a bright cold day in April, and the clocks were striking thirteen"—came into the world as the far less compelling "It was a cold, blowy day in early April, and a million radios were striking thirteen." Those radios became "innumerable clocks" and then finally, brilliantly, just "the clocks," while "blowy" became "bright."[218] Manuscripts show a similar amount of self-editing through the entire novel. For Orwell, it was most important to secure the hunk of clay first and worry about sculpting it later.

Orwell arrived at his spare style by reading the work of many other authors, internalizing the styles of his favorites. He drew on the their work in many ways, often blatantly. From a very early age, Orwell appreciated literature with a political bent, especially Jonathan Swift's *Gulliver's Travels*, which he read at least seven times during his lifetime, starting on the eve of his eighth birthday.[219] Both men—Swift in the eighteenth century and Orwell in the twentieth—were geniuses of the political novel, and *Gulliver* served as a clear template for *Animal Farm*, less in actual content than in style and intent, with its satirical suspicion of European governments and man's inherent corruptibility. "He is one of the writers I admire with least reserve, and *Gulliver's Travels*, in particular, is a book which it seems impossible for me to grow tired of," Orwell wrote in the essay "Politics vs. Literature: An Examination of *Gulliver's Travels*" in 1946.

Years earlier, Orwell took even more direct inspiration in the writing of *Down and Out* from Jack London's *The People of the Abyss*, which he first read as a teenager.[220] To create his book, London had taken to the slums of London's East End, just as Orwell would do three decades later, masquerading as one of the downtrodden in order to offer a firsthand account of the sad conditions.

For his last great masterpiece, Orwell looked to Yevgeny Zamyatin's dystopian novel *We*, translated into English in 1924, set in a future city built entirely of glass, enabling the government to easily monitor its citizenry. The novel contains a Big Brother–like figure called the Benefactor, a protagonist who comes to rebel against the dehumanizing totalitarianism of the country's leaders, and even, yes, a clock that can strike thirteen. Orwell read *We* in 1946 when he reviewed it for the *Tribune*, and he published *1984* three years later.[221] The influence is unmistakable and borderline controversial. One can easily imagine that in our current litigious age, a lawsuit would have been filed within hours of *1984*'s appearance on the bestseller list. Oprah has ended careers for lesser sins.

But it's no surprise. Orwell never had trouble with the writing part of writing. It was the subject matter that tied him in knots.

He relied on historical events for inspiration as well. *1984* was shaped in part by a 1944 meeting of the Allied leaders, near the end of World War II. He already had the book in mind, but watching that meeting he became convinced of a plot among the leaders to divide the world,[222] crystallizing the cynicism that defined the novel in Orwell's mind.

The Newspeak of *1984* was inspired largely by the work of the linguist and philosopher C. K. Ogden, who created a simplified version of English that he believed would become a universal language. Early on, Orwell was a proponent of Basic English, as Ogden named it—it satisfied Orwell's admiration for straightforward, clear language. But in the years just before writing *1984*, Orwell came to denounce Basic English as a negative force on nuanced thinking, then caricatured it with the propagandizing Newspeak.

Orwell held his works in progress close to the vest, rarely allowing anyone to read them. In his nascent writing days in London, he allowed only Ruth Pitter to review his work—he was writing bad poetry at the time, and it was she who encouraged him to turn to prose.[223] Later, his wife often lamented that he did not use her as a sounding board while he worked. Only during the writing of *Animal Farm* did he share his progress, reading his work to her at the end of the day in bed—the only warm place in their frigid flat—and encouraging her suggestions.[224]

Orwell wrote his books on a typewriter, but his handwritten journals proved as critical to his writing process as the writing itself. His trim cursive—illegible despite its tidiness—covered page after page in notebook after notebook, informing his books with their firsthand record of events. He kept one such diary during his research in the coal-mining towns of northern England for what would become *The Road to Wigan Pier*.[225] The journal became another tool for drawing on life experiences. He wrote in journals consistently over the course of his life, often keeping several going at once on different subjects: one for politics, one for home life, and so forth. The entire first draft of *Down and Out*, in fact, was written as a diary, subsequently undergoing several revisions before being accepted by a publisher.[226]

Orwell's intensity, with regard to his journals, his many drafts, and his research, is perhaps unmatched. Ultimately, his fanatical dedication to his writing, alongside a life of self-imposed hardship, may have killed him—Orwell died of a tuberculosis infection that most believe he could have easily prevented, just seven months after *1984*'s publication and acquired during the writing of that novel in the harsh, unforgiving confines of Jura. He was forty-six years old.

A DAY IN THE WRITER'S LIFE . . .

George Orwell wrote what he knew, after he'd gone out and lived it, always keeping a notebook along the way. He might spend months in the research phase, rising each day to unknown adventures. After finally returning to whatever barren room he inhabited at the moment—a chair, a table, and nothing more if he could help it—he'd write almost constantly. He wrote upon waking, in the afternoon, and in the dead hours of the night. If he took breaks, it was to tend his garden. If the writing atmosphere ever became too cheery, he dampened it. The first drafts poured out of him. They invariably needed work, but their faults didn't concern him, so long as he had completed the work. He'd then revise it over and over until, when things went well, he had a masterpiece on his hands.

PLOTTING AHEAD

about literature, and exposed her to London literary circles. Leslie was steeped in London's literary life (his first wife was William Thackeray's daughter; his second was Virginia's mother), which seeped into the Stephen home, bringing a string of renowned writers like Henry James and James Russell Lowell into their drawing room.

Reading became the only activity in Woolf's life to rival in importance the writing itself. For her, reading and writing were very nearly one in the same, twin passions that sustained the other. She tended to latch on to writers who fell into one of two categories: those who simply wrote beautifully, and those who challenged the rules of fiction or other conventions in ways that appealed to her own goals to experiment with words through fiction and to use fiction to probe consciousness—conventional plot was never a primary component of her work. But it was the act of reading itself, more than any one or two or seven writers, that influenced Woolf, as a daily exercise in intellectual stimulation and as a means of revving the engine for her own work. "Reading makes me intensely happy, and culminates in a fit of writing always," she wrote in 1905, at the age of twenty-three.[228] Decades later, she echoed the earlier sentiment in a diary entry dated December 8, 1929: "To begin reading with a pen in my hand, discovering, pouncing, thinking of phrases, when the ground is new, remains one of my great excitements."[229]

But it was not a seamless evolution from Woolf's book-filled childhood to her book-filled adult life. After her mother's death when she was thirteen years old and her father's subsequent descent into a mad and permanent sort of mourning, the mood of the Stephen home changed dramatically. Virginia and her sister Vanessa, in the absence of the parental guidance they'd relied on before, clung to each other, growing extremely close. They began to work out their ideas for their chosen careers together, Virginia as a writer, Vanessa an artist.[230] Virginia exploited this less supervised time in her life by taking on her own curriculum of study, especially in the classics.[231] She started keeping a diary around age fifteen—along with a household "newspaper" published by her and her siblings, it was her first written work.

After her father's death when she was twenty-two, Virginia moved to Gordon Square with her three siblings. From there, she tapped her wide net of literary connections to start writing book reviews, the first appearing in 1905.[232] At the same time, as a writer still learning the craft, she gave herself assignments, for instance writing "lives" of people she knew well.[233]

During this time Virginia developed friendships with many of her brother Adrian's friends from Cambridge University, and the Bloomsbury Group was born. She was a central member of this loose collection of intellectuals that favored the pursuit of art, knowledge, and enjoyment over the time's prevailing values, in which bourgeois propriety and public service ruled the day. The Bloomsbury Group meant that she was immersed in a literary scene that gave her constant inspiration and feedback. As a young adult, Virginia found it natural to host literary gatherings in her own home, and the activity stoked her writing. John Maynard Keynes, Desmond MacCarthy, E. M. Forster, Roger Fry, Lytton Strachey, Duncan Grant, and Clive Bell, among others (including her future husband, Leonard Woolf), became the guides and stirrers of her thinking and writing. She grew especially close to Clive Bell, who would soon marry Vanessa. "We met regularly," remembered Bell of this time, "once a week I dare say, to talk about writing generally and her writing in particular."[234] This is an early example of Woolf using conversation to learn about other characters, to accumulate ideas for her writing, and to crystallize her narratives.

The Bloomsbury Group also met collectively on at least a weekly basis, first in the Gordon Square house and later in one in Brunswick Square, where the doors were thrown open to Thursday-night salons and at any moment one might be "launched into a terrific argument about literature; adjectives? associations? over-tones?" as Woolf recalled.[235] At Bloomsbury get-togethers, Virginia didn't talk much, especially in the early days, but she absorbed worlds full of material. She also rarely drank, during these younger days as well as later on. "I listened—with the deepest curiosity," she remembered of the nights when E. M. Forster showed up, "for he was the only novelist I knew."[236] She was observing, learning how she, too, might become a novelist.

Woolf always counted herself among those lucky aspiring writers whose independent means enable them to never work outside of their writing pursuits. She famously believed that financial means were a prerequisite for a literary career, especially for a woman (and even if Woolf strikes many as exactly the kind of personality who might have benefited from having to work just a little harder for her sustenance). She spent her days in the comfort of her home, and home became the setting for all of her writing pursuits. Her financial security enabled her to take her time perfecting her writing—she didn't publish her first novel until age thirty-three.

That famed room of her own (actually, several different rooms over the years, and most often two at once—a city and a country version) invariably overflowed with books, papers, and manuscripts, plus, according to Leonard, "old nibs, bits of string, used matches, rusty paper-clips, crumpled envelopes, broken cigarette-holders, etc."[237]—arranged not so much for easy retrieval as left haphazardly in the place where they'd lost her attention. More than one person who knew her well referred to the conditions as squalid. Vita Sackville-West recalled the "incredible muddle of objects" in a letter to her husband after a visit to Woolf's writing room.[238]

Despite the importance she attached to having a space of her own, Woolf's requirements for the ambience of that space were minimal, if nonexistent. Her most famous writing room, the "writing lodge" in the back garden of the Woolfs' country house in Sussex, appeared charming, with its many windows, its warm light, and its French doors opening onto a brick patio and the English countryside. The surviving photographs of Virginia entertaining Keynes or the Bells on that patio in the afternoon sun only increase the sense of her idyllic surroundings. But the writing lodge contrasted starkly with the writing room she kept at the same time in their London house, set up in a large and otherwise abandoned room in the basement that her husband believed once to have served as a billiards room. John Lehmann, for a time the managing director of Hogarth Press, the publishing house founded by Virginia and Leonard and run out of their basement, remembered in particular the "dusty top light,"[239] bringing to mind a dodgy backroom poker game. There, she sat among the mounds of unsold books produced by Hogarth—essentially working in the press's storeroom.

There was always a desk in these rooms, although Woolf rarely sat at them to write, at least her first drafts. For these, she chose a well-worn armchair, where she placed a plywood board fitted with an inkstand on her lap to serve as a writing surface. She always wrote her first drafts out with pen and paper, thus seated, her formal handwriting crossing the page, reminiscent of calligraphy.[240] Every morning, no matter where she'd left off, she started on a fresh piece of paper.[241] With a draft complete, she'd then type it out, making a first revision as she went. Woolf revised relentlessly. Even though she most often professed a real horror at the ritual, and even as it took a toll on her mental health, the perfectionist in her kept her going, through five or six or seven miserable revisions.

But the writing itself (along with reading) came as a joy and became the means through which she could remain busy and healthy. She often found herself in "the restless state most safely to be appeased by writing."[242] In less euphemistic terms, writing for Woolf was a tool for fending off madness. In this way, it became an absolutely necessary crutch, in a strange way not an end in itself, but a means of accomplishing something else, in her case a sane and salubrious existence. While so many writers struggle to force words onto the page every day, Woolf seemed to have the opposite problem—the pull toward writing was so strong that she could become frantic in her enthusiasm for it and then wear herself down.

This pull meant that Woolf didn't struggle with a traditional type of writer's block. Which isn't to say that the writing always came easy. Although she always wrote something, the words emerged with varying ferocity; sometimes she found the work frustratingly slow, sometimes it poured out. She wrote alternatingly in a three-month period in her diary of "the creative power which bubbles so pleasantly in beginning a new book," then how "I ought to be writing *Jacob's Room*; and I can't," and then a few weeks later, "Really I think my scribbling is coming back."[243] When she began working on *To the Lighthouse*, the first twenty-two pages came out in less than two weeks, then she went months unable to figure out what to do next, then resumed, writing about two pages a day.[244]

As frantic about writing as Woolf could be, she was equally as regimented. Duncan Grant remembered her in her twenties writing always for two and a half hours every morning, but never more than that for her day's work.[245] This pattern would evolve after Leonard entered the picture.

Once she finally went through with marrying Leonard, he played a fundamental role in the organizing of her writing process. "The marriage made a frame and a space for the work," wrote Woolf biographer Hermione Lee.[246] Out of concern for keeping her busy and thus healthy, as well as respect for her particular genius, Leonard took the structuring of Virginia's days very seriously, and she let him. In a letter to a friend in 1913, Leonard chronicled the couple's shared workday as follows: "In the morning, we write 750 words each; in the afternoon we dig; between tea and dinner we write 500 words each."[247] In his autobiography, he recalled a slightly different approach: "Every morning . . . at about 9:30 after break-fast each of us, as if moved by a law of unquestioned nature, went off and 'worked' until lunch at 1."[248] Either way, when Virginia was well, she rarely took a day's break unless on an "authorized" holi-day, and Leonard estimated that they both spent roughly 330 days per year writing (a number that was surely lower in the years when Woolf fell ill).[249] It's also certain that she never wrote at night, a time of day when she found her "head full of pillow stuffing."[250]

Not mentioned by Leonard in those rundowns of their days were Virginia's walks, which cleared her head and helped her think through her current (and future) writing. She undertook one nearly every afternoon, rain or shine.[251] "Two weeks ago I made up *Jacob* incessantly on my walks," she wrote in 1920. "An odd thing, the human mind!"[252] She particularly enjoyed wandering by foot around London, which, she wrote, "perpetually attracts, stimulates, gives me a play and a story and a poem without any trouble, save that of moving my legs through the streets."[253]

When she fell into mental illness—often believed to have been bipolar disorder—Leonard did not allow her to write. Only as she began her recovery did he permit a half hour per day of writing, an allotment that might steadily increase as her health improved. Virginia seems to have gone along with the instructions.[254] In her diaries, she reported going weeks without writing. Leonard recalled that it could, at its most extreme, become months. "One hour's writing daily is my allowance for the next few weeks," she wrote on January 20, 1919, like a modern-day child whose television watch-ing has been limited; "and having hoarded it this morning I may spend part of it now."[255]

Often during convalescence, she'd come back first to her diary. Woolf believed strongly in the benefits of keeping a diary, in which she typically wrote in the afternoons. "The habit of writing thus for my own eye only is good practice. It loosens the ligaments. Never mind the misses and the stumbles," she wrote on April 20, 1919.[256] She used the diaries not only to practice her writing, but also to work out the logistics, plotting it out weeks and months in advance, and setting a timetable for completion of the multiple projects she often had running at once, as in this diary entry from May 26, 1924:

> I am now saying that I will write [*Mrs. Dalloway*] for 4 months, June, July, August and September, and then it will be done, and I shall put it away for three months, during which I shall finish my essays; and then that will be—October, November, December—January; and I shall revise it January, February, March, April; and in April my essays will come out, and in May my novel.[257]

As she progressed, she'd track her progress against the timetables, making note if she fell behind, goading herself to pick up the pace. On the following August 2, for example, she expressed her wish to write more quickly, "instead of hacking at this miserable 200 words a day." On August 15, she noted she had "never worked so hard," but at the same time, "I see that *Mrs. Dalloway* is going to stretch beyond October. In my forecasts I always forget some most important intervening scenes." In the end, she finished the novel on October 9.[258] All in all it took her about a year to complete the draft. (It's one of the few novels she completed without a break because of illness.)

Woolf also used her diaries to work out her novels before starting. Entire plots, characters, and even the eventual titles would be in place before the first word of the first draft sprang from the pen. Of the prospect of *To the Lighthouse*, for example, she wrote:

> This is going to be fairly short; to have father's character done complete in it; and mother's; and St. Ives; and childhood; and all the usual things I try to put in—life, death, etc. But the centre is father's character, sitting in a boat, reciting We perished, each alone, while he crushes a dying mackerel.[259]

An idea for a novel often sprung from a thought previously and nonchalantly recorded in her diary; only in hindsight and with reflection would she realize that the seed for the story was in the throwaway remark. On September 18, 1927, for example, Woolf mused about writing "sketches" of all her friends. Going through the list, she imagined that Vita Sackville-West "should be Orlando, a young nobleman." On October 5, she wrote of "instantly" coming up with the next project now that her last article for the *Tribune* was complete: "a biography beginning in the year 1500 and continuing to the present day, called *Orlando*: Vita; only with a change about from one sex to another." Other times, the idea for a novel came seemingly out of nowhere. In her diary in 1927, she explained "the odd horrid unexpected way in which these things suddenly create themselves—one thing on top of another in about an hour. So I made up *Jacob's Room* looking at the fire in Hogarth House; so I made up the *Lighthouse* one afternoon in the Square here."[260]

Sometimes those sparks came from personal memories that had remained and festered over the years, eventually finding their way into her novels. *To the Lighthouse*, for example, was a fictional version of her childhood days at St. Ives, a seaside town in Cornwall where the Stephen family spent holidays during Virginia's youth. A single memory might show up in several different works—versions of a memory of lying in bed, looking through yellow blinds, and hearing the water lap up against the sand and then the blinds' "little acorn" slide across the floor, appeared in her autobiographical writing and in both *Jacob's Room* and *The Waves*.[261]

Once the idea had taken root, Woolf often reported finding novel writing to be a joy. "I can write and write and write now: the happiest feeling in the world," she observed while working on *Mrs. Dalloway*.[262] There was a notable exception to her enjoyment, however: She almost always found the final chapter a slog. "Always, always the last chapter slips out of my hands. One gets bored," she wrote on February 11, 1928, while struggling to finish up *Orlando*.[263] She may have been all too aware that the last chapter directly preceded the revision process, which she loathed.

Between her writing and her husband and her reading, Woolf also found time to become preoccupied with a string of women who would become important influences on her work. Her sister Vanessa became the seminal muse, a woman with whom she developed not only the closest of relationships, but also a rivalry that would propel both women throughout their professional lives. Visitors to a young Virginia Stephen might have noticed the tall desk in her workroom, the perfect height to write standing up. What they might not have known was that the desk was purchased only after, as Clive Bell recalled it years later, someone mentioned how hard it must be for Vanessa to stand for so many hours to paint: "Virginia, outraged, I suppose, by the insinuation that her sister's occupation was in any way more exacting than her own, went out at once and bought a tall desk at which she insisted on standing to write."[264] Woolf would not make a lifelong habit of writing on her feet, but the unchecked competitiveness would endure.

Her attachment to Vanessa was the first of a string of competitive, intellectual, and sometimes romantic relationships that would fuel Woolf's own ambitions. With Katherine Mansfield in the late teens, for example, Woolf shared and developed her interest in breaking down the traditions of fiction—both women wanted to explore consciousness and expand the limits of narrative in their work, and their friendship was based on this mutual and unique view of writing.[265] Likewise, Woolf's intense and romantic relationship with Vita Sackville-West, author of the novel *The Edwardians*, inspired her book *Orlando*, as well as a number of other works, and Vita's exotic life, her unconventionality, and her own writing had a profound effect on Woolf.[266]

This appropriation of a muse for the sake of literature echoed Woolf's tendency to appropriate memories, some of them long past, in her novels. Memories of her homes, memories of the books within them, memories of a husband so central to her writing process, and always, always, an unyielding passion to put words on the page.

A DAY IN THE WRITER'S LIFE ...

Virginia Woolf awoke early every morning, either at her home in London or the country house in Sussex, and breakfasted with her husband. Around 9:30 a.m., they both retreated to their respective writing rooms, hers an explosion of muddle—books, papers, odds and ends— where, assuming she was well, Woolf would sit in her armchair, plywood board on her lap, to work on her latest piece of fiction until 12:30 or 1 p.m., when she would break for lunch. In the afternoon, she would almost always take a walk, write in her diary, or work on an essay. Teatime came in the late afternoon. Then, before dinner, she would sometimes make revisions, sometimes read, or sometimes even see friends. The nighttime hours were for reading or socializing—her mind, she claimed, was no longer fit for writing after the sun went down.

VLADIMIR NABOKOV

It was always a matter of what was available. No room for a desk in his two-room flat? Vladimir Nabokov wrote in the bathtub. Financial constraints required that he work all day? Vladimir Nabokov wrote all night. The market for Russian literature all dried up? Vladimir Nabokov switched to English. Had he been a less adaptable writer, or a more neurotic one, the near-constant volatility of Nabokov's adult life most likely would have suffocated his creativity, and we would not have *Lolita*, *Pale Fire*, or *Speak, Memory*. His writing thrived even as he fled with his formerly aristocratic family to Europe in the wake of the 1917 Russian Revolution, even as he escaped Europe during the events leading up to World War II (living in Germany and married to his Jewish wife, Véra, in the 1930s), and finally even as he struggled to gain a foothold in America. Time and again Nabokov demonstrated that those two mainstays of the typical writing life, the right time and place, simply didn't matter much. Armed with a confidence in his own abilities that bordered on hubris, Nabokov never wavered. Ironically, it was that very hubris ("I write like a genius") that kept him steadily at work from one decade to the next.

At a very young age, Nabokov knew that he would be a writer. By age fifteen, he was writing every day, even if it was mostly bad, derivative poetry.[267] His fabulously wealthy family spent the colder months steeped in St. Petersburg's early twentieth-century intellectual fervor, and the warmer ones in their country home, Vyra, both of which inspired him intellectually. His parents doted on him as the oldest child and instilled in him the boundless faith in his own abilities that would come in so handy later in life. It's no surprise that his childhood memories became so important to his writing. "Memory is, really, in itself, a tool, one of the many tools that an artist uses," he said.[268]

His idyllic childhood ended with a slap in 1919 when his family went into exile. World War I was drawing to a close, and after the move to Europe, Nabokov would soon enter Cambridge University. Upon graduating he settled in Berlin, a major hub for Russian émigrés at the time. There, even as his literary efforts blossomed, he began taking work outside of writing, tutoring or teaching tennis out of a necessity that would remain with him until he'd nearly reached retirement age, when the publication of *Lolita* at last allowed him to bookend those impecunious middle decades with the life of a rich man.

Nabokov became flexible in his writing routine because he had to in order to accommodate his irregular working life, but also because it suited his temperament. During a spell of time unencumbered by outside work, he might write all night, then not rise until noon.[269] Or he might rise early to get started, such as during an extended holiday in the South of France, when he wrote his Russian novel *The Gift* from 7 a.m. to 10 a.m. every morning, then took a break for the beach and lunch, then resumed writing from 3 p.m. to 11:30 p.m. At other times in Berlin, he worked during the day around tutoring or caring for his young son, then wrote into the night.

Once he moved to America, again fleeing war, Nabokov almost

always had teaching obligations. He took a position teaching Russian language and literature at Wellesley College soon after moving to America, and later taught literature at Cornell for a decade, along with temporary stints at Stanford and Harvard. At one point in 1945, between teaching at Wellesley and working at Harvard as a lepidopterologist (his passion for butterflies rivaled that for literature), Nabokov reported to his sister that he wrote only on the weekends.[270] He'd sometimes stay in bed all day on Sundays, working on a novel.[271] At another point, he wrote all night after working two other jobs.[272] Such habits were helped by the presence of an insomnia that he never shook (and by the looks of it, never really tried to).

Nabokov was capable of marathon writing sessions, although they took a toll on him. "Sometimes I write for twelve hours nonstop. I grow ill when I do this and feel very badly," he once said.[273] In his mad rush to finish the novel *Bend Sinister* before preparing for the next year's teaching duties, Nabokov almost had a nervous breakdown and was ordered to take a vacation by his doctor.[274] Most of his novels were written not in these forced outpourings, however, but at a slower and steadier clip, and often with a greater speed and intensity during the summer months, when his teaching obligations ceased. The biographer Andrew Field put Nabokov's typical output at 280 pages per year.[275] Nabokov himself put it at 200 pages of "final copy" per year.[276] This pace, along with his tendency to take on several projects at once, could make for slow going. *Speak, Memory* took him three years;[277] *Lolita* took five.[278] A translation of Aleksandr Pushkin's *Eugene Onegin* took him ten full years to complete.

Even when they found themselves in one city for a long time, Vladimir and Véra never settled down in any traditional sense. During the émigré years in Berlin, they switched flats continually. Decades later, during their ten years in Ithaca, they lived in ten different houses, preferring the vacated homes of professors on sabbatical to securing one of their own.[279] In his entire adult life,

Nabokov never owned a home. As such, he never created a personalized writing space, except during the last phase of his life, living in the Montreux Palace hotel in Switzerland, with his greatest writing already behind him. He could live anywhere, and anywhere he lived, it seemed, he could write, so long as there were no classes to teach or butterflies to chase.

"Place does not matter much, it is the relationship between the brain and the hand that poses some odd problems," Nabokov once wrote.[280] At Cambridge, he wrote poetry on his bed.[281] After graduating, he wrote his first book on the "moth-eaten couch" of a Berlin boardinghouse.[282] In the 1930s, also in Berlin, Véra secured a job, leaving Nabokov to serve as a very modern sort of stay-at-home dad. He took good care of his son, Dmitri, and then stole time for writing in the apartment's empty bathtub, a wooden board propped against the sides to form an improvised writing desk.[283] While living briefly in a one-room apartment in Paris, it was to the bathroom again, where he sat on the bidet, a suitcase propped up to serve as a desk.[284] Later, in America, he wrote a large portion of *Lolita* while traveling across the country by car with his wife. In motels with thin walls and loud highways nearby, he'd head to the parking lot, climb into the backseat of the car, and work on *Lolita* there.[285]

There were desks, too. During an extended trip in the Pyrenees, he sat at one covered by a checkered tablecloth to work on *The Defense*, a pained look of concentration bearing down on the paper.[286] During his golden years in Montreux, Nabokov began his writing day standing at an ornate wooden lectern he found in the basement of the hotel. Next to it he placed an armchair, where he'd continue to write once his legs grew tired. When his back started hurting, he'd lie down on the nearby couch and keep going.[287]

Despite the constant change, Nabokov did maintain a few long-term habits in his writing routine: For twenty years he used the same oak penholder, well chewed and well loved.[288] And, being a male product of his day, he never learned to type, writing everything out by hand and relying on his wife or, later on, a hired typist. For decades, he wrote in notebooks, until, with the writing of *Lolita*, he famously began writing his novels on index cards. Until his Cornell days, Nabokov was a smoker and kept an ashtray next to him as he worked. It's easy to see when he finally quit—photographs show a man in Ithaca sixty pounds heftier than the lean young man toiling in Berlin. If alcohol never gets mentioned alongside Nabokov's name, it's because he had little interest in it. He had a distinct disrespect for drugs as well—he wouldn't even try sleeping pills despite his decades of insomnia.[289] The most important constant might have been Véra, who read and advised on all of his novels at least twice before they reached their published state.[290]

Nabokov's novelistic ideas didn't usually emerge at his desk (or couch or bathtub or bidet), though. He often sensed a nebulous idea on the horizon, which after a few days would come to him in an instant as a novel—he called that moment of conception a "pang" or a "shock." In the case of *Pale Fire*, that pang came on board a ship from New York to France—"a rather complete vision of its structure in miniature."[291] Of his novel *Ada*, he recalled the moment when the "entire novel leap[ed] into the kind of existence that can and must be put into words."[292] Immediately following that particular pang, he wrote the following amorphous paragraph:

Sea crashing, retreating with shuffle of pebbles, Juan and beloved young whore—is her name, as they say, Adora? is she Italian, Roumanian, Irish?—asleep in his lap, his opera cloak pulled over her, candle messily burning in its tin cup, next to it a paper-wrapped bunch of long roses, his silk hat on the stone floor near a patch of moonlight, all this in a corner of a decrepit, once palatial whorehouse, Villa Venus, on a rocky Mediterranean coast, a door standing ajar gives on what seems to be a moonlit gallery but is really a half-demolished reception room with a broken

outer wall, through a great rip in it the naked sea is heard as a panting
space separated from time, it dully booms, dully withdraws dragging its
platter of wet pebbles.[293]

This scene ultimately unfolds midway through *Ada*. But it is the initial burst that made the rest of it possible. The first working title, in fact, was "Villa Venus."

Even with a fully formed vision in place, though, there might be six months of mental gestation before he put pen to paper. All the while, he'd be working on other projects, short stories or final revisions for another book. Sometimes he'd start and complete an entire other novel while mulling the first one over.[294] Such was the case as he wrote *Speak, Memory* with *Lolita* lurking in his mind.

Occasionally an idea spanned several works, evolving each time he used it. In one paragraph in his novel *The Gift*, written in the 1930s, Nabokov wrote about a man who married a woman to get to her daughter. Around 1940, the paragraph became a short story about a man's obsession with a young girl. In the 1950s, he moved the story to America and expanded it into the novel that would become his masterpiece.[295]

A young Nabokov wrote linearly, more or less starting from page one and proceeding in succession, chapter by chapter.[296] Starting with *The Gift*, his process became more piecemeal. "I don't write consecutively from the beginning to the next chapter and so on to the end," he said at age sixty-three. "I just fill in the gaps of the picture, of this jigsaw puzzle which is quite clear in my mind, picking out a piece here and a piece there and filling out part of the sky and part of the landscape and part of the—I don't know, the carousing hunters."[297] This switch happened to coincide with his decision to write on index cards, which enabled easy sorting and rearranging—and less rewriting to do if a "page" needed to be done over (three index cards amounted to one typed page)[298]—as well as his switch from pen to pencil, which allowed for more orderly editing as he went along.

Despite the great care that went into drawing out his work, Nabokov was a compulsive, impulsive, relentless reviser. "I have rewritten—often several times—every word I have ever published. My pencils outlast their erasers," he told an interviewer in 1962.[299] And in *Speak, Memory*, he compares his own "mousy hand and messy drafts, . . . the massacrous revisions and rewritings, and new revisions," unfavorably with his father's "flawless handwriting."[300] When he was younger, he rewrote every page three or four times, crossed out and inserted and crossed out again ad nauseam. He'd recopy the entire thing a couple of times before his wife would type it up.[301] His first drafts could be unruly—information highways of crossed-out phrases, arrows indicating rearrangement, circled notes, and arcane symbols. When he would revise the typed manuscript, there would still be plenty of room for name changes, details deleted or added, descriptive words replaced.[302]

Once Nabokov completed his own revisions, he considered the work done and had little tolerance for the changes suggested by editors, whom he referred to alternately as "limpid creatures" and "pompous avuncular brutes."[303] The one exception proved to be Katharine White, the fiction editor at the *New Yorker*, whose edits he more often than not took issue with, but who could sometimes convince him to accept a change.

Though his confidence seldom wavered, he threw in the towel completely on two of his greatest novels before being coaxed back from the brink. Once, feeling that *Lolita* was progressing too slowly and perhaps worried that it would never find a publisher anyway, he carried the first draft out to the garden incinerator, only to be intercepted by his wife before it was too late.[304] And in 1959, he contacted his publisher to arrange for the return of the $2,500 advance for *Pale Fire*, writing, "The work has not been advancing . . . I am not sure I shall ever write it."[305] Two years later, of course, the novel would be finished.

These stumbles were rare. More common was Nabokov's stone-cold belief in his own genius. He claimed never to have learned a thing from another writer, taking everything he accomplished from somewhere inside him. "As for influence, well, I've never been influenced by anyone in particular," he said at the age of sixty-nine.[306] History suggests otherwise. It was during college at Cambridge that Nabokov came across a copy of the nineteenth-century lexicographer Vladimir Dahl's *Explanatory Dictionary of the Living Great Russian Language*. Once it was in his possession, he recalls in *Speak, Memory*, he "resolved to read at least ten pages per day, jotting down such words and expressions as might especially please me."[307] The volumes would stay with him for decades, a talisman of the Russian language for the man who was no longer in Russia; he even took the tomes with him on holidays.[308] During his university years, other literature proved formative to his evolving style—he mentioned, in particular, the anonymous Slavic epic poem *The Song of Igor's Campaign*, Pushkin's and Tyutchev's poetry, and Gogol's and Tolstoy's prose. Those Russian poetic influences would color his early work, but by the time he emerged as a great prose writer, he'd largely shaken them (although Gogol and Tolstoy would stick). Later, in America, Nabokov developed a crucial friendship with Edmund Wilson, who would serve as an advocate of Nabokov's work in this country until the relationship broke down over Wilson's negative review of Nabokov's translation of *Eugene Onegin*.

But his own life may have been the biggest literary influence of all. "Imagination is a form of memory," he said.[309] The inverse of that statement might apply even more perfectly to Nabokov's work. Indeed, he was a relentless borrower from his own life for his fiction. His first sighting of the love of his teenage years, a girl named Valentina who appeared to him sitting in an apple tree, reappears in *Ada*.[310] A professor at Cambridge reappears in his novel *Glory*.[311] One of the Nabokovs' houses in Ithaca became that of Lolita.[312] And there are echoes of the childhood romance with a ten-year-old French girl in Biarritz that he recounted in *Speak, Memory* in Humbert Humbert's remembered childhood love. Memory for Nabokov was a resource, there to be mined.

Of course, Nabokov did his research on the present, too. In Berlin, he once went so far as to visit a lung specialist for advice on how the murder of the heroine in *King, Queen, Knave* might best be carried out.[313] Especially after moving to America and beginning to write about that country, memories could no longer provide him with the background information he needed. For *Lolita*, he took copious notes during summer drives across the country, staying in the cheap motels that would find their way into the novel. He read scientific books about adolescent girls. He read teen magazines and Girl Scout manuals. In order to master American schoolgirl slang, he rode on buses and took notes on conversations he overheard.[314] For a Russian man with European sensibilities, dialogue such as the following, between Humbert Humbert and the young, thoroughly American Lolita, could not be so perfectly rendered had his research not been so thorough:

> "Now I do hope that's all, you witty child."
> "Yep, that's all. No—wait a sec. We baked in a reflector oven. Isn't that terrific?"
> "Well, that's better."
> "We washed zillions of dishes."

This later work in America finally made Nabokov rich. In his sixties, no longer required to work outside of writing, Nabokov moved to a luxurious hotel in Switzerland and achieved something approaching a conventional routine, waking at 7 a.m., lying in bed for a while thinking and brainstorming, and finally rising around 8 a.m. for a "shave, breakfast, enthroned meditation, and bath—in that order."[315] Then he'd enter his study to write until lunch at 1 p.m., with a brief break possibly for a walk with his wife by Lake Geneva. After a short lunch, he'd be back to writing until 6:30 p.m., when he'd head to the newsstand for the day's papers and then back home for dinner at seven. "No work after dinner," he said of that period in his life. He still struggled with insomnia but usually managed to be asleep by 1 a.m. By 1968, that routine remained, with slight variations, including a hot bath around 11 a.m. and a nap in the afternoon.[316] Finally, after more than four decades, he'd established a writing schedule on his own terms.

A DAY IN THE WRITER'S LIFE . . .

On any given day, Vladimir Nabokov more than likely rose in the morning to head to some job that did not involve writing: tutoring or teaching tennis or lecturing college students. Writing filled in the time between those bills-paying activities. And when he did find time for it, he was as likely to be found writing on a couch, in bed, or in the bathtub as at a writing desk, and it was as likely to be 4 a.m. as 4 p.m. Puffing on a cigarette (or later, sucking on a molasses candy), eyes boring into the page, he'd continue as long as he could, whether that be for three hours or twelve, his wife, Véra, always nearby, poised to assist in any way necessary. For Nabokov, the only certainties in his writing life would be his faith in his ability, the support of his wife, and the unpredictability of his schedule.

WINGING IT

(9)

SALMAN RUSHDIE

Salman Rushdie, alone in a quiet room, eyes intent on his laptop screen, fingers popcorning against the keyboard. It's hardly the image that we've come to associate with one of the world's most famous living authors. Instead, we latch on to Salman Rushdie the exile; Salman Rushdie the man on the scene; Salman Rushdie, dater of models and hobnobber with the glitterati. If these personas are indeed part of the larger truth—and Rushdie does little to dispel the myths surrounding them—then they coexist in harmony with the man who approaches writing as a very serious endeavor, undertaken in quiet solitude. The tabloids cover the parties and the liaisons while the man's quiet working days are all but lost in the commotion. But every day by midmorning, there's Rushdie, shut up in his writing room, working without fanfare.

In a quite literal way, the writing comes before everything else, first thing every morning. "I've learned that I need to give it the first energy of the day, so before I read the newspaper, before I open the mail, before I phone anyone, often before I have a shower, I sit in my pajamas at the desk," he told the *Paris Review* in 2005.[317]

(Presumably by now he has added the Internet and social media to that list.) That first energy generally comes sometime between 9:30 and 10:30 in the morning—an early riser he is not.[318] Rushdie then writes for four hours or so, during which he might write two to four pages[319]—over the years, he's learned that beyond that chunk of time, the output becomes mush.[320] There's the occasional exception, and if he finds himself in the rare position of being on a roll, Rushdie takes full advantage: He once went fourteen straight hours working on the lecture "Is Nothing Sacred?"[321] And he sticks relentlessly to a project once he's all in, rarely seeing daylight when he's working,[322] and often going home to work more at night after one of his infamous social outings.[323]

He also doesn't take weekends off. "I'm not saying I don't go out for Sunday brunch, but I do think that the rhythm thing is important," he says, "that you have to just get into the rhythm of it and not get out of it."[324] At the same time, that Sunday brunch (or late-night club) plays an important role in its own right, and it's not for nothing that he allows himself that release. "I always had a very high requirement for [interacting with] other people," he says.[325] A busy social life for Rushdie serves as an antidote to long hours of solitude spent writing.

His writing life wasn't always the two-toned existence he enjoys today. In the early days in London, Rushdie needed to earn money outside of his writing, which wasn't yet providing enough to live on, even after he had a novel under his belt. He took a job in advertising, a career he'd toy with on and off until the success of *Midnight's Children* enabled him to abandon it for good in his midthirties. He never loved advertising, but he did carry a couple of important lessons from it over to his fiction. His years in the industry solidified the discipline of writing first thing in the morning—"not pacing around waiting for the muse to descend"—and the discipline of using words sparingly, of not overwriting.[326]

Leading up to the writing of *Midnight's Children*, Rushdie decided that in order to do it properly, he needed to immerse himself in the India he planned to write about. He quit the advertising job and, with his future first wife, Clarissa, spent five months traveling around the subcontinent, keeping a journal along the way that would prove a handy reference for more than one future novel.[327] When he arrived back in England, he began work on the novel immediately, returning to advertising part-time—two or three days a week—in order to have money coming in. He spent the remaining days of the week at work on the novel.[328] It was, like most of his novels, slow going. In this case, the time from start to finish spanned five years, with two and a half years spent on the first draft alone,[329] which ran twice as long as the final product of five hundred or so pages. This was typical of his early career. Later, his writing became more refined out the gate. "When I was younger, I would write with a lot more ease than I do now, but what I wrote would require a great deal more rewriting," he said in 2005. "Now I write much more slowly and I revise a lot as I go. I find that when I've got a bit done, it seems to require less revision than it used to."[330]

On Valentine's Day 1989, the prosaic customs of Rushdie's daily routine were interrupted in a way that most writers can hardly imagine. On that day, the Iranian ayatollah issued a call for his death for alleged crimes against Islam committed by writing *The Satanic Verses*. Rushdie immediately went into hiding under the protection of the British government, and was clandestinely relocated to at least thirty different houses and flats over the following few years. The challenge for Rushdie became how to get on with things in the most basic ways. In one of the first houses that he and his then wife, Marianne Wiggins, lived in (an old cottage in Wales), Rushdie "managed to find a small upstairs room where he could shut the door and pretend to work."[331] Writing would always be difficult under these circumstances, but over time, the pretending ceded to doing, as living in hiding became the new normal. Rushdie learned to re-create the atmosphere he needed to write in every new place. Realizing that he found it grueling to work without his own possessions around him, he had friends bring things from his house, arranging them around whatever room he happened to be working in to create a sense of the familiar and the constant.[332] These little ruses worked: In the near decade that Rushdie spent in hiding, he wrote five books.

Disorienting as it must have been, the transient way of living forced upon Rushdie during the fatwa was not entirely new to him. Even before, he was a man always on the move. Born in Bombay (now Mumbai), Rushdie lived there until he turned fourteen years old, when he left for boarding school in England. While away, his parents moved to Pakistan. After graduating from Cambridge University, he joined them in Pakistan for a stint and then came back to London, where he moved into a shared house with his sister and a few others. He began writing here in earnest, if in secret. He was not yet ready to proclaim himself a writer, even an aspiring one. In 1967, he also lived in a friend's flat in London's Chelsea for a time.[333] In 1973, he moved into Clarissa's flat with her and another lodger, and wrote the first novel that would see publication, *Grimus*.[334] In 1976, he moved yet again after marrying. As a writer, he was comfortable with transience.

Though there was never a truly permanent space, he always carved out a writing room for himself, and this was a key to his success. Just before the fatwa, it was the attic of his Islington row house.[335] At a much earlier point in his life, it was the bedroom of one of his roommates, unused by her during the day.[336] He often kept items for reference around him in these spaces. While writing *The Satanic Verses*, for example, it was a note pinned to the wall above his desk that read: "To write a book is to make a Faustian contract in reverse. To gain immortality, or at least posterity, you lose, or at least ruin, your actual daily life."[337] The note kept him focused—not to mention that it portended the impact the book would have on his life in a way he couldn't have foreseen at the time.

His nomadic lifestyle would endure well after the fatwa. When Rushdie came out of hiding and moved to New York City, he again wandered from place to place, living in a series of "borrowed apartments." He made one attempt to put down roots by buying an apartment in a co-op, but the board rejected him, after which he abandoned the notion of securing a space of his own.[338] But Rushdie did finally find a place to settle into: He's been living in the Union Square area of Manhattan for well over a decade now.[339]

This continually improvised existence has come to define Rushdie's writing and inform his knack for finding the universal in every particular: "My subject is the way in which the stories of anywhere are also the stories of everywhere else," he says.[340] This was true from the outset. Aside from the ever-present desire to "simply tell stories,"[341] Rushdie became fascinated early on with the implications of being a migrant. In his early novels, including *Midnight's Children* and *The Satanic Verses*, he dealt with those implications, first by taking his Indian identity head on, and then by attempting to reconcile what was Indian and what was English in him. Within this context, it's no surprise that Rushdie's work also ruminates on the past and its interplay with the present. And as a history major at university, he learned to approach fiction with the techniques of the historian. "I have always used a kind of historical method in the completely unmethodical way which is the luxury of fiction," he says.[342] His reverence for history reflects Rushdie's persona as a novelist—concerned with big topics like national identity and the legacy of colonialism, willing to be a public figure, and willing to let the public see his zest for life. He conducts his writing life the way novelists were known to do a couple centuries ago, using his craft to engage in the public debates of the day.

Rushdie may be a novelist in the grand nineteenth-century sense, but he's no Luddite, and has been quick to incorporate new technologies into his routine. He wrote his first novels on a type-writer in the seventies and early eighties, as the times dictated, but eagerly switched to a desktop for 1995's *The Moor's Last Sigh*, and then to laptops as they became available. Apple devotees can count a titan of literature among their ranks.[343] Rushdie welcomed the transition, finding computers more amenable to the editing and revision process. "In my view, my writing has got tighter and more concise because I no longer have to perform the mechanical act of re-typing endlessly," he says. "So there's no doubt in my mind that the computer's improved my writing."[344]

As for Twitter and other social media, Rushdie has to a large extent embraced these new communication forums. He joined Twitter in 2011 and explained to the *New York Times* that "it allows one to be playful, to get a sense of what is on a lot of people's minds at any given moment."[345] Topics he covers in his tweets are wide and varied, a reflection of his interest in the entirety of the world around him. He also started a Tumblr and famously went to war with Facebook over its refusal to let him use the name Salman, which is not his real first name (Rushdie won). Rushdie even started an Instagram. But more recently he has claimed Twit-ter fatigue,[346] and he hasn't updated his Tumblr since February 2012. For Rushdie, social media has proven to be a vehicle for pro-motion more than one for cultivating the writing itself.

Which doesn't interfere with his lifelong love of consum-ing words the old-fashioned way. During his childhood in India, Rushdie was an inveterate bookworm, devouring P. G. Wodehouse and Agatha Christie.[347] A fifteen-year-old Rushdie became obsessed with J. R. R. Tolkien's *The Lord of the Rings* and spent time meant for studying reading that and science-fiction novels instead.[348] These authors undoubtedly seeped into the subconscious of the budding writer, who later referred to *The Lord of the Rings* as "an infection he never managed to shake off."[349] The influence shows up in his work; Rushdie's towering literary reputation is due in no small part to his extraordinary ability to weave a fantastical story.

He has cited Shakespeare, Joyce, and Bellow as major influences. Despite frequent comparisons to Gabriel García Márquez, Rushdie says he was not an early influence. He loves writers who "understood the unreality of 'reality'"—Rabelais, Gogol, Kafka.[350] As he began work on *Midnight's Children*, Rushdie found inspiration in Dickens, Swift, and Laurence Sterne, all writers with a comedic and/or satirical approach to social commentary in their fiction.[351] For *The Satanic Verses*, he took direct influence from William Blake's *The Marriage of Heaven and Hell*, for the way it intertwines the concepts of heaven and hell, and Mikhail Bulgakov's *The Master and Margarita*, which gave him a template for what he calls the "interpolated narratives" in his own novel.[352]

Alongside literature, Rushdie finds inspiration for his writing in film. He wrote his first story at the age of ten after seeing *The Wizard of Oz*,[353] which presaged the inspiration he took from film later on, especially from those European art-house directors of the sixties and seventies. "I think I learned as much from Buñuel and Bergman and Godard and Fellini as I learned from books," he says.[354] He emulated the way they broke down the constructs of filmmaking, the way they incorporated surrealism without losing their sense of reality. Rushdie finds inspiration in all forms of creative media: As he prepared to write *The Ground beneath Her Feet*, he was "reading Rilke, listening to Gluck, watching on blurry VHS the great Brazilian movie *Orfeu Negro*, and being happy to discover, in Hindu mythology, an Orpheus myth in reverse."[355]

While he's entrenched in work on a book, though, Rushdie prefers to read poetry. "When you're writing a novel," he says, "it's so easy to have odd bits of laziness slip in. Poetry is a way of reminding myself to pay attention to language."[356] His strategy here echoes the lesson he took from advertising, that each word needs to matter, that it's best to be economical with one's choices.

Rushdie keeps journals, but does not appear to be an obsessive notetaker. He lets ideas float around in his head and waits to see which ideas stick. "My books . . . often sit in my head for a long time before I write them . . . In fact, the fact that they stay in my head is one of the things that tells me that I want to write them. So in a funny way it chooses you—it sticks in your head."[357] This isn't to say that the journals play no role—there were, of course, the India diaries that he drew on for *Midnight's Children* and again in writing *The Moor's Last Sigh*.[358] There have been other notebooks for other novels, and throughout his life Rushdie has kept a diary.

But Rushdie only really discovers his novels after he begins writing them. He has called his typical writing day "exploratory."[359] While writing *Shalimar the Clown*, he remembers, "Moment by moment in the writing, things would happen that I hadn't foreseen."[360] Earlier on, he abandoned an entire and never-published novel, keeping just one idea from it—a character named Saleem Sinai—that became the germ for *Midnight's Children*.[361] He completed the entire first draft of it in the third person, then for the second switched to the first person, at which point the voice of the novel became obvious as if by magic.[362] It was sometime after this that he finally wrote what would ultimately become the first page of the novel. Likewise, in *The Satanic Verses*, it was only after one hundred pages that he wrote a page about a plane breaking apart in the sky, felt it didn't belong where it was, and moved it up to page one.[363]

For Rushdie, a key part of that exploratory process involves finding the right title for the work. "When you know the name, you know what the book is about," he says.[364] Early on during his work on *Midnight's Children*, for example, Rushdie started struggling with the hunch that he wasn't actually sure what the book was about or where he was going with it. He stopped writing it altogether and turned instead to spending his days jotting down potential titles. "I wrote down hundreds, pages and pages and pages, a whole week," he says. Every day he'd whittle the list down, until finally, there on the paper, were two titles: *Midnight's Children* and *Children of Midnight*. He wrote each title out a hundred more times and decided he preferred the former.[365] With the title chosen, the novel became clear to him—it elucidates for him the core subject, which had previously been swimming in a sea of potential themes. In other words, the title helps him clarify his point of focus.

Other times, a single sentence will reveal itself to be the foundation for the entire novel. "There were sentences that one knew, when one wrote them, contained or made possible dozens or perhaps even hundreds of other sentences," Rushdie wrote in his memoir, *Joseph Anton*. One such sentence came months into his work on *Haroun and the Sea of Stories*:

> There was once, in the country of Alif bay, a sad city, the saddest of cities, a city so ruinously sad that it had forgotten its name. It stood by a mournful sea full of glumfish.[366]

When he wrote that sentence, he had his book.

How does Rushdie know when the book is ready to go out into the world? "Embarrassment is a good test," he says. "When you feel you wouldn't be embarrassed by people reading what's on the page, then you can let people read it."[367] Rushdie doesn't typically let anyone read his works in progress, although he made an exception at least once, while writing *Shalimar the Clown*—a deliberate experiment to see if it would have an impact on the finished product.

After he finishes a novel, Rushdie enters a sort of recovery period. After *Midnight's Children*, he hardly wrote at all for eight or nine months.[368] But these times remain full of artistic energy.

"Some of my most creative moments are the moments between books," he says, "when I don't know where I'm going, and my head freewheels."[369] He ultimately throws a lot of the work away when he doesn't know where he's headed, but he still gets up and does it, and in those unformed moments, he discovers somewhere amid the cacophony of thought the germs of his next book.

A DAY IN THE WRITER'S LIFE . . .

A late riser, Salman Rushdie goes straight from the bed to the writing desk sometime between 9:30 and 10:30 in the morning. Seated in his pajamas, he gets to work, spending four or so hours intent on the page, always cognizant of finding the universal in his unique Anglo-Indian legacy, always aware of history. By 3:30, he's done for the day. Particularly adept at balancing the solitude of the writing life with the buzz of his social life, in the evenings Rushdie often heads out for fun, conversation, and the kind of intellectual stimulation that can only come from social interactions. Then, if he's in the throes of a novel, he'll come home and review his day's work, maybe even write a few more words, before drifting off to bed.

10

JOAN DIDION

Joan Didion sat in the Riviera in Las Vegas at one o'clock one early morning in the 1960s and watched a minor actress she'd met once cross the casino floor. Upon hearing her name called on the PA system, the minor actress, "a young woman with long hair and a short white halter,"[370] strode in sharp relief against the backdrop, rendered in softer colors and less intrusive lighting than the casino floors of today's Vegas. When she stopped at the house telephone, then picked it up, Didion wondered who had paged her and why, and what she was doing on the casino floor of the Riviera at one in the morning anyway. As the action unfolded before her, a scene began to coalesce in her mind, a scene that would become the seed for her most famous novel, *Play It as It Lays*, the protagonist of which is a minor actress named Maria who vows never to cross the floor of the Sands or Caesar's after midnight:

> Maria made a list of things she would never do. She would never: *walk*
> *through the Sands or Caesar's alone after midnight.* She would never: *ball*

at a party, do S-M unless she wanted to, borrow furs from Abe Lipsey, deal.
She would never: *carry a Yorkshire in Beverly Hills.*

Didion's stories always sprout from scenes such as this, some witnessed firsthand, others read about or seen in the paper, then enhanced, metastasizing in the mind. In her first fictional effort, the novel *Run River*, published when she was twenty-eight years old, the scene came from a blurb in the *New York Times* about a man on trial somewhere in the Carolinas for killing his farm's foreman. The resulting novel opens with a similar murder on the banks of a California river. For *A Book of Common Prayer*, she incorporated a number of events taken from real life: There was the photo in the newspaper of "a hijacked 707 burning on the desert in the Middle East"; there was the view at night from a hotel room in Colombia, in which Didion spent a deliriously sick week while her husband made the rounds at a local film festival; and there was that most crucial shimmering image, the Panama airport at 6 a.m.—a similar airport becomes a central setting in the novel.[371] In writing workshops, participants are often provided with a "writing prompt," a picture or trinket that can be used as the catalyst for a story. For Didion, this concept is key.

An admittedly shy woman, Didion was never good at inserting herself into situations, social or otherwise. To compensate, she became exceptionally adept at observing them. She has said of herself as a writer that she is "so physically small, so temperamentally unobtrusive, and so neurotically inarticulate that people tend to forget that my presence runs counter to their best interests."[372] Because no one is paying attention to the diminutive woman loitering around the edges, she can witness as things unfold unaffected by her presence. In the 1980s and 1990s, she wrote some of the most compelling coverage ever published on the Democratic conventions not by interviewing anyone present, but by watching from the sidelines as the events revealed themselves to be meaningless affectation.

Didion's pictures may not become the central theme of the particular work they inspire—Maria never even enters the casino, only thinks about how she never would, in the end. Yet even a picture as inspiration or muse can be enough to crystallize a character.

These pictures—or the desire to understand them—are what made Didion want to write in the first place. "I write entirely to find out what I'm thinking, what I'm looking at, what I see and what it means," she says in her oft-quoted lecture "Why I Write." A little later on, she explains that the pictures determine the words, not, as one might expect, the other way around: "The arrangement of the words matter, and the arrangement you want can be found in the picture in your mind. The picture dictates the arrangement." That picture of the Panama airport at dawn inspired Didion to place a woman there, of whom she as yet knew nothing, other than she was wearing an emerald ring and was ordering a tea and insisting the water be boiled in front of her. Didion began asking herself questions about the woman: Why was she there? Where has she been? What neurosis led to her strange demand? Answering those questions provided her with the earliest lines of *A Book of Common Prayer*.

Even with the foundational pictures in place, though, the writing does not begin immediately. The note-taking phase comes first and can, in fact, go on for years. Didion keeps notes all the time, even more so when she is writing a book. In her essay "On Keeping a Notebook," she writes: "See enough and write it down, I tell myself, and then some morning when the world seems drained of wonder, some day when I am only going through the motions of doing what I am supposed to do, which is write—on that bankrupt morning I will simply open my notebook and there it will all be, a forgotten account with accumulated interest, paid passage back to the world out there."

She says this as though she were skeptical of the power of her notes, and yet, given everything she's said about them over the decades, one gets the sense that they are indeed her paid passage. Wherever she's gone—and she's gone seemingly everywhere—she's brought a notebook with her. Her husband, the writer John Gregory Dunne, took it so seriously as to scold her when she forgot it. She remembers him saying that "the ability to make a note when something came to mind was the difference between being able to write and not being able to write."[373] Without the notes, the writing cannot even begin.

One such note was transcribed onto a map of Central America, informing *A Book of Common Prayer*, which takes place in that region. The note was this: "Surface like rainbow slick, shifting, fall, thrown away, iridescent." As she explained in a 1977 interview, "I wanted to do a deceptive surface that appeared to be one thing and turned color as you looked through it."[374] For the duration of writing *A Book of Common Prayer*, the map and its note stayed up in the office of her Malibu home, where she had a panoramic view of the ocean but also a number of cool, dark corners. They were accompanied by postcards from those countries, a newspaper photo of a janitor cleaning up blood, and other knickknacks that informed the work. Once, trying to work on the novel in Berkeley, she found it nearly impossible without the map, even if at that point it was more of a talisman than a true point of reference.

In her nonfiction, the notes loom even larger. Didion relies and draws on them for the entire structure of the piece—the notes "shap[e] the research into the finished thing," she says of nonfiction (whereas in fiction the notes provide only "background").[375] After her husband's death at the end of 2003, for example, she began writing down notes about him and their life together. She thought she was too stricken with grief to work, but unbeknownst to even herself, she was indeed working on her next book. The notes in this case were the foundation of what eventually became *The Year of Magical Thinking*. "After a few days of making notes, I realized that I was thinking about how to structure a book, which was the point at which I realized that I was writing one," she said.[376] The very first notes she took down, four of them, became the opening lines of the book and a recurring motif over the two hundred plus pages:

> *Life changes fast.*
> *Life changes in the instant.*
> *You sit down to dinner and life as you know it ends.*
> *The question of self-pity.*

Didion repeated those lines throughout the book. It's a technique she's used often, as if trying to drill a specific idea into the reader via simple repetition. "Technically it's almost a chant. You could read it as an attempt to cast a spell, or come to terms with certain contemporary demons," she has said.[377]

Pivotal though they were, those four lines don't quite reflect the depth of Didion's note-taking. Work on *The Year of Magical Thinking* didn't begin for ten months after these first lines were written, which seems like quite a bit of time until you learn that for *Play It as It Lays*, it would be several years.

Putting actual words on the page never came in as magical a package as those easy, nascent images. Didion has called the process "fraught" and "an occasion of daily dread."[378] Ten pages into a novel, she told the *Paris Review* in 1978, she's "already blown it," and finds herself hating the book.[379] She never really stops hating the book, if it's the one she's currently working on.[380] In a later interview with that journal, she referred to the "blank terror" of facing the Royal typewriter in the morning (these days, it's a computer). "There is always a point in the writing of a piece when I sit in a room literally papered with false starts and cannot put one word after another and imagine that I have suffered a small stroke, leaving me apparently undamaged but actually aphasic," she wrote in the preface to *Slouching towards Bethlehem*.

And then what? How does she go on in the face of what would appear to be total paralysis? With blind faith, it turns out—that if she just goes into her study every morning, eventually she'll break through what she calls the "low dread." Not that the low dread ever disappears completely. It's there waiting for her every morning, she told the *New York Times Book Review*. But off she goes into her study, today located at the end of a hallway in her Upper East Side apartment, and after an hour or so, the dread is gone: "once you're in there, you're there and it's hard to go out."[381]

In her office there is a bulletin board where Didion keeps fragments of a story that will fit somewhere eventually, but nowhere yet—an index card with a single sentence typed on it, perhaps, or even a couple pages of a novel. "Toward the beginning of a novel I'll write a lot of sections that lead me nowhere. So I'll abandon them, pin them on a board with the idea of picking them up later."[382] The bulletin board becomes a physical representation of Didion's nonlinear approach to writing. When she started *A Book of Common Prayer*, "I wrote the first paragraph and continued for about three pages. Then I got scared and started skipping around and writing odd things"[383]—many of which presumably ended up on the board. And when everything from the board has finally been included, holes often remain. When she turned the draft of *Play It as It Lays* in to her editor, for instance, "it was quite rough," she says, "with [several] places marked 'chapter to come' . . . For example, I didn't know that BZ was an important character . . . until the last few weeks I was working on it. So those places I marked 'chapter to come' were largely places where I was going to go back and pull BZ through, hit him harder, prepare for the way it finally went."[384]

At that point, she draws on the scenes and images accumulated in her own mind. But no one else's—Didion keeps the writing of others at an arm's length from her workspace. "I once tried to work in John's office here and I was beside myself," she says. "There were too many books. I mean there was this weight of other people's opinions around me."[385]

To mitigate the paralysis that continually plagues her, Didion retypes her own sentences every day from the previous days' work, to create continuity and incorporate edits. "Towards the beginning of a book, I will go back to page one every day and rewrite. I'll start out the day with some marked-up pages that I have marked up the night before, and by the time you get to page, maybe, 270, you are not going back to page 1 necessarily anymore, but you're going back to page 158 and starting over from there."[386] This approach harkens back to her earliest fascination with literature, when as a teenager, before she even knew she wanted to be a writer, she copied out Hemingway's stories word for word in order to internalize the rhythm of his prose. When she rewrites her own work, she's doing the same thing, maintaining her own rhythm, giving continuity to her tone, and perfecting her own deceptively simple sentences. She does this over and over during the creation of a single work. Didion started *A Book of Common Prayer* more than twelve times, for example, a number that shocked even her when she discovered the many discarded manuscripts years later.

Didion also maintains continuity by writing every day of the week, every week of the year. "Sometimes I don't accomplish anything every day, but if I don't work every day, I get depressed and get afraid to start again. So I do something every day," she has said.[387] Another daily event, at least during her New York years: a morning walk in Central Park. Before her husband died, they'd walk together, sometimes splitting up for part of the walk, but rejoining before the return to the apartment. After his death, Didion has continued the ritual on her own.[388]

Despite the daily anxiety she experiences in the face of writing, once she starts, the books seem to come out quickly. The actual writing of *Play It as It Lays*, after those years of making notes, took ten months. She finished *The Year of Magical Thinking* in eighty-eight days. *Run River* took longer, but as is often the case with a first book, it was written under a far different set of circumstances from her later ones. Written at night out of necessity, during her off-hours at *Vogue*, it was the only book she completed before meeting her husband, while still living in an uptown apartment furnished with someone else's discarded belongings.[389] With *Play It as It Lays*, once she'd been struck by the initial images (the minor actress, the Riviera, the phone call at 1 a.m.), Didion had the luxuries of money, time, and a husband who understood the intricacies of writing. She had her own office, set up exactly as she wanted it. In their house in Brentwood in the 1980s, that was a small, white, organized room, a cheery contrast to the anguished work she created there.[390] A decade earlier, the office in her Malibu home was described as cluttered, suggesting that Didion may have grown tidier over the years.[391]

While her office may be devoid of other authors' work, Didion admits to taking influence from a certain few writers as she prepares to write a book. She actively courts just a select group, a carefully curated virtual advisory board composed of great works of literature. After her first novel, she never started another without rereading Joseph Conrad's *Victory*, using the novel to set the mood the way a restaurateur might use a lighting scheme—she says, "It opens up the possibilities of a novel. It makes it seem worth doing."[392] Other writers she lists as influential for her own work include V. S. Naipaul and Edmund Wilson. She points to the latter's essays in *The American Earthquake* as particularly useful in ridding oneself of the off-putting "authoritative tone." She took influence from Norman Mailer's *The Executioner's Song* for *The Year of Magical Thinking*, impressed by the "flatness" of the prose that opened the book. "And then suddenly at the end of the first chapter you hear his own voice, which is very effective. I wanted to get some of that flatness."[393]

But once a project is under way, Didion avoids the work of others, and not just in the physical space of her office. "When I'm working, I don't read much at all," she has said. "If it's a good book, it will depress me because mine isn't as good. If it's a bad book it will depress me because mine's just as bad. I don't want anybody else's speech rhythms in my dream."[394]

After the dread of writing is dealt with, overcome, and finally conquered, Didion comes to the end of the day. She welcomes it with one drink, an hour before dinner, which she sips while reviewing her day's work—earlier in life it was whiskey, more recently a glass of wine. She has called this her most important writing ritual. "The drink helps. It removes me from the pages," she says.[395] Her nightly review includes marking the pages up in preparation for the rewriting she'll take on the following morning.

As the writing process for each book nears its conclusion, Didion retreats, not quite to the womb, but as close as she can get. For each of her first three novels, she returned to her childhood home in Sacramento, where her mom cooked her breakfast and her dad fixed her early-evening review drink, and where she spent the rest of those days writing the last one hundred pages.[396] "It's very easy for me to work there. My concentration can be total because nobody calls me. I'm not required to lead a real life. I'm like a child, in my parents' house," she has said. She liked to work in her childhood bedroom, a carnation-pink but also cavelike sanctuary, made so by the vines and trees that grew over the windows. She called it her finishing room.[397]

Didion has shown a tendency to place great trust in her editors. She named an entire book after her first editor: *After Henry* features some of the first essays she wrote without Henry Robbins's guidance after he died in 1979. More recently in 2006, she called the *New York Review of Books* editor Robert Silvers the "person I trust more than anybody."[398]

Another source of comfort in her process: From 1963 until his death at the end of 2003, Didion never wrote a piece that wasn't edited by her husband, John Gregory Dunne, her trusted first reader. During most of their forty-year marriage, they both worked from home, in adjoining offices, every day. Their writing styles differ—Dunne inserts a grittier, more tongue-in-cheek wit into his work than Didion, with her refined detachment from her subjects. But their working relationship was so extraordinarily close that when several surprised readers asked if John had read one of her famous lines, which appears near the beginning of the nonfiction essay "In the Islands"—"We are here on this island in the middle of the Pacific in lieu of filing for divorce"—she scoffed. "Did he know I was writing it?" she wrote rhetorically. "He edited it."[399]

A DAY IN THE WRITER'S LIFE . . .

Joan Didion wakes up and spends the breakfast hour dreading writing. She ultimately forces herself to enter her study, where most often, after an hour or so, the words find her. She begins by rewriting her own work from previous days, capturing the rhythm of her own prose and eventually breaking new ground, progressing further into the book. At some point in the morning, she takes a walk. And at the end of the day, just before dinner, she retreats with a single drink to review her day's work, marking it up for the next day's revisions. Finally, for most of her adult life, she'd then dine with her husband, maybe see friends. And always, she is looking for the next picture to present itself.

THE AUTHOR AS PROTAGONIST

JACK KEROUAC

A three-week creative frenzy in a Manhattan loft, resulting in a single 120-foot-long scroll. The origin myth of Jack Kerouac's novel *On the Road* is today embedded in the popular imagination as the singular act of the Beat generation, a distillation of its freewheeling, free-spirited ethos, its questioning of the status quo via drug-fueled experimentation in both life and literature. The uninhibited way of life he wrote about inevitably informs our understanding of how Kerouac worked, but it ultimately misleads. Kerouac was in reality hardly a free spirit, plagued by his search to find the right way to live; he was not so much unhinged as he was meticulously organized; and finally, the 120-foot scroll was not the first draft of *On the Road*, but rather the culmination of a couple years of work—these are the true realities of Jack Kerouac's writing days.

Kerouac spent much of his adult life chasing an exalted existence through his travels across America, Mexico, and beyond. But life for him started out on a small scale. Until Kerouac won a football scholarship to Columbia University—which included a year at the Horace Mann prep school in the Bronx, where he published his first clumsy story in the school's literary journal[400]—life was pointed toward his working-class hometown of Lowell, Massachusetts. But already, he told his disapproving parents, he had the urgings of the artist, and specifically, a calling to write.[401] During his high school years, Kerouac pored through the great works of literature at the library and began keeping a journal. He developed an intense friendship with a schoolmate, his "mad poet brother"[402] Sammy Sampas, with whom he spent a summer obsessing over Walt Whitman and, later on, Dostoyevsky.[403]

At Columbia, Kerouac dabbled with short stories in the style of his early literary heroes like William Saroyan, a then-popular novelist who fell largely out of favor after World War II, and Hemingway. Henry David Thoreau, Thomas Hardy, and Emily Dickinson would leave an impression on the young Kerouac as well.[404] That his budding interest in literature coincided with his first major adventure—to New York City—presaged the very close relationship his writing would always have to journeying out in the world.

After breaking his leg midway through his freshman season playing football, Kerouac began hobbling over to the West End and Lion's Den bars, reading Thomas Wolfe over cheap beer.[405] Wolfe was Kerouac's first true literary god, and his first novel, *The Town and the City*, clearly emulates Wolfe's autobiographical approach to American mythmaking in fiction and also his often saccharine style. "Wolfe was a torrent of American heaven and hell that opened my eyes to America as a subject in itself," Kerouac reflected many years later.[406]

In the fall of his sophomore year, Kerouac dropped out of Columbia suddenly, and after wandering to Washington, DC, and back and sailing twice with the Merchant Marine, he returned to New York City and moved in with his eventual first wife, Edie Parker. She introduced him to a friend of hers, Lucien Carr, who in quick turn introduced him to Allen Ginsberg, then only seventeen years old to Kerouac's twenty-two.[407] Soon after, Carr brought William Burroughs around, too. At thirty years of age, Burroughs became a different kind of friend than Ginsberg, and yet the entire ragtag group coalesced as the core of what would come to be known as the Beats.

Kerouac, so sure he was a person who thrived on quiet and solitude, fed off the artistic forces of his writer friends. They spent their time talking incessantly about their "New Vision," the nebulous theory for literature and life they developed to challenge societal conventions, and imitating Rimbaud's poetic mutiny. Kerouac stayed in Ginsberg's dorm at Columbia, spending all his time reading and writing (he destroyed all of his work from this time).[408] He then lived with Burroughs and others, all the while in thrall to the soon-to-be-christened Beats, who would cross-pollinate one another's writing for years to come and become Kerouac's principal creative point of reference.

And then he met the charismatic but troubled Neal Cassady in 1946, and everything changed for Kerouac again. *On the Road* opens with that meeting, and there's an easy argument to be made for it being the definitive event of Kerouac's life as a writer. At the time, he was working on *The Town and the City*, still besotted by Thomas Wolfe, but beginning to look to other sources of inspiration. Kerouac wrote that first novel at a more conventional pace as well, over the course of two years.[409] He found Cassady's crude charisma and intellectual zeal captivating, and made a clear effort to incorporate Cassady into his writing scene. In a 1947 letter to Cassady, Kerouac wrote, "I'm particularly anxious that you and Allen and Bill get together so that you may form a permanent friendship and keep things boiling for me to enjoy when I get back—purely selfish."[410] Even though Cassady didn't turn out to be a great writer, he inspired others with his feverish enthusiasm for life, "desirous of everything at the same time," as Kerouac wrote of him in *On the Road*.

Kerouac would write two novels with a protagonist modeled on Cassady (*On the Road* and *Visions of Cody*), and Cassady would figure prominently in three others.[411] The two tape-recorded their conversations so Kerouac could capture "the secret of LINGO in telling a tale" that he felt Cassady revealed.[412] Parts of *Visions of Cody*, in fact, came directly from transcriptions of Cassady speaking, and sections of *On the Road* were lifted from Cassady's letters to Kerouac.[413] When Kerouac spent time living in the Cassadys' attic in San Francisco, every night was given over to emotive, crazy banter, which fueled Kerouac's imagination. And, of course, it was Cassady who got Kerouac out on the road in the first place. (In one of the great ironies of literary history, Kerouac went to his grave having never learned to drive.)

At the same time Cassady was blowing Kerouac's mind, though, Burroughs was there to serve as an antidote to the unshackled, stream-of-consciousness style. The opening pages of *On the Road* focus on Cassady, but it was Burroughs's novel *Junky* that inspired the tenor of Kerouac's spare opening:[414]

> I first met Dean not long after my wife and I split up. I had just gotten over a serious illness that I won't bother to talk about, except that it had something to do with the miserably weary split-up and my feeling that everything was dead. With the coming of Dean Moriarty began the part of my life you could call my life on the road.

With its frank tone and measured upfront reporting of personal troubles, the passage is a clear echo of Burroughs's opening for *Junky*:

> My first experience with junk was during the War, about 1944 or 1945. I had made the acquaintance of a man named Norton who was working in a shipyard at the time. Norton, whose real name was Morelli or

something like that, had been discharged from the peacetime Army for forging a pay check, and was classified 4-F for reasons of bad character.

A female friend of Burroughs's taught Kerouac one night how to extract Benzedrine from inhalers.[415] "Bennies" would serve as a writing aid for the rest of Kerouac's life. He most often worked at night, powered by the Benzedrine, after whomever he was living with had drifted off to bed. It was the Benzedrine that kept Kerouac going for three nonstop weeks when he wrote *On the Road* on the single scroll of paper in April 1951, although years later he claimed to have written it fueled by coffee alone.[416] In 1960, he wrote in a letter to his agent, Sterling Lord, that he was ready to begin his new novel, but was "waiting for my supply of benzedrine to start on it. Once I have the benzedrine it'll be done in 10 days or less." Later in the same letter, he wrote, "I haven't had any benzedrine for 2 years and I realized that's why I haven't written any new novels."[417] The Bennie habit, plus his aversion to steady employment, meant that Kerouac was never an early riser, preferring instead to sleep in and ease into the day.

Kerouac's reliance on substances in his writing did not end with Benzedrine. He wrote *Doctor Sax* with the aid of marijuana and morphine.[418] Mescaline, Seconal, and mushrooms played a role both in the experience chronicled in *Big Sur* and in the writing of it. Drugs, for Kerouac, were a means for tweaking one's perceptions, a key element in his creative philosophy.

By the time he finished *The Town and the City* in 1948, Kerouac was no longer impressed with his own approach to it—the conventional structuring, the third-person narrative. Still, he sent the manuscript off to publishers, and after a few rejections, Robert Giroux at Harcourt Brace agreed to publish it, and the book was released in 1950. By that time, Kerouac's new friends had displaced

Wolfe as his literary touchstone. Still, two enduring features of Kerouac's novels can be credited to Wolfe: his autobiographical plots and American mythmaking. After Kerouac's own life, America became his most important subject. As he was planning his first trip across the country and thinking of *On the Road*, he wrote to a friend, "My subject as a writer is of course America, and simply, I must know everything about it."[419] Going out on the road became his way of conducting research.

In the beginning, *On the Road* seemed to be taking the shape of a more conventional novel, in the vein of *The Town and the City*. Kerouac came up with the idea a few years before writing the scroll draft in April 1951. "I have another novel in mind—'On the Road'—which I keep thinking about: two guys hitchhiking to California in search of something they don't really find, and losing themselves on the road, coming all the way back hopeful of something else," he wrote in his journal in August 1948.[420]

Early versions differed dramatically from the one the world knows. One, titled "The Road" and written in 1950, was typed on regular sheets of typing paper. It opened with a romanticized historical account of the American West, followed by a list on page two of roads that span the United States ("Route 6, Route 50, Route 66, Route 40, Route 54, Route 30").[421] Another, from the fall of 1950, was written by hand as a mock newspaper called *American Times*, with three chapters of *On the Road* representing editions for October 2, 3, and 4. This version opens in a bar in Lowell, Massachusetts.[422]

After two years of experimenting with the concept of the novel, Kerouac received a letter (now lost) from Cassady, said to have run forty thousand words in length, about a Christmas weekend spend carousing around Denver.[423] It provided what he called "the flash"— he suddenly understood the kind of prose he would use for *On the Road*, describing Cassady's writing in the letter as "all first person, fast, mad, confessional, completely serious, all detailed."[424] The first time he engaged in this new style came one evening after he sat in a Manhattan restaurant with a friend, who suggested he write like a painter. Kerouac thought the idea over, let it meld with his impressions from the Cassady letter, then took the subway back to Ozone Park and stood on Cross Bay Boulevard with a notebook in hand, writing everything that came to him about the window of a bakery—painting it with words, so to speak.[425] He called his new style "spontaneous prose," and with it, he felt he had hit upon his genius.

As his life expanded outward, the constant in Kerouac's life became his mother's house. His parents moved from Lowell to New Haven, Connecticut, then in 1943 to Ozone Park in Queens, establishing a permanent base in New York City that proved useful to Kerouac. After his father died, his mother moved to nearby Richmond Hill, also in Queens. He wrote *The Town and the City* in Ozone Park—during the days, he cared for his dying father; at night, the only time he could create the right quiet conditions, he took Benzedrine and worked at the kitchen table. At intervals, he settled into other workspaces—Cassady's attic in San Francisco, or a room above a friend's house in Mexico City, where he often lit a candle, then worked continuously until the candle burned out, signaling the end of his session[426]—but he invariably returned to his mother's house. He never did establish a home apart from her, even during his three inconsequential marriages, and her kitchen table was his most consistent writing space. The scroll draft for *On the Road* proved an exception, written in the Chelsea loft of his second wife, Joan Haverty, whom he left two days after finishing the manuscript.

Kerouac didn't write his novels while out on the road, where the constant hustle for a ride or a bed, the perpetual lack of personal space and sleep, and the thirst for adventure kept any attempt at sustained writing at bay. Instead, he kept notes for later use. Kerouac started keeping a journal as a teenager and over his life accumulated more than two hundred volumes (commonly steno notebooks).[427] During his travels with or without Cassady, he carefully recorded his experiences. He often gave titles to the covers such as "Boog of Spring 1960" or "Benzedrine Vision Mexico City 1952."[428] Sometimes a notebook served as a catchall for his thoughts and observations; other times he took down entire stories.[429] He also kept one notebook to record his dreams, writing in it every morning.[430] Once he'd secured a house for himself and his mother, Kerouac set up a contraption by his bed that he called his "bedside sheets," a sheaf of paper attached to the headboard that he could easily access in the middle of the night.[431]

He also wrote frequent letters to his artistic kindred spirits. More than one scholar has likened Kerouac's note-taking and letter writing to rehearsals before a performance, the performance being the feverish, spontaneous composition of his novels. Visiting Bixby Canyon near Big Sur in the summer of 1960, for example, Kerouac went out every night to sit on a cliff and write about the ocean, writing stream-of-consciousness interpretations of the Pacific in a small spiral-bound notebook that became the poem "Sea." He later told Ginsberg he'd written it with his eyes closed, and the haphazard nature of the notebook, the large writing that doesn't adhere to the lines on the pages, supports that. Back home on Long Island, he wrote letters memorializing the experience to many people.[432] A little over a year after the trip, with the idea sufficiently massaged, he wrote the novel *Big Sur* in a typical Kerouacian burst. The poem "Sea" became the novel's conclusion.

The notes and letters proved useful, but so did Kerouac's immaculate memory. His ability to recall events from decades previous with pixel-like detail became one of his most important writing tools. Kerouac could remember scenes from his childhood or his times on the road with Cassady on a dime, and those memories poured into his writing. "He really had a memory like few men that you meet," said Lucien Carr, recalling that back home in Lowell Kerouac had earned the nickname Memory Babe.[433]

Without the appearance of any particular logic, Kerouac alternated between handwriting and typing. "Certain kinds of stories seem to deny the rackety typewriter," he said.[434] *Visions of Cody* and *Visions of Gerard* were among his handwritten works, taken down with pencil in a handwriting that could be almost freakishly neat, leaning to the right as if in a hurry to get somewhere. Writing in pencil allowed him to erase words and replace them without cluttering the page. *On the Road*, *The Dharma Bums*, and *Big Sur* were more famously typed on scrolls in a single sustained burst.

After inventing spontaneous prose and feeling the rush of success with the writing of *On the Road*, Kerouac entered the most prolific phase of his life. He failed to get *On the Road* published for six years, but the state of limbo turned out to be perfect for his creative process; he wrote eleven books between 1951 and 1957, *Visions of Cody* and *The Subterraneans* among them. He was on a seemingly perpetual high. "I'm getting even better," he wrote to the poet Gary Snyder in the summer of 1957, just months before *On the Road* was finally published, "like Stan Getz the tenor jazz man—there is no real repetitiousness in my work . . . I love to do it."[435]

Kerouac bested his frenetic pace in *On the Road* with subsequent novels, writing *The Subterraneans* in three nights, *Big Sur* in five, and *Visions of Gerard* in ten, "midnight to dawn," he said.[436] But as with *On the Road*, such outpourings were not quite as spontaneous as that pace would suggest. "When the time comes to pay the rent again you force yourself to sit at the typewriter, or at the writing notebook, and get it over with as fast as you can . . . and there's no harm in that because you've got the whole story lined up," he said. "All of it is in my mind, naturally, except that language that is used at the time that it is used."[437]

A strict monitor of his literary output, Kerouac approached his daily word count as sport, determining his cumulative "batting average" at the end of every day through what he called "an intricate mathematical thing which determines how assiduously I'm getting my novel typed and revised day after day. It's too complicated to explain."[438] In a journal entry on June 3, 1948, he determined that if he hit as well as Ted Williams, he'd finish *The Town and the City* that very month. In his journals, he alternately praised or admonished his progress. Kerouac always kept austerely organized—visitors to his house were always surprised to see how meticulous he was in keeping records and files.

Yet he wanted his writing to stand as a document of spontaneous thought. As such, Kerouac rejected the very notion of revision. In 1957, he wrote to his editor of *The Subterraneans*: "I can't possibly go on as a responsible prose artist and also a believer in the impulses of my own heart and in the beauty of pure spontaneous language if I let editors take my sentences . . . and riddle them with commas, cut them by half, in threes, in fours, ruining the swing, making what was reasonably wordy prose even more wordy and unnaturally awkward (because castrated)."[439] But in the end his novels invariably succumbed to some editing before publication. The famous *On the Road* scroll itself betrays his tendency to revise, peppered as it is with crossed out words, notes to make changes, and other indications of revision.[440] "I approve of the few cuts you made," Kerouac wrote to his editor Malcolm Cowley years later, leading up to the novel's release date.[441]

The sudden success of *On the Road* in 1957 after so much time and struggle changed Kerouac's life overnight, giving him a measure of financial security for the first time. With the money from this second novel, he bought a house for his mother and himself on Long Island and, also for the first time, had a room dedicated to his writing. A reporter for the *Long Island Newsday*, who visited him in the second of the two Northport houses he lived in in 1964, described a room with "a thousand books on the shelves, and everybody's there, from Aristophanes to Allen Ginsberg. Two of the walls blaze with abstract paintings from many lands."[442]

But *On the Road* also made Kerouac a celebrity, and only once it was pointed squarely at him did he understand how uncomfortable he was in the spotlight. His already-heavy drinking intensified, and his journals reflected a man who had become disillusioned, bored, and depressed. His writing suffered accordingly. Kerouac finished *The Dharma Bums* in the few months after *On the Road*'s release, and then didn't complete another book for four years.[443] This one, *Big Sur*, was his last major work and the only one written about his life after success—tellingly, about a nervous breakdown. He finally had everything at his disposal for a stable writing life, and he could no longer make the writing happen. Kerouac passed away at age forty-seven from internal bleeding caused by alcoholism. For Jack Kerouac, the journey was clearly preferable to the destination.

A DAY IN THE WRITER'S LIFE . . .

Most of Jack Kerouac's days passed in the service of *preparing* to write a novel. He wasn't an early riser—wasn't necessarily even a morning riser. He might spend months or even years out conducting his particular brand of research before writing the first word of a novel. Out on the road, he followed a generally conceived itinerary but let the day take him where it would. Every day, he took notes, kept his journal, wrote letters. But the time reserved for novel writing came in sporadic bursts, during which he would take Benzedrine and then write night and day until the work was finished, often at his mother's kitchen table.

ERNEST HEMINGWAY

In the spring of 1918 Ernest Hemingway, who would not turn nineteen for two months and didn't have to go anywhere near World War I on account of his poor eyesight, abandoned a nascent journalism career to sign on as an ambulance driver for the Red Cross in Italy. A couple of months in, during a trip to the front to deliver coffee and cigarettes, Hemingway fell into the line of mortar fire. Gravely wounded, he spent the next six months in a Red Cross hospital. There, in what would become a Hemingway trademark, near disaster became riveting material for fiction. He fell in love with his nurse, Agnes, and while the affair did not last, it became the genesis for *A Farewell to Arms* a decade or so later. For Hemingway, danger, adventure, and novel writing went hand in hand. He invented the writer as hero, and in doing so reinvented what it meant to have a literary life in America. Getting out in the world, running up to death and then teasing it—in Hemingway's conception, this was the life of the writer.

Growing up in well-off Oak Park, Illinois, just outside Chicago, Hemingway's father encouraged outdoor activity over whiling away an afternoon with a book. Hemingway was happy to indulge in the fishing trips and other fresh-air adventures; at the same time, he enjoyed reading books on the side. But even curled up reading, Hemingway's tastes bent toward adventure, and the books of his youth skewed not to cerebral literature but to journey and action, such as that in the historical adventure novels of the now largely forgotten G. A. Henty.[444] When he started writing in his teen years, he emulated the satirical sports writer Ring Lardner.

At age eighteen, uninterested in attending college, Hemingway decided on something more audacious when he took a job through a family connection as a cub reporter at the *Kansas City Star*. He hadn't quite settled on the idea of writing as a career—a point he contradicted later in life, saying both that he always knew he wanted to be a writer and also that he realized when he was twenty, after he'd left the *Star*. (It has been the burden of all Hemingway biographers to extract the self-made myth from the facts of his life.) Still, at the *Star* he began to learn the kind of economical writing that came to define his later work. "On the *Star* you were forced to learn to write a simple declarative sentence," he said.[445] The paper's style guide gave him a template for succinctness and clarity that would stay with him forever.

With a foundational approach to writing in place, Hemingway began toying with fiction, which immediately emerged as a way of reinterpreting his own life experiences. The subject that most fascinated Ernest Hemingway as a writer revealed itself to be Ernest Hemingway, and his fiction started off and remained intensely autobiographical. In early short stories, he invented the character of Nick Adams as a stand-in for himself. Nick Adams provided Hemingway with a sort of buffer, shielding him from having to acknowledge self-criticism and also allowing him to create a per-haps more pleasing version of himself: Adams is more optimistic and less flawed than his creator.

The extent to which Hemingway wrote autobiographically is more obvious in his early drafts than his published work. Many first drafts of his novels contained not the eventual character name but the names of the real people upon whom they were based. Between the first draft of *The Sun Also Rises* and the final manuscript, for example, the real-life Harold Loeb became Robert Cohn, Hem (short for Hemingway) became Jake Barnes, his friends Bill Smith and Don Stewart were conflated into a single character, Bill Gorton, and so on.[446]

After his eight months in Italy, Hemingway returned to America for a stint as a war hero back in the Midwest and lived briefly in Toronto, where he did some work for the *Toronto Star*. He met and married his first wife, Hadley, then almost immediately moved to Paris, a home base from which he embarked on a series of adventures in Europe that would fuel his fiction, most notably to Spain to see the bullfights. It was on one of these trips that the idea for *The Sun Also Rises* came to him, and he began writing the novel on the very trip that inspired it. Later journeys would be used to similar ends: *To Have and Have Not* tells the story of a man who runs contraband between Key West and Cuba; Hemingway kept houses in both places at the time. *The Old Man and the Sea* is about an old fisherman fighting a marlin in the seas near Cuba, where Hemingway was living and growing old himself. *For Whom the Bell Tolls* was based on Hemingway's own experiences reporting on the Spanish Civil War. Arguably his greatest short story, "The Snows of Kilimanjaro," was inspired by his travels in Africa. There's an argument to be made that *A Moveable Feast* is not a memoir at all, but a fictionalized account of his time in Europe.

In Paris, Hemingway eventually began to feel that his journalistic work was adversely affecting his creative writing. His newspaper assignments not only commanded chunks of time he would have rather devoted to fiction, but also put him in the wrong frame of mind for producing creative work—many writers can engage in only one style at a time, and Hemingway fit that bill. He stayed on as a correspondent for the *Toronto Star* because it paid well, but felt increasingly embittered by the demands it put on him. Once he gained confidence in his prospects as a novelist, Hemingway chose the life of a poor fiction writer over a well-paid journalist, although true penury was never a risk: his wife's trust fund ensured that.[447]

Hemingway's love of reading continued in adulthood—his fourth wife, Mary, once counted 4,623 volumes in their house, which Hemingway claimed to have read all but one of.[448] Once he'd established his own style, though, he used reading not to inform his own writing, but to escape from it. "When I was writing, it was necessary for me to read after I had written . . . If you kept thinking about it, you would lose the thing that you were writing before you could go on with it the next day," he wrote in *A Moveable Feast.*[449] Although Hemingway revered legendary writers like Tolstoy, one never gets the sense that he was emulating any one of them. The young Hemingway seemed to always be inventing his writing style from within, even when he accepted the odd piece of advice. The older Hemingway felt that he alone wrote like he wanted to write.

Nonetheless, a few key writers influenced Hemingway early on. Before moving to Paris, he met Sherwood Anderson in Chicago and quickly had him convinced of his potential—not through his writing, but through the sheer charm of his personality. Anderson armed Hemingway with letters of introduction to eminent writers in Paris, which helped him to meet Ezra Pound, from whom he learned to "distrust adjectives," among other stylistic principles.[450] He later told Pound that he "learned more about how to write and how not to write from you than from any son of a bitch alive." He also met Gertrude

Stein, who urged him along and deployed useful advice. Hemingway transcribed much of Stein's novel *The Making of Americans* and almost certainly absorbed some of her rhythms during the process, especially her avoidance of complicated words and the beat of her sentences.[451] And there was, of course, F. Scott Fitzgerald, a man in whom Hemingway recognized the same stroke of genius that he saw in himself. Fitzgerald sometimes served as an early reader—at his suggestion, Hemingway cut portions from the early pages of *The Sun Also Rises*.[452] He didn't always react so well to Fitzgerald's critiques, though: "Kiss my ass," Hemingway wrote in the margins of one of Fitzgerald's letters containing a criticism of *A Farewell to Arms*.

That Hemingway managed to meet and befriend so many important writers before he himself had published much of anything speaks to his other great ability. Rivaling his talent with the written word was Hemingway's knack for networking, which had as much to do with his success as anything. At the same time he was working so hard to develop his writing chops, he made sure that those who might further his career knew him and liked him. Hemingway possessed a potent charisma and deployed it strategically.

But Hemingway genuinely loved to see people, too, and bore none of the reclusive habits common to some writers. In his Paris days especially, he took to the cafés some mornings to work on his writing surrounded by the collective human bustle. He always maintained a series of close friendships with other men. (Relationships with women, on the other hand, he felt ambivalent toward and at times even considered them a hindrance.) He derived an intellectual and creative energy from his interactions with friends, especially those engaged in some artistic pursuit: He said he learned as much from painters as he did from other writers, and he tried specifically to translate Paul Cézanne's brushstrokes into the sweeps of his sentences. He also aspired to the "harmony and counterpoint" achieved by great composers of music.[453]

His social nature had a down side, however. Hemingway found himself easily distracted by the prospect of a good conversation (or a good fishing outing, or a good war to cover). Especially after he became famous and even strangers sought out his company, Hemingway understood that discipline was necessary and that he was the only one capable of enforcing it. He thus gradually learned to keep would-be visitors at bay.

Hemingway kept the lifelong habit of rising with the sun—he claimed his unusually thin eyelids made it impossible to sleep any later. Already at age twenty, long before he could call himself a real writer, he spent mornings writing in Michigan, where the family had a summer home, and the afternoons chasing local girls.[454] He typically got down to writing by 7 a.m. or so, first rewriting the previous days' work to get back in the right headspace, and then continued on writing new material until roughly noon, after which he completely cast off the writing life for the rest of the day. A writer was no good at it after six hours, he firmly believed, and for him the stopping point was the most important moment of the writing day: "The best way is always to stop when you are going good," he said. "If you do that you'll never be stuck . . . That way your subconscious will be working on it all the time, but if you worry about it, your brain will get tired before you start again."[455]

Hemingway liked to track his daily progress. During the writing of *The Sun Also Rises*, he claimed to average 2,000 words per day.[456] While working on *A Farewell to Arms* in Wyoming, he kept a daily log of pages written along with his other activities: "worked 4 pages, fished with Bill Horne, caught 12," read one entry.[457] In his later years, he kept a chart in his workroom showing his daily output, which could range from 450 words to well over 1,000.[458] His lifetime norm fell between 500 and 1,000 words per day.

Typically a slowish but steady worker, Hemingway could also be prone to the occasional burst of creativity, which he took full advantage of. "My head . . . can go most of the time like a frozen cabbage and then it can give you hell when it starts going," he wrote to Gertrude Stein and Alice Toklas in 1925.[459] He wrote the draft of *The Sun Also Rises* in six weeks, for example, and once completed two important short stories in a day. More typical perhaps was *A Farewell to Arms*, on which he spent eight months writing a first draft. At any rate, he believed in the importance of simply getting that first draft down: "You put down the words in hot blood, like an argument, and correct them when your temper has cooled."[460]

He enjoyed those mornings spent writing and felt the gratification of accomplishment after. "The worst time is just before," he said.[461] And despite his reputation for hard living, Hemingway didn't drink while writing, although he did tend to commence pretty quickly after stepping away from his desk. In his younger days especially, he could get away with it, go out drinking late into the night and function fine as a journalist the next day. Later on, even though he became a problem drinker, he usually stopped before the early-morning hours rolled around and still rose at daybreak for a daily writing session.

Writer's block didn't hit Hemingway often, but when it did, he wrote copious letters instead of fiction. During one three-month period in 1925 when things weren't going great, he managed just one two-page short story and one short essay—and at least thirty-three letters.[462] Conversely, if he was on a roll with his writing, friends learned not to hold their breath waiting for correspondence from him.

With the threat of writer's block perhaps always in the back of his mind, Hemingway could be superstitious about his work. He never worked on two writing projects at once. When he was young, he carried a rabbit's foot in his pocket for luck with his literary endeavors. He was suspicious of writing on Sundays: "It's very bad luck . . . Sometimes I do it but it's bad luck just the same."[463] And he hated discussing works in progress with anyone, especially the media. "Though there is one part of writing that is solid and you do it no harm by talking about it," he said, "the other is fragile, and if you talk about it, the structure cracks and you have nothing."[464]

Hemingway often took notes on his trips and other adventures—he annoyed everyone by doing so incessantly on one particular fishing trip in the Pyrenees in his twenties—but never named note-taking as a central device in his process. He didn't make a point of taking notes or making outlines before starting a novel. He did, however, emphasize the importance of constant observation. "If a writer stops observing he is finished. But he does not have to observe consciously nor think how it will be useful. Perhaps that would be true at the beginning. But later everything he sees goes into the great reserve of things he knows or has seen."[465]

A complete story would often have come together in his mind before Hemingway wrote the first word. Other times it came to him as he went. In this sense, Hemingway had no consistent process for conceptualizing the story itself. Some novels emerged as he envisioned them, while others began as short stories that became much, much longer. A couple of novels were abandoned altogether partway through. *The Old Man and the Sea* was in his mind for many years before he finally put it to paper, while he began *The Sun Also Rises*, his first published novel, nearly the moment the idea occurred to him.

When Hemingway was young and had few possessions, his writing spaces tended to be spare, a reflection of his living arrangements. By the time he had settled in his house on the outskirts of Havana as a Nobel Prize winner, though, his work desk had become, as George Plimpton once described it after a visit, "a square foot of cramped area hemmed in by books on one side and on the other by a newspaper-covered heap of papers, manuscripts, and pamphlets."[466] Hemingway wrote at that messy desk standing up. In his Key West home before that, he kept a writing studio in a carriage house out back, this one with a small desk and austere wooden chair placed in the center of a sun-filled second-floor room. But Hemingway was not too particular about his writing spaces. "I have worked well everywhere," he said. "I mean I have been able to work as well as I can under varied circumstances. The telephone and visitors are the work destroyers."[467]

He often kept two writing spaces going at once. In Paris, he wrote both at home and in a hotel room he kept for that purpose, as well as in the cafés on occasion. In Cuba, he had a writing space in the bedroom and another in a tower on the property. During his frequent travels, he worked at a table in a rented room or a bar down the street. Once he had enough money to own a boat, he liked to anchor it "in the lee of some bay" and get down to writing. He worked better there than anywhere else, he said, mostly because distractions had been left on land.[468] No matter the location, he alternated between the typewriter and writing in pencil with his unvarying handwriting, curiously globular and almost feminine, in a blue-covered notebook.

With a first draft done, Hemingway entered an intense period of revision and rewriting. He tended to cut a lot from the first draft—no surprise for a writer with no tolerance for superfluous words. "The test of a book is how much good stuff you can throw away," he said. "When I'm writing it, I'm just as proud as a goddam lion. I use the oldest words in the English language"—the very words that disappeared by the final version.[469] He claimed to have rewritten the ending of *A Farewell to Arms* precisely thirty-two times,[470] and likewise claimed to rewrite first chapters of his novels forty to fifty times.[471] The extensive rewrites helped him achieve perfect openings, like this justly famous one from *A Farewell to Arms*:

In the late summer of that year we lived in a house in a village that looked across the river and the plain to the mountains. In the bed of the river there were pebbles and boulders, dry and white in the sun, and the water was clear and swiftly moving and blue in the channels. Troops went by the house and down the road and the dust they raised powdered the leaves of the trees. The trunks of the trees too were dusty and the leaves fell early that year and we saw the troops marching along the road and the dust rising and leaves, stirred by the breeze, falling and the soldiers marching and afterward the road bare and white except for the leaves.

Only with the extensive rewrites behind him and the final version in place did Hemingway come up with names for his novels. With the story or book completed, he then made a list of titles—"sometimes as many as a hundred"[472]—and then whittled it down to the eventual winner, the chosen one always seeming as though it were the only title the book ever could have accommodated.

The completion of a novel from start to finish, including the rewrites, usually took a couple of years or so, although some novels, like *The Sun Also Rises*, he finished much more quickly, while others, like *The Old Man and the Sea*, took longer. And on the other end of a job well done, Hemingway had no problem indulging in some time off. "I take a long time to write a book and I like to have fun in between," he told the *New York Herald Tribune* in 1959, explaining why he'd written "only" thirteen books.[473]

Not long after that interview, Hemingway suffered the sudden onset of a mental deterioration, probably hereditary, that left him confused, paranoid, and suicidal. It was a departure from the Hemingway the world knew. A stretch at the Mayo Clinic didn't help and may have made matters worse. In 1961, Hemingway took his own life in a dismal act that stood in stark contrast to the rest of his robust life.

A DAY IN THE WRITER'S LIFE . . .

Every day, Ernest Hemingway rose with the sun and by 7 a.m. got straight down to writing. Where didn't particularly matter—at different times in his life, he wrote in a hotel room reserved for that purpose, at café tables, standing up at a cluttered desk in his bedroom, and on his anchored boat near Cuba. Wherever he was, Hemingway started by rewriting the previous days' work, then moving forward, always going until around noon, at which time he was done entirely, both mentally and physically. Afternoons were often spent outdoors, in the company of his many male friends, or reading the work of others to clear his mind of his own efforts, a drink invariably in hand.

SLOW AND STEADY

13

JAMES JOYCE

Legend has it that one day in the early twentieth century, a friend found James Joyce in despair at his desk toward the end of the afternoon. He asked Joyce how much he'd managed to write that day. *Seven words,* Joyce replied. *That's not so bad,* said the friend, adding, *for you.* But Joyce's response is the real kicker: *But I don't know what order they go in!*

The story seems to show a man deliberating over his work to the point of paralysis, seven words away from total writer's block. The reality, though, was not quite so pained: Joyce was not one to despair over his writing; his unwavering confidence in his own genius saw him through most writing sessions, and it turns out he averaged far more than 7 words per day—a full 90, based on the eight years it took him to write *Ulysses*'s 265,000 words. It may have taken him three days to write a full page of text, yes, but the pace didn't worry him. Joyce maintained a clear vision of where he was slowly headed.

Joyce was remarkably consistent in his sluggish, patient progress. Before *Ulysses*, he worked on his first two books, *Dubliners* and

A Portrait of the Artist as a Young Man, for ten years collectively. By the time he arrived at his final work, *Finnegans Wake*, the pace had slowed even further: He gave a full fifteen over to that book,[474] and never during that time felt inadequate, or that his talent may have slipped. Just the opposite, in fact: "I have discovered I can do anything with language I want," he is said to have told Samuel Beckett late in his career.[475] Joyce even took some joy in his plodding progress and liked to tally the hours spent on a particular work. By his measure, the twenty pages of the "Anna Livia Plurabelle" section of *Finnegans Wake* took him 1,200 hours to complete, or 60 hours per page.[476] He likewise calculated that the "Oxen of the Sun" chapter of *Ulysses* required 1,000 hours.[477] It's no surprise, given these protracted timelines, that Joyce completed only three novels and one book of short stories in his fifty-eight years (along with a play and a modest number of essays).

Joyce maintained a singular dedication to his writing career, but on a daily basis that devotion manifested itself imprecisely and at different hours. He often found himself taken up with other activities, required or diversionary. And often, those other activities stemmed from struggles with money that began in his childhood. Joyce came into the world as the eldest surviving son of a large and well-off Irish family, living in material and intellectual abundance in the Dublin suburb of Bray. His profligate father managed to remain well off long enough to start the six-year-old Joyce on the path toward an elite education, but the wealth was soon squandered, and the Joyce family began moving from house to house, always one frantic step ahead of creditors. It was a piecemeal existence that allowed Joyce to experience Ireland in a less sheltered way, exposing him to the ordinary, hardscrabble lives that would become central to his fiction. But it also meant that he had to work for his money when it wasn't coming from his writing, which was often. After graduating from University College Dublin and a brief stint in Paris to purportedly study medicine, Joyce returned to Dublin to see his dying mother and then stayed on awhile. During this time he met his wife, Nora, and the two soon moved to Trieste, Italy.

At one point while living in Trieste in 1910, he'd wake around ten in the morning, sit in bed for an hour or so skipping from thought to thought, then rise and, after some attempt at grooming, make his way to his piano, where visitors (or creditors) often interrupted him. At 1 p.m., he'd break for lunch and then teach English lessons for the rest of the afternoon and into the evening. He might keep giving lessons into the night, or he might take in a play with Nora.[478] Just as likely, he'd make his way to one of Trieste's cafés for a bout of drinking. Joyce also loved to take walks, alone or with company. In his high school days, he wandered the streets of Dublin daily, exploring obscure nooks and observing obscure people. Later, in Trieste, he often took evening strolls to mull over the phrasing of his current work. It's hard to see where he fit the writing in, and the struggle only intensified during the frequent times that he held full-time teaching positions, or for one brief period, worked in a bank.

On a couple of occasions, Joyce took as much as an entire year off from work on a novel. While living in Rome for seven months in 1906 and 1907, he did little if any writing, struck dumb by his dislike for that city and overwhelmed by his work at the bank and giving private English lessons.[479] He also wrote nothing from April 1908 until early in 1909. This time, it took an unexpected and gushing letter from a respected student to rouse him from his literary inertia.[480] In 1913, a failed extramarital affair with a student was just the thing to snap him out of a writing malaise after another extended break from his work. Joyce also benefited from living and working in the age of novel serialization. At points during the writing of both *A Portrait of the Artist as a Young Man* and *Ulysses*, the imminent serialization of the novel spurred him into action—the magic of the deadline touched Joyce just like it touches mere mortals.

The necessities of his daily routine changed significantly in 1917, when an anonymous patron, later revealed to be the English publisher Harriet Shaw Weaver, enabled Joyce to stop giving English lessons and organize his days exclusively around his writing. From this time on, first in Zurich and then after settling in Paris, he was known to stick to his home for most of the day—although the pace of his output never did pick up. At night, he remained an inveterate socializer. Despite his skepticism toward people in general and his taciturn self-presentation, Joyce liked to throw a good party, and he liked to attend them. He was a borderline problem drinker for most of his adult life, despite abstaining into his university years for fear of ending up like his drunkard father. Even on quieter nights he liked to sit with a friend and discuss literature over his favorite white wine, "St Patrice."[481]

As he got older, Joyce spent fewer of those evenings with a good book. He read insatiably in his teenage years and young adulthood; less so by the time his eyesight began to fail him. He began writing in earnest as a teenager as well. At first, Joyce focused on poetry, inspired by fellow Irishman William Butler Yeats. He filled several exercise books with his poetic compositions; his brother Stanislaus remembered one he titled "Moods" and another called "Shine and Dark."[482] At university, with his gift for poetry proving limited, Joyce's thirst to write evolved in other directions. He spent many nights in the National Library absorbing the works of others. *The Odyssey* emerged as the most obvious influence, serving as the model for *Ulysses*, although that work was less a stylistic influence than a framework with which to give structure his own peculiar style. The Norwegian playwright Henrik Ibsen sparked Joyce's lifelong love of the theater and, more important, became the first writer to truly light a literary fire under Joyce. He especially revered Ibsen's decision to feature not heroic figures but everyday people in his plays.[483] In his enthrallment, Joyce decided to become a play-wright and wrote a play before he ever attempted a novel. He later destroyed it, unpublished and unperformed.

Other strong influences included the French novelist Édouard Dujardin, whom Joyce credited with introducing him to the con-cept of writing in stream of consciousness and using "interior monologue";[484] Honoré de Balzac, whose own portraits of a young artist loomed over the writing of Joyce's first novel;[485] and the Ital-ian author Gabriele D'Annunzio, with his novel *The Flame*, in which the author fictionalized his own life and focused on lyricism over plot, an approach that would become quintessential Joyce.[486]

While at University College Dublin, Joyce began working on a series of sketches that he called "Epiphanies." These were short profiles and observations that helped him develop his approach to writing longer works, when the time came. Stanislaus observed that the Epiphanies "served [Joyce] as a sketch-book serves an artist."[487] While some were abandoned, twenty-five made their way into his later published work.[488] Joyce was clearly moving toward the life of a writer, but didn't yet seem ready to go all in. He halfheartedly enrolled in medical school, first in Ireland, then Paris, as a sort of backup plan, but the studies never took. He later took singing les-sons with an eye toward performing professionally. When Joyce began to experiment with writing about his own artistic ambitions, he finally hit on the thing that convinced him he was a writer. As biographer Richard Ellmann put it, he "found he could become an artist by writing about the process of becoming an artist."[489]

Ultimately, Joyce had to leave his native country in order to write about it the way he wanted, and he never set foot in Ireland again after 1912, the year he turned thirty.[490] Not even his father's death and funeral in 1931 could lure him. Despite an adulthood lived in Continental Europe, Dublin remained Joyce's artistic focal point. Although in some ways he qualified as an autobiographical author, Joyce's dedication to writing about the Ireland he knew meant that he wrote about a fixed moment in time. David Norris, a director of the James Joyce Centre in Dublin, put it this way: "For Joyce, Dublin was always the Dublin of 1904. The clock stopped. That meant he had stable material with which to work as an artist."[491] *Ulysses* famously takes place over the course of just one day, June 16, 1904—the day Joyce met Nora. But it also contains vastly more than that day, as does each prosaic day in a person's life. And over the course of writing about that day, Joyce's autobiographical focus shifted from one protagonist, Stephen Dedalus, to the other, Leopold Bloom, making each character both autobiographical and not.[492]

In the nascent phase of writing a novel, Joyce took haphazard notes on any available surface. "I make notes on stray bits of paper which I then forget in the most unlikely places, in books, under ornaments and in my pockets and on the back of advertisements," he once explained to one of his typists.[493] His wallet, too, was usually bloated with such scraps, collected while out and about. He'd later transfer those notes, assuming he hadn't lost them, into one of his notebooks. He rarely filled a page, but rather recorded one thought or concept per sheet. In one book of notes for *Ulysses*, page topics include "Stephen," "Recipes," "Art," and "Jews," all topics that factored in his novel.[494] As he sculpted his notes into a work of literature, he color-coded them—text struck through with the same-colored pencil was destined to link up in the novel's final form.[495] Very little from his initial drafts failed to make it into a final version—Joyce was not a man to place words on the page indiscriminately. Every word he put on the page, even on a first draft, had to be the perfect one.

Joyce never typed his own work, and his abominable handwriting often required that, even after writing one draft, he recopy his work into another one more carefully so his typists would be able to decipher it (although his brother remembered his writing as "neat" and "firm" in their university years).[496] In addition Joyce, always eager for a moneymaking scheme, came to realize after he gained acclaim that each additional draft could potentially be sold to a collector and was happy to produce another, whether truly necessary or not.

Despite the care he took in getting the right words on the page the first time, Joyce made endless minute revisions to all drafts, filling the margins and even the spaces between the lines with additions and changes, so that a passage starting out as:

By Bachelor's walk jogjingle
jaunted Blazes Boylan, bachelor.
In sun, in heat, warmseated,
sprawled, mare's glossy rump
atrot. Horn, Have you the ?
Horn. Have you the ? Haw
haw horn.

might finally appear in the published version of *Ulysses* as:

By Bachelor's walk jogjaunty jingled Blazes Boylan, bachelor, in sun, in heat, mare's glossy rump atrot with a flick of whip, on bounding tyres: sprawled, warmseated, Boylan impatience, ardentbold. Horn. Have you the ? Horn. Have you the ? Haw haw horn.[497]

The gist of the passage remains, as it usually did from conception to publication, but several tweaks give it an inspired sheen that was just barely missing in the first go at it. Joyce's obsession with details thus displays itself. "I've got a grocer's assistant's mind," he once said.[498]

Joyce also demanded that the facts upon which his stories were propped be unerringly accurate. He often wrote to a friend or family member back in Dublin to have some point or other verified. One typical letter to Stanislaus during his work on *Dubliners* requested answers to such questions as: *Can a priest be buried in a habit? Can a municipal election take place in October?* And, *Are the police at Sydney Parade of the D Division?*[499] And it wasn't just Dublin that he wanted to represent accurately: After giving *Ulysses's* Molly Bloom a childhood in Gibraltar, Joyce, having never visited the territory, researched it so extensively that years later when he met a man from Gibraltar, the man could hardly believe that Joyce had never set foot there. As Joyce worked, he often kept relevant references around him to help with accuracy. While writing the "Oxen of the Sun" episode of *Ulysses*, for example, about the fertility and incubation of both humans and language, he kept a diagram of fetal ontogeny in front of him to help keep the facts straight.[500]

He used every encounter in life as potential fodder for his fiction and respected few boundaries in doing so. Joyce had no qualms about putting friends and loved ones into his work, regardless of potential embarrassment or offense; he in fact left a trail of resentment among family and friends with each published work. His friend Oliver St. John Gogarty was apparently terrified of how Joyce would represent him in his work. Stanislaus accused his brother of taking unauthorized peeks into his diary and lifting portions for *Stephen Hero*, Joyce's early novel that he later rewrote as *A Portrait of the Artist as a Young Man*.[501] Interestingly, Joyce never kept a diary of his own, more concerned with putting his experiences directly into the context of fiction than with recording them for his own recollection.

Joyce might even go so far as to manipulate reality for literary ends. Friends sometimes noted that Joyce seemed to be steering conversations in a deliberate way.[502] "While one talked to him one could not help but feel, at times, that he was using the conversation as a sort of counterpoint to his own thoughts, which ran in an altogether different vein as he mentally composed 'Work in Progress' (published as *Finnegans Wake*)," wrote his friend Arthur Power.[503] He took such manipulation to perhaps its most egregious extreme when he urged his wife, Nora, to sleep with other men so he could write about it.[504]

Never shy about letting early readers go over his work, Joyce nonetheless discouraged harsh criticism, and if he received it, he looked elsewhere for praise. Especially during the writing of *Finnegans Wake*, about which so many people expressed doubt, Joyce pressed for encouraging words. Even his patron, Harriet Shaw Weaver, admitted to him that she feared he might be "wasting [his] genius."[505] Joyce was so dismayed by her doubt that he went to bed and stayed there for a couple of days, emerging finally to consult other friends about his work in progress. He ultimately stayed the course, choosing to rely on his inner sense of direction over the opinions of others. But the doubts had shaken him, however fleetingly.

Nora, however, never served as an early reader and was in fact hard-pressed to read her husband's work even after it was published. In a fit of exasperation, she once asked him, "Why don't you write sensible books that people can understand?"[506] Nora's role in Joyce's writing life was indirect, as she wasn't particularly interested in literature. Her biggest contribution was in providing him with the rough model for *Ulysses*'s Molly Bloom.

Joyce calculated that he worked on *Ulysses* from twenty different homes. In other words, he never achieved a consistent writing space. This was largely Joyce's own fault; his money management skills rivaled those of a shopping addict with a gambling problem. What could have been a comfortable income as an English teacher was squandered on ill-advised purchases, extravagant nights at the opera (he once attended *La Bohème* eight times in ten nights), and new clothes for the children (Nora threw them all out with the change of every season). As a result, the Joyces were constantly hearing the knock of creditors at the door and often evicted from their apartments. Joyce had a choice between cultivating a writing space and living a spendthrift lifestyle. Without a thought, he chose the latter.

In one apartment in Trieste, Joyce wrote at the kitchen table because the light in that room was better than elsewhere in the apartment.[507] In another apartment, he worked in the dining room, a smattering of his notes and manuscripts overwhelming the table.[508] After his eyesight worsened, he often wrote lying across his bed wearing a white jacket, which he hoped would aid his vision with its reflective powers.[509] In some apartments, he kept his books and workspace hidden from almost everyone. At the same time, he didn't like to be too secluded, worried that if he grew accustomed to an ideal work environment with total silence, he'd no longer be able to concentrate when he inevitably found himself in that next, less ideal space. "When I am working I like to hear noise going on around me—the noise of life," Arthur Power remembered Joyce telling him.[510] This partially explains why Joyce spent his entire life living in cities, thriving off their energy.

To make ends meet, Joyce proved himself more than willing to lean on the financial generosities of friends and family. While living in Paris just after university, he allowed his family to pawn treasured belongings in order to enable his writer's existence. When his brother Stanislaus came to live with him and Nora in Trieste, the move was made at Joyce's behest and seemed motivated more by the quest for financial support than the desire to be close to his brother. Indeed, Joyce used his brother with a jarring lack of respect. "A brother is as easily forgotten as an umbrella," he wrote in *Ulysses*, after Stanislaus had spent years propping up Joyce and his family.

As the years progressed, Joyce's overall health worsened. He was forced to take breaks from writing because of his increasingly debilitating eye problems, which may or may not have been helped or intensified by the dozens of operations meant to improve his sight. There were stretches of time Joyce spent nearly blind. In order to see his own work, he began writing in a comically large hand. He continually refused the suggestion that he dictate his work, insisting until the end, which came after surgery for a perforated ulcer at age fifty-eight, that he be the master of his own gradual progress.

A DAY IN THE WRITER'S LIFE . . .

For a man whose very being revolved around writing, James Joyce's days tended to get filled up by any number of activities other than writing. Consistency of routine was not one of the skills that made him great. Joyce tended to sleep late, until 10 a.m. or so, then lounge for an hour, easing into the day. He was easily distracted by music, a visitor, or a drink, and he spent many days teaching English in order to pay the bills. Yet he was always thinking about his writing, always playing with the next turn of phrase he'd write down. At night, Joyce's spendthrift ways tended to get the better of him; he and his wife, Nora, often headed out to the opera or one of the finer restaurants in town, or Joyce might head out on his own to spend a small fortune in the local pubs.

JUNOT DÍAZ

Junot Díaz dashed off the first seventy-five pages of his only novel to date, *The Brief Wondrous Life of Oscar Wao*, soon after his first book of short stories, *Drown*, came out in 1996. Fifty or so of those pages appeared in the *New Yorker* in 2000 as a long short story bearing the same name. The story was a promising start to an ambitious project. But then Díaz lost his handle on it. "Nothing I wrote past page 75 made any kind of sense," he later wrote. Díaz tried to abandoned it and start other novels, but they turned out even worse. Efforts at short stories, previously his go-to, failed as well. He felt compelled to continue on *Oscar Wao*, not because it was working, but because those first seventy-five pages were really good, worth turning into something, and also for reasons he didn't quite understand. But nothing worked: "I wrote and I wrote and I wrote, but nothing I produced was worth a damn."[511]

Díaz kept on like this not for a few months but for five whole years. At the end of those five years, with progress still stymied, he considered quitting writing altogether, came to think maybe he'd had only one book in him. He put the manuscript in a box, put the box in a closet, and decided to go back to grad school. Then, during a sleepless summer night, he succumbed to a familiar compulsion. He brought the pages back out and set about reading them over. With the fresh perspective brought by the passing of time, he discovered everything after page seventy-five to be even worse than he'd remembered. Díaz nonetheless found himself intrigued all over again, pulled back into the project almost against his will. The slog resumed; he did not enroll in the grad school program. Díaz worked on the novel for two more years before it began to resemble something worth finishing, not to mention publishing. Three years after that, he was done with the book. Ten years total to write a single novel.[512] *The Brief Wondrous Life of Oscar Wao*, a complicated work about a nerdy Dominican kid growing up in New Jersey and the forces of history that got him there, won the Pulitzer Prize for Fiction in 2008.

If a natural ease with the written word were the sole criteria for an author, needless to say Junot Díaz never would have become one. Prone to false starts, full stops, and gauging the uneasy passing of time, Díaz writes plenty of drafts for stories that in his estimation simply aren't good and never come close to publication. A story called "Primo," for example, took Díaz six months to write. Intended as the closing to *This Is How You Lose Her*, his book of interconnected short stories published in 2012, he couldn't get from it what he wanted and ultimately abandoned it. "That was a miserable botch . . . and it never came together," he says.[513] He spent another year on a story meant again for the end of the same book. "Santo Domingo Confidential" suffered the same fate as "Primo." Díaz has reached many points during which it seemed like the right words would never find him. "I worry all the time about never writing again," he says.[514]

Díaz suffers not so much from writer's block as from an inability to write as he wants to on demand. The result can be an agonizingly slow progression from start to finish, and it largely explains why he has published just three books in two decades. His slow pace is not a matter of failing to find a work-life balance, or of carving out time to write every day. It doesn't seem to be a matter of succumbing to distractions. It's merely that Díaz finds writing extremely difficult. And yet he knows that he's capable of plodding on through that difficulty to produce something exceptional. One story in *This Is How You Lose Her*, "Miss Lora," for example, he tried to start a dozen or so times over the course of a decade, never getting past the first page. And then, once, maybe on the thirteenth try, it hit on all cylinders and he finished it in a day.[515] Díaz recognizes the irony in his situation. "I think it might sound ridiculous . . . but I seem to be good at something I find very difficult," he says.[516]

Just how good is evidenced by what happened when he finally put his hard-won work out there. Díaz finished an MFA in creative writing at Cornell, where he wrote a large chunk of his short-story collection *Drown*. For a total of three years while he was there and just after, he also worked on what would become his first published short story, writing and rewriting. Díaz finally submitted it, and within four months he published it, signed with a literary agent, and had a book deal.[517] *Drown* was published when he was twenty-seven years old to universal acclaim.

But from there, nothing was seamless, and nothing came quickly. As with any struggle, there were deep-seated reasons for Díaz's slow progress. He has struggled periodically with depression, which has stopped him from working many times. On the other hand, he's managed to harness the low times as a motivating force. "Well if I have to deal with being fucking depressed," he says, "I'll figure out some way to make some art out of it."[518] His particular art, though, isn't the kind that comes with a blueprint. Díaz follows in no one's footsteps and strives to do things with his writing that haven't been done already. "If you feel familiar and you feel comfortable, you're in mapped territory," he says. "What's the use of being in mapped territory?"[519] Mapping uncharted territory, full of wrong turns and dead ends, by definition isn't fast work.

Díaz also suffers the plight of the perfectionist: Nothing is ever good enough. This principle can grind things to a halt, and for Díaz, sometimes that's exactly what happens. He throws out twenty unsatisfactory pages for every one he keeps.[520] He rewrites twenty, thirty, forty times. When he types a draft and then prints it out, its flaws become even more apparent to him. And even after a book is done and published, he continues to harp on it, wishing he could work on it more, make it even better. Of writing the female characters in *This Is How You Lose Her*, for example, he said, "I wish I had another 10 years to work those muscles so that I can write better women characters."[521] His perfectionism leads him to solicit feedback from any number of early readers and to incorporate critiques as the work develops. "Much is gained by admitting one's limitations, by seeking help around those limitations," he says.[522]

In the earliest stages of a project, Díaz finds nascent inspiration in baubles collected through his everyday life: a photo of his father dressed in a fascist uniform during Rafael Trujillo's three-decade reign over the Dominican Republic, which informed *Oscar Wao*; another photo of the steel mill he worked in during college, a topic he has tried to write about, so far unfruitfully. He collects newspaper clippings and saves wayward scraps of paper on which he's written ideas as they come to him.[523] Although, in his telling of it, Díaz doesn't produce nearly enough of those scrap pieces. "I think 90% of my ideas evaporate because I have a terrible memory and because I seem to be committed to not scribble anything down," he says.[524]

He also finds that it's more important to be out and engaged with the world in an unencumbered way than it is to obsess over taking it all down. Díaz doesn't want to see everything through the lens of looking for material. From his perspective, living life is at least as important as writing about it. Having that in mind after *Drown* gave Díaz a certain amount of financial freedom for the first time in his life, he prioritized traveling over writing for a while. After he finished *Oscar Wao*, he didn't write at all for at least several months, preferring instead to catch up on sleep and reading.[525]

There's no tried-and-true approach to conceiving a book for Díaz—with each one so far, it's been different. He does prepare and plot and plan, but never in the same way. "My material starts of my unconscious," he says,[526] and of course, once he starts, "stuff changes on the fly."[527] He likes it this way. Even as he begins to more deliberately consider a story, he tries to let it evolve organically: "If I observe too much control over my material, I destroy it."[528] With *Oscar Wao*, his initial idea was "to chart the political and sexual terror of the Trujillato and how this haunted a family across three generations."[529] But the book evolved in the direction of telling the story of Dominican American Oscar, a hopelessly nerdy and unattractive kid straddling two cultures, with his family's Dominican history as a backdrop.

Although he's written a couple of the most striking characters in contemporary fiction, including Oscar Wao, the characters themselves are not necessarily the genesis for each story. "It all sort of builds up," he says. "Maybe I'll start by describing a house, or a bad mood. Characters accumulate; emotions accumulate; events accumulate. Slowly, over time, the confusion comes into focus, and I have this set of characters and conflicts."[530]

For Díaz, little research is required to place his stories in the historical context that permeates them. He accumulates this kind of information by nature. "I had this enormous amount of historical knowledge [already] in my head," he says of writing *Oscar Wao*.[531] That knowledge ultimately overflowed into the copious footnotes attached to the novel, which form a sort of secondary narrative.[532] But Díaz did need to research another theme of that book, what he calls "nerdy stuff." Even though he was into science fiction and other "nerdy" pursuits as a child, he needed a refresher. Díaz watched the kinds of movies that his protagonist would be obsessed with, obscure films like *Zardoz*, an early John Boorman work, and *Virus*, a postapocalyptic Japanese film. He read *The Lord of the Rings* three times in a row, so that his knowledge of it would be as detailed as a true fanboy's.[533]

Díaz also draws prodigiously from his own life. Born in the Dominican Republic in what he describes as "a super-gangster neighborhood"[534] in Santo Domingo, he moved to New Jersey at age six—English is his second language. His characters are likewise shaped by their immigrant experience, products of both Dominican and American culture. Like him, they tend to have absentee fathers. Growing up, Díaz was obviously smart, but he learned to be street-smart in his tough neighborhood, too. The mix of the Spanish and English languages is a trademark of his work, along with a mash-up of cultural influences: Caribbean, African American, nerd- and academic-speak. He is fearless in his use of the divergent dialects and cultures that he's been exposed to in life, which come together in passages like this one from early in *Oscar Wao*, describing the teenage Oscar's inability to fit in:

> [He had] none of the Higher Powers of your typical Dominican male, couldn't have pulled a girl if his life depended on it. Couldn't play sports for shit, or dominoes, was beyond uncoordinated, threw a ball like a girl. Had no knack for music or business or dance, no hustle, no rap, no G. And most damning of all: no looks. He wore his semi-kink hair in a Puerto Rican afro, rocked enormous Section 8 glasses—his "anti-pussy devices," Al and Miggs, his only friends, called them.

Those words are spoken by the novel's narrator, Yunior, a character who has served as a Díaz alter ego from the beginning. He appeared in the short story Díaz used in his application to MFA programs and is central to the short stories in *Drown*. Yunior is the largely passive narrator of *Oscar Wao* and is again the central character in the connected stories of *This Is How You Lose Her*. The character and the author share similar backgrounds, similar interests, and similar intelligences. They both have had a brother with cancer. They both have their troubles with women. They both worked delivering pool tables in their early twenties. They both end up teaching and writing in Boston.

But Yunior differs from Díaz in a key way. Of Yunior, Díaz says, "I find someone like him very difficult because as a construct inside me he rarely talks about the things that emotionally matter to him most."[535] In "The Cheater's Guide to Love," the opening short story in *This Is How You Lose Her*, for example, Yunior documents the five-year period after his fiancée dumps him for cheating on her, and yet the most salient loss in Yunior's life—the woman he loved—is the very facet of the story that remains least discussed, as if Yunior doesn't know how to approach the real source of his unhappiness. The things that Díaz's characters aren't willing to say, it turns out, say a striking amount about them.[536] The silences, or what isn't said, are a crucial element in Díaz's work.

Knowing the narrator's audience is critical to Díaz in deciding what to leave out. Given that all people wear what he refers to as different masks, depending on whom they're interacting with, it's important for Díaz to understand the persona a character is trying to project at any given time. In *Oscar Wao*, for example, "Yunior talks always like he's in a car with his best friends on their way to the Shore."[537] The choice of that persona is a reaction to his perceived audience, and there are certain things he'd omit when talking to those friends.

In contrast to Yunior, Oscar Wao was a relative breeze of a character to write. "I must have had him in my mind a long time because he emerged, like Athena, almost fully formed out of my skull," he says. "His sections of the novel were the easiest for me to compose. It was the rest of it that took years."[538] Still, like Yunior, Oscar Wao bears similarities to his creator. Díaz describes his childhood self, and would describe Oscar, too, as "a ghetto nerd supreme: a smart kid in a poor-ass-community."[539] The young Díaz, like Oscar, read like crazy, making clandestine trips to the library and devouring fantasy novels, the more epic the better: *The Lord of the Rings, Watership Down*, the Lensman series.[540] The difference between the two is that Díaz also had the ability to present himself as non-nerd, knew how to project a certain amount of cool and machismo. More like Yunior in that regard.

Despite the clear line from his life to his fiction, Díaz's work doesn't cross the line into autobiographical. Unlike a writer such as Jack Kerouac, Díaz's life informs his fiction, but his fiction isn't directly based on it. The way he describes it, his real life serves the same function as a theater set: The scene is recognizable from his life, but the minutiae of what happens within it comes from the imagination.[541] He can't faithfully write about major life events until they're a decade or two behind him, and once he does get them down, by the time they've gone through the numerous rounds of the editing process, what may have been autobiographical has morphed into something else completely.[542] "I know that the work transforms utterly any attempt I make at subtle autobiography. By the time the work gets done with it, it's unrecognizable."[543]

Naturally, as he grew up Díaz discovered a broader range of literature. He remained interested in the fantastical, however, finding straight realism unable to relay the disjunction he experienced as a kid displaced from one culture and thrust into an alien one. The French Caribbean writer Patrick Chamoiseau's *Texaco*, a novel that like Díaz's work weaves the personal with the historical, "blew my head off," he says.[544] In a public discussion at the New York Public

Library, Díaz told Toni Morrison that when he read her 1977 novel *Song of Solomon*, "the axis of the world shifted for me."[545] He loves Octavia Butler and Samuel Delany, two writers who examine social issues through science-fiction stories. He also loves James Joyce for his ability to comprehensively represent his culture, although he has never exactly strove to emulate him.

For Díaz, the pure love of reading when he was young eventually bred the compulsion to write. He started writing while still in high school, but not seriously. After his brother's diagnosis with a particularly pitiless form of leukemia, Díaz began writing things down. His brother's illness, he says, "was an excuse to now participate in the form I loved so much. So that's how I started actually, writing letters to someone in a hospital."[546] When he read Toni Morrison and Sandra Cisneros during freshman year at Rutgers, his desire to write solidified. He started coming into contact with the literary world and applied to MFA programs soon after graduating. He ended up at Cornell, where he quickly became disillusioned with the program. The lack of diversity didn't cultivate the kind of writing he wanted to do. But he stuck it out, from stubbornness more than anything.[547]

Today, Díaz splits his time between the Boston area, where he teaches at MIT, and his Harlem apartment in New York City. In both homes, he rises early, usually by 7 a.m. He checks his e-mail first, but tries to keep it brief, then works on his writing until lunch. Only if he's on a real roll does he keep going later into the day.[548] His writing days often get broken up by his teaching schedule, which Díaz enjoys. He finds the minds of a younger generation intriguing, and on a basic level, "you also just want company. I mean, it's nice."[549] On the other hand, the time allotted for teaching means that he writes even more slowly: "[It's] very time-consuming and works exactly the muscle you use when you write—the language muscle."[550] Díaz is a social person in general and enjoys spending time out in the world, running into people or stopping by a place where he knows he'll see a friend.

He likes to listen to music while writing, but none with lyrics. Movie sound tracks have thus become favorites. *Drown* was written while "listening to the soundtrack to the movie *Conan the Barbarian* on a loop," for example.[551] These days, Díaz writes standing up or lying down, never sitting at a desk. But this is less a creative strategy than a function of his bad back, on which he had major surgery in 2012. When he needs complete isolation, Díaz shuts himself in the bathroom with a notebook.[552] He doesn't demand a certain number of words from himself in a day, and he is more likely to throw away the morning's work than add it to a running total. Díaz wrote *Oscar Wao* in a series of notebooks, working by hand in a sharply slanted cursive, and then organized it using colored tabs.

Still a voracious reader today, Díaz plows through a book a week almost without fail. There are heaps of them stacked precariously around his apartment, and by now he has three storage units full of volumes. But he's careful about his approach to reading and recognizes a tendency to use it as a crutch. "I'm old enough and experienced enough to know when I'm reading to avoid . . ." he says. "And I also know—you get old enough, you know when you're forcing the writing, so you need to go hit the books."[553] He does read strategically, picking a book that he expects to relate to his current writing effort. But he also makes sure to just read, letting unexpected sources seep into his mind.[554] Rick Moody's *The Ice Storm* is one example of this. When Díaz was working on *Oscar Wao*, it was this novel that crept in out of nowhere and, as he puts it, "gave me the idea for the deep structure of the book."[555] Both feature largely absent narrators who begin to figure more prominently in the story late in the novel, and both, in different ways, draw on the family-like friendships in *The Fantastic Four* comic books. Díaz continually thinks as a reader in his approach to writing. "I don't write because I know a lot about writing, I write because I know a lot about readers," he says.[556]

Either way, the writing continues at its glacial pace. The future looks to be proceeding at a similar tempo to his past. As of fall 2013, Díaz had been at work on a second novel for five years—"and I still don't have a first chapter," he says. "This one is taking a lot longer and is a lot worse than the other one. It's not heartening."[557]

A DAY IN THE WRITER'S LIFE . . .

Junot Díaz is up by 7 a.m. most mornings, and after a brief session on the Internet, he gets down to writing. He works through the morning with a movie soundtrack playing in the background, standing up or lying down—never sitting, ever since back surgery in 2012—and when he breaks for lunch around noon, he's done with writing for the day. While for Díaz not every day is a writing day, every day *is* a reading day, and his daily routine often also involves teaching creative writing at MIT. A social creature, Díaz tends to find the time to get out and see people, frequenting one or another of his favorite haunts, especially in New York City, where he lives when school's not in session.

THE SOCIAL BUTTERFLY AND THE LONE WOLF

15

F. SCOTT FITZGERALD

In a late essay titled "Early Success," F. Scott Fitzgerald lingered over a writing career that began explosively with the publication of his first novel, *This Side of Paradise*, at the age of just twenty-four. The book was an instant success, but was more notable for turning him overnight into a celebrity, a poster boy for what Fitzgerald himself would soon dub the Jazz Age. He was carried along in those early days, it felt to him, by fate—discipline had so far proven itself unnecessary. He wrote, "Premature success gives one an almost mystical conception of destiny as opposed to will power."[558] By the time most writers just begin to harness their talent, Fitzgerald, at age twenty-eight, had already published four books, among them *The Beautiful and Damned* and *The Great Gatsby*. All were written, it seemed, in the spare moments between cocktails.

Fitzgerald's talent came too easily, in the beginning enabling him to cultivate both a writing career and a lifestyle that any thirty-year-old could have told him would be impossible to maintain. Together with his glamorous wife, Zelda, he drank too much and flouted conventional decorum. "The dream had been early realized and the realization carried with it a certain bonus and a certain burden," he wrote. He continued: "I had fair years to waste."[559] Fitzgerald never maintained a regular writing routine. Instead, he worked in periodic coffee-fueled bursts that often coincided with a need for income. The first draft of *Paradise*, with an early working title of "The Romantic Egotist," took shape during Fitzgerald's stint in the army (he never saw action), written at the officers' club at Fort Leavenworth, Kansas, on his free weekends. It took only three months.

Then, after a transfer from Fort Leavenworth to Camp Sheridan, outside of Montgomery, Alabama, Fitzgerald met Zelda, who would not marry him until he could afford the lifestyle she required. Thus motivated, Fitzgerald wrote his short story "Camel's Back" in fourteen straight hours in 1919, sold it promptly to the *Saturday Evening Post*, and immediately bought a $600 platinum-and-diamond watch for Zelda with the earnings, but was $100 short in paying for it. He was not proud of the story, but it served its intended purpose and established Fitzgerald's lifelong approach to writing short stories for the money rather than the art of them. The watch helped his cause, and Zelda finally married Fitzgerald once he'd secured publication for his first novel.

In Fitzgerald's time, the short story enjoyed its role as a dominant form of entertainment, and magazines like the *Saturday Evening Post* and *Scribner's* were willing to pay small fortunes for stories by popular writers. For a time, Fitzgerald was one of the most popular, at his peak commanding $4,000 per story—about $55,000 in 2014 dollars. But the difference between the short "commercial fiction" in these publications and the longer "serious work" that Fitzgerald yearned to associate himself with would become the defining creative struggle of his life. He developed a theory that short stories, less important than his longer work, must not take up too much of his time: "Stories are best written in either one jump or three, according to length," he wrote to his daughter in 1940, months before his untimely death at age forty-four. "The three-jump story should be done in three successive days, then a day or so for revise and off she goes."[560]

Fitzgerald strove to find a balance between writing lucrative short stories and working on his novels. That he completed only four novels and left another behind unfinished at his death, while he published in the neighborhood of 175 short stories in that time, demonstrates which form generally won out. (He planned and began a number of other novels that were for various reasons abandoned.) His ever-present plan was to write enough short stories to fund a six-month period of uninterrupted work on a novel. Had Fitzgerald any sense of economy or money-managing skills, the strategy may have worked out for him. But as soon as the waves of money came in, they went out again, spent on lavish accommodations, luxurious things for Zelda, and endless liquor-fueled nights, which in turn further compromised his efforts at establishing a regular writing routine. On at least one occasion, though, the approach worked: Between the end of 1923 and March 1924, Fitzgerald completed ten stories, bringing in enough money to focus on *Gatsby* through the following summer.

It's impossible to consider Fitzgerald's writing life without also considering his drinking life. In the beginning, alcohol was part of the celebration of his youth and success. Fitzgerald always cultivated a robust social life; he liked to see people and be amused by them and was easily lured from his work by the prospect of a good time. He became drunk easily and didn't hold his liquor well, which can be charming only when one is very, very young. Over time, Fitzgerald found himself unable to strike a note of moderation, and his days became an increasing and continual struggle to remain sober enough to write worthwhile material.

Fitzgerald made careful note of the stretches during which he managed to stay on the wagon—a term he defined loosely. In his estimation, restricting his drinking to beer and wine qualified as often as not, and he had a talent for rationalizing his frequent returns to the harder stuff. His favorite was gin, apparently because he thought it couldn't be detected on his breath. Fitzgerald eventually concluded that he could manage short stories while drinking, but couldn't keep a novel together in his head while inebriated.[561] This may explain why at one point in 1934 he made the decision to spend the days working on his novel and the evenings on short stories. The plan failed, and he ended up not working on short stories at all, too burned out at night after a day's work.[562]

There was never a permanent or even long-term home in Fitzgerald's life. The haphazard writing space he carved out for himself at the officers' club to write *Paradise* turned out to be typical. To write the third and final version of *Paradise*, he hid out in the top floor of his parents' house, avoiding parties and drink, until it was done.[563] In his Great Neck, Long Island, home—the model for Nick Carraway's house in *Gatsby*—he absconded to the "large bare room"[564] above the garage every day to settle in to work. While living in St. Paul, Minnesota, around the time his daughter, Scottie, was born, he rented an office downtown.[565] When he lived at La Paix, an estate on the outskirts of Baltimore near Zelda's sanatorium, he wrote "alone in the privacy of my faded blue room with my sick cat, the bare February branches waving at the window, an ironic paper weight that says Business is Good."[566]

For all of his association with New York City and Paris, Fitzgerald couldn't write much in either city; too much distraction. During the couple's time living in Paris, Fitzgerald commonly rose at 11 a.m. and didn't get down to writing until around 5 p.m. He claimed that he'd then continue into the early hours of the next day, although it's safe to say that as often as not he was lured away by some alcohol-fueled occasion or other. Then, around the time Fitzgerald turned thirty, Zelda began experiencing episodes that would eventually result in a complete mental breakdown—she spent her last fifteen or so years, until her death at age forty-seven, living in a sanatorium. They never again lived in New York or Paris. Especially during the time of Zelda's decline, Fitzgerald often went months without writing.

Although Fitzgerald saw his short stories and novels as separate lines of work, in reality the line between his commercial and serious fiction was fluid. Some of Fitzgerald's short stories have gone on to become classics of the genre—"The Ice Palace," "Bernice Bobs Her Hair," and "The Rich Boy" among them. And he regularly absorbed lines, sections, or entire completed works from his short stories into his novels. For example, in the early stages of contemplating what would become his masterpiece, he wrote the short story "Winter Dreams," a *Gatsby* in miniature, with a story line and characters that differed only slightly from the eventual novel. Fitzgerald lifted the description of the home of Daisy Buchanan's counterpart, Judy, wholesale into *Gatsby*.[567] The converse was true as well: His short story published as "Absolution" was originally written as an early chapter of *Gatsby* detailing Jay Gatsby's boyhood that was cut from the final version of the novel.[568]

That boyhood differed but was not unlike Fitzgerald's own youth, growing up in a comfortable but undistinguished family in St. Paul, Minnesota. He was never a good student, a general rule that held from early childhood through Princeton University, from which he more or less flunked out and never graduated. But he displayed keen powers of observation and creativity early on. He loved to read, claiming to have completed Thackeray's oeuvre by the age of sixteen,[569] and learned to appreciate poetry from his father, who read Poe and Byron to him.[570] Growing up, he kept a "character book" describing the people around him that would prove prescient, as the adult Fitzgerald incorporated so many real-life characters into his work.[571]

Early literary influences included Oscar Wilde, Booth Tarkington, Compton Mackenzie, and H. G. Wells—authors with literary cred who were also highly accessible. In college, he read two novels that centered on the decline of a once-promising character, a central theme that would evolve in Fitzgerald's fiction: Stephen French Whitman's *Predestined* and Charles G. Norris's *Salt* (both little read today). Also around that time, *The Notebooks of Samuel Butler* became a go-to read that he would come back to again and again, including Butler's theories on the impact of wealth on a person's soul. Fitzgerald even organized his own notebooks using Butler's as a template. Keats also became an early and enduring influence. Although Fitzgerald wrote prose, he emulated the rhythms of Keats's poetry throughout his career, the movement that one can feel in his sentences, the way he used verbs to bring things alive.[572]

At Princeton, Fitzgerald's literary ambitions accelerated. He met Edmund Wilson there, and the two developed a friendship that was equal parts reverential and antagonistic—Wilson found Fitzgerald's work lacking intellectually, while Fitzgerald flaunted his natural abilities to Wilson. Still, Wilson became a valued early reader for Fitzgerald, who much later called him the "intellectual conscience" of his writing career.[573] He also befriended John Peale Bishop during his Princeton days, and for the first time had a friend as committed to his literary proclivities as Fitzgerald himself was.[574] He spent a formative summer month in 1917 at Bishop's house in West Virginia writing, reading, and discussing literature.

Other mentors included Father Sigourney Fay, a trustee at the prep school Fitzgerald attended and one of the first to encourage his writing; the Irish writer Shane Leslie, who took an early interest in Fitzgerald; and George Jean Nathan, coeditor of the *Smart Set* and the first person to purchase a Fitzgerald short story. Fitzgerald developed intense loyalties to his mentors and others involved in getting him published, especially his agent Harold Ober and editor

Maxwell Perkins; despite receiving attractive offers elsewhere, he published his books with Perkins at Scribner's for the duration of his career.

Fitzgerald never stopped studying the work of others in service of his own. After finishing *Paradise*, Fitzgerald read Samuel Butler's *Notebooks* and studied Joseph Conrad's technique in preparation of his next novel, *The Beautiful and Damned*.[575] Later, as he began work on *Gatsby*, Dostoyevsky provided the new novel with an element that Fitzgerald called "masculine."[576] He was already a famous author when he met the still-unknown Ernest Hemingway in Paris and was early to recognize his genius. The two embarked on a great, fraught friendship that had them critiquing each other's works in progress for years down the line. For all of Fitzgerald's admiration of Hemingway, though, he did not seek to emulate him, and in fact stopped reading him altogether at one point out of fear that Hemingway's rhythms were infiltrating his own work.[577]

Sharing his work with others as it developed appealed to Fitzgerald. In a 1924 letter he explained of his typescript to *Gatsby*, "I've read it to everyone with hearing."[578] Fitzgerald took thoughtful criticisms seriously, whether they came from the likes of Hemingway or from housewives he barely knew, and used them to inform the direction of his work. Perhaps no early reader loomed larger in shaping Fitzgerald's work than the legendary editor Maxwell Perkins. Perkins was the first to consider "The Romantic Egotist." He rejected it but expressed interest in seeing a rewrite. Fitzgerald obliged, only to have the second version rejected as well. Perkins finally accepted the novel for publication after Fitzgerald rewrote it a third time.

Later, after reading the manuscript for *Gatsby*, Perkins wrote to Fitzgerald with three major suggested revisions: to make Gatsby's physical presence less vague, to provide more hints about how Gatsby acquired his wealth, and to revise sections in chapters 6 and 7 that seemed to Perkins to depart from the flow of the narrative.[579]

Fitzgerald took each criticism to heart and rewrote the manuscript accordingly.[580] He also, in the end, deferred to Zelda and Perkins's preference for the title *The Great Gatsby* over a short list of others that he favored.

Although a compulsive planner in his work, Fitzgerald rarely followed through on his own agendas. He loved the idea of order—his letters to Perkins and Ober are filled with plans, timelines, and self-prescribed deadlines. And he also planned his novels out, especially later on. Fitzgerald wrote a sixteen-page summary of *Tender Is the Night* before beginning it, plus character sketches and a work schedule for it.[581] He also wrote a complete synopsis of *The Last Tycoon* before starting it, partially in the hope of securing an advance that way (and incidentally providing scholars with a template of what the completed work might have looked like).

He was also a compulsive list maker. Fitzgerald kept a ledger starting in 1919, when his first work was published, until 1938, two years before his death; in it he documented every piece of work he published and when, along with the outlet and money it brought in. The ledger also included a line-long summary of each year in his life: "Revelry and Marrige [*sic*]. The rewards of the year before. The happiest year since I was 18" for the year he was twenty-three years old; "A Year in Lausanne. Waiting. From Darkness to Hope" for the year he was thirty-four.[582] He also made lists of potential titles for his novels, which often got sent around to friends for opinions. He had a tendency to favor lines of poetry for his titles—*This Side of Paradise* comes from a Rupert Brooke poem,[583] and *Tender Is the Night* is a line from Keats. The lists even infiltrated the fiction itself: Arguably his most famous one is a two-page list detailing all the questionable characters who attended Gatsby's extravagant parties.

Fitzgerald kept journals from childhood on as well and put them to work in his fiction. In them, he wrote down ideas for stories, unused excerpts to be recycled in other work, overheard snippets of conversation, and references to interesting events in his life. He drew from them heavily to write *This Side of Paradise*, an almost entirely autobiographical first novel that covered his years at Princeton and just after. In *Paradise*, his characters were based on real-life models: the protagonist Amory Blaine is based on himself, while he made Zelda the model for Rosalind.[584] His first love, a young Chicago woman named Ginevra King who eventually rejected him, was the model for Isabelle, and John Peale Bishop the template for Amory's friend Thomas.

After *Paradise*, Fitzgerald's novels became less purely autobiographical with each step. *The Beautiful and Damned* was loosely based on his relationship with Zelda, but in a speculative way, prophesying how they *might* turn out (he would be sadly close to accurate). *The Great Gatsby* was the first novel in which Fitzgerald achieved what he'd been working toward: transmuted autobiography, meaning he was able to suffuse characters that were not him with his own emotions. Jay Gatsby, unlike the protagonists in *Paradise* and *The Beautiful and Damned*, is not Fitzgerald. Instead, he's a man with a similar disposition to Fitzgerald who has lived an entirely different life.[585] In this way, the genesis of each story Fitzgerald wrote was not a plot or a character. "I must start out with an emotion," he said, "one that's close to me and that I can understand."[586] He could write characters that were not him, but the emotions that brought life to them had to be his own.

Yet the habit of basing characters on real people would continue: Edith Cummings, a woman he knew in Chicago through Ginevra King, became the model for Jordan Baker in *Gatsby*.[587] MGM studio head Irving Thalberg was the model for the protagonist Monroe Stahr in Fitzgerald's last, unfinished novel, *The Last Tycoon*. The list goes on. Real events, too, made their way into his work. In *The Great Gatsby*, Fitzgerald borrowed Jay Gatsby's backstory of working on the yacht of a man who taught him how to make his sketchy fortune from a friend, Robert Kerr, who worked a similar job after warning a man about the dangers of bringing his yacht into Brooklyn's Sheepshead Bay.[588] A trip during a college break to the Montana ranch of a Princeton friend provided the setting for his great short story "The Diamond as Big as the Ritz."[589] A rich neighbor in Great Neck made his fortune as a bootlegger and called people "old sport."[590]

Fitzgerald wrote his drafts in pencil on unlined, legal-sized sheets of paper, in a beautiful small cursive that became sloppier as he got older.[591] He wrote subsequent drafts by hand as well, marking them up here and there, crossing out a word as he proceeded, less often an entire paragraph. He sent drafts to the typist when they were ready for later-stage edits and liked to have these typescripts triple-spaced to allow for marking up. There were often many drafts—at least five for *Gatsby* and twelve for *Tender Is the Night*—and he was prone to radical alterations from one to another. The plot could change completely, or be told from a different perspective. The first attempt at *This Side of Paradise* was written in the first person, for example, but he finally rewrote it in the third person, likely at the suggestion of Maxwell Perkins.[592] Likewise, Nick Carraway was not the narrator of the first draft of *Gatsby*.[593]

Even his early attempts, though, contained Fitzgerald's unique stroke of genius. The famous closing lines of *Gatsby* originally appeared early on in a handwritten manuscript, in a shorter, less developed form:

> And as I sat there brooding on the old unknown world I too held my breath and waited, until I could feel the motion of America as it turned through the hours—my own blue lawn and the tall incandescent city on the water and beyond that the dark fields of the republic rolling on under the night.[594]

In a later draft, also handwritten, that paragraph had been expanded into the following:

> And as I sat there, brooding on the old unknown world I thought of Gatsby ~~wonder~~ when he picked out the green light at the end of Daisy's dock. He had come a long way to this blue lawn but now his dream must have seemed so close that he could hardly fail to grasp it. He did not know that ~~he had left it behind long before, it lay somew~~ it was all behind him, ~~somewhere~~ back in that vast obscurity on the other side of the city, where the dark fields of the republic rolled on under the night.
>
> He believed in the green glimmer, in the orgastic future that year by year recedes before us. It eluded us then but never mind—tomorrow we will run faster, stretch out our arms farther . . . And one fine morning—
>
> So we beat on, a boat against the current, borne back ceaselessly into the past.

He then moved this passage to the end, using it to close out the book. But beyond that, he hardly changed a thing from this draft to the published version; he reinserted the word "wonder"; "on the other side of the city" became "beyond the city"; the second paragraph opens with "Gatsby" instead of "He"; "never mind" became "that's no matter"; and "a boat" became "boats."

For all of his careless behavior in life, Fitzgerald was a perfectionist in his writing, and he often had trouble leaving off editing, requesting changes after the type had already been set. When *Gatsby* was finally ready, he set it aside for a week in order to give it one more read with a fresh mind before sending it off to Perkins. And even then, he would have many ideas for revision.[595] In his short fiction, on the other hand, Fitzgerald showed less concern, as long as the price was right. If, after he dashed off a story, the *Saturday Evening Post* complained about an ending, he would rewrite it to the editors' specifications.[596] If a story needed thousands of words cut in order to fit the space allotted for it, he would happily oblige.

Fitzgerald eventually made the ultimate concession to money for a serious writer of his time: He accepted a contract with a movie studio and headed to Hollywood. By this time, he no longer held out much hope that he and Zelda would resume a life together. The studio provided him a steady income and brought him back from the brink of true penury. In California, he met the gossip columnist Sheilah Graham and settled into a life with her. She helped him to finally curb his drinking, but it came too late. Fitzgerald died of a heart attack in Graham's Hollywood apartment at the age of forty-four.

A DAY IN THE WRITER'S LIFE . . .

F. Scott Fitzgerald's evenings tended to dictate his days. Never one to resist the lure of a party, his nights often devolved into drunken fiascos from which he awoke embarrassed the next morning. He might not rise until 11 a.m., and not get down to writing until 5 p.m., with an intention to work through the evening that didn't often pan out. When he needed money, though, Fitzgerald could hole up reliably and write a lucrative short story, at least in his younger years. But he never kept to a consistent daily writing routine. Fitzgerald's success came instead thanks to a spectacular talent that triumphed despite his lack of discipline.

(16)

PHILIP ROTH

Philip Roth was looking for trouble. From the grounds of an eighteenth-century clapboard house in rural Connecticut, cossetted in the idyllic writing studio he had used for nearly four decades, what he needed was a problem. Having long outgrown inviting trouble into his own life, Roth still required it of his fiction—the crisis, the resistance, the disconnect between his character and the world. "My hero has to be in a state of vivid transformation or radical displacement," he said.[597] He needed an Alexander Portnoy frothing against his repressive Jewish upbringing or a Nathan Zuckerman acting out against his newfound notoriety. Without understanding a character's particular beef with the world, Roth could write a hundred pages, working day after day, to aimless effect. Over time, he learned the best strategy for avoiding that fate: a peaceful, secluded existence of his own, which enabled him to home in on the crucial problem.

But it wasn't always that way. As a young man in his twenties, Roth had indeed sought out the kind of drama that he would later eschew. He moved to New York City for the stimulation it provided and married a volatile woman disastrously ill suited for him. Roth never felt as free to experiment with his writing as he did in New York in the 1960s and has even speculated that staying in the city would have been better for his career, given the wealth of material to be found there. New York also helped him discover the comic side of his talent as he fell in with a group of friends there with whom he spent frequent boisterous nights filled with food, drink, and conversation. To his delight, Roth found that his quips were well received, and he began to incorporate them into his writing.

Leading up to the release of his fourth book, *Portnoy's Complaint*, Roth showed signs of settling into a quieter existence. During this time he was living in Manhattan with another girlfriend, keeping his own apartment but using it primarily as a writing studio.[598] The notoriety that came with the publication of *Portnoy's Complaint* soon drove Roth to abscond to the Yaddo writers' colony in upstate New York for a full three months at the age of thirty-six. He would soon decide that rural living suited him better than did New York City, and ultimately found an agreeable plentitude of quiet and hours in the clapboard house in rural Connecticut, where he has lived since 1972, notwithstanding stints in London and, in his later years, winters spent in Manhattan. For much of that time, he shared the house with the actress Claire Bloom, his second wife, whom he divorced in 1995.

The cosmopolitan scene in general, Roth can do without. "By and large, I don't get anything from being in the literary world," he says.[599] Plus, he loves living in the country too much to abandon it and derived ingredients for his writing there that are more crucial than those available in the city. What he gained from being immersed in city life ultimately didn't stack up against the benefits of the country. "I enjoy solitude the way some people I know enjoy parties," he said. "It gives me an enormous sense of personal freedom and an exquisitely sharp sense of being alive—and of course it provides me with the quiet and the breathing space I need to get my imagination going and my work done."[600]

In the serenity of the country, Roth spent his days in his writing studio, standing at a wooden lectern next to a pair of latticed windows, facing away from the room with its towering fireplace, leather couch, and reclining chair, a portrait of Kafka looking over him.[601] It was only in the early 1990s that Roth, so famous for writing standing up, began to in fact do so.[602] Motivated by severe back problems to try it out, he found that it worked for him. "My mind was freer standing up," he says.[603] For years, Roth wrote on an IBM Selectric typewriter, although he eventually made the switch to a computer, which he found a great facilitator of the editing process.[604]

Roth thrived on the rote consistency of his writing routine, regularly working straight through both the morning and the afternoon.[605] "I work seven days a week. I need lots of quiet. I need lots of hours," he said.[606] He estimated that he put in full work sessions 340 days per year. The long hours didn't necessarily result in a lot of daily output, though, and Roth didn't necessarily want them to. If he managed a page in a day, he could be pleased with it, while if he wrote four or five pages, he might find it necessary to spend a few more days working on them before they became something worth keeping.[607] And no matter the speed of the first draft, Roth spent a lot of time rewriting it later. "The book really comes to life in the rewriting," he said. "The first draft is extremely crude, but at least it's down. So when I have a first draft, I have a floor under my feet that I can walk on."[608]

With a day of writing behind him, Roth intermittently enjoyed the company of friends. During his many years in Connecticut, he maintained a few friendships with people living nearby and met with one or the other of them for dinner a few times per month. And even now that he's retired from writing, he still keeps up friendships with a number of writers and kindred spirits around the world, most of whom he manages to see occasionally. Not a pure recluse, then; just a guy who found that he thrives on solitude. More often than with friends, throughout his writing career Roth passed the evening with a good book, a not only enjoyable activity, but one that he found useful in terms of keeping the mind working. "It's a way of keeping the circuits open," he said. "It's a way of thinking about my *line* of work while getting a little rest from the work at hand."[609]

Early on, Roth had to discover reading more or less on his own. Books weren't a part of the Roth household when he was growing up, and it wasn't until his older brother went away to college and returned for visits bearing copies of titles like *A Portrait of the Artist as a Young Man*, *Winesburg, Ohio*, and *Only the Dead Know Brooklyn* that Roth gained his first exposure to what he calls "adult reading."[610] His first short stories were written in thrall to his early literary heroes, composed during college at Bucknell University and often published in the campus literary magazine. Still unsure of his own style, in these stories Roth replicated, in his own words, the "cloying come-on" of J. D. Salinger, the "gossamer vulnerability" of Truman Capote, and the "self-pitying self-importance" of Thomas Wolfe.[611]

Roth hadn't yet come to understand that his own life and background could be a source for material and continued to imitate the material of others instead. "How could Art be rooted in a parochial Jewish Newark neighborhood having nothing to do with the enigma of time and space or good and evil or appearance and reality?" he remembers believing early on.[612] It took Saul Bellow to change that outlook. Roth read *The Adventures of Augie March* his senior year of college and discovered that anything at all could be grounds for fiction, that there were no limits.[613]

At a certain point in his efforts, Philip Roth emerged as a singular voice. "After the first ten years the influences fall away," he said, even if reading in general still fueled his literary passion.[614]

As he moved into the recalcitrant style of *Portnoy's Complaint*, he freed himself from an adolescent fascination with the more formal styles of writers like of Henry James and Gustave Flaubert,[615] at the same time he became intrigued by Kafka's ability to turn the grotesque into a sort of entertainment—"hideous, but funny."[616] He was intrigued, yes, but his writing was no longer consequently derivative. Over time Roth found himself reading less and less fiction, and as he's aged, he has come to prefer history and biography.[617] There are two exceptions to that general rule, however: Around the time he retired from writing in 2010, Roth decided to revisit the fiction that had most affected him decades earlier, and then to reread his own entire oeuvre.[618]

Until well into college Roth thought he'd become a lawyer, and he was twenty-three years old when he decided definitively to pursue the career of a writer, a decision made easier by having his first story published in the *New Yorker*. Roth chose to teach as well, because in terms of things he might do to make money—he never expected to make his living as an author—it allowed the most free time for writing. He taught first at the University of Chicago while also earning a master's degree and doing some work toward a PhD, then at the Iowa Writers' Workshop, Princeton, and the University of Pennsylvania. He continued to teach, even after financial concerns ceased to be a factor, as a way to get himself out of the house on occasion and to discuss literature with others on a regular basis.

So often perceived to be an autobiographical writer, Roth's life experiences are not central to his fiction in the direct way readers might assume. Although he did draw on his own life for material, Roth is careful to point out that there's as much in his fiction that has no connection to his own personal history as there is that's drawn from events that really happened. Roth has never been one to keep a diary or journal, which is perhaps a reflection of his disinterest in true autobiography.[619]

What he got from drawing on real life, more than characters and plots, is the verisimilitude that makes his novels feel so completely alive. The mien of reality courses through stories that are products of his imagination. Reality is a foundation for the subject matter, not the subject matter itself. "[Reality] provides something against which to measure what you make up, so that in the end the invented experience and the real experience will have the same kind of life," he explained.[620] His success here is the very reason that his protagonists are so often mistaken for thinly veiled representations of himself. Roth once described *Portnoy's Complaint* as "a novel in the guise of a confession [that] was received and judged by any number of readers as a confession in the guise of a novel."[621]

Examples of these "half-imaginary" scenarios abound. Roth was in psychoanalysis when it occurred to him to put the protagonist of his next book in the analyst's office, although the session described in the novel resembles none that Roth himself ever undertook. And a major theme in *Portnoy's Complaint* is Jewish American repressiveness, which Roth had experienced, but not in the context readers may have assumed. The condemnation he received from the Jewish community in response to his debut book, *Goodbye, Columbus*, exposed him to the repressiveness. He took that treatment and inserted it into the Portnoys' family dynamic. Roth's own childhood home was a far more accepting environment.

In other novels, we find similar half-truths. For example, Roth dated a middle-aged former lesbian, just as the protagonist of *The Humbling* did. But whereas in fiction that relationship ended in tragedy, in real life Roth remained friends with his former girlfriend, both parties having emerged unscathed. And while writing *The Ghost Writer*, in which one of the characters believes she is Anne Frank, Roth kept a picture of Frank on his desk next to one of his then girlfriend, Claire Bloom, at the same age; their resemblance was striking. Yet even Bloom, upon reflection, doubted that this or any of Roth's characters were fundamentally based on her.[622]

It was thanks to Bloom, who is British, that from 1977 until around 1989, Roth spent half the year in London and the other half tucked away in Connecticut. In both locations, he had little contact with America at large. This living situation gave him some needed distance from home, a renewed perspective, and ultimately a reinfusion of energy with which to tackle the subject of his home country. "And when I came back, I was thirsting for America," Roth says. "And what I discovered was that I had a new subject, which was an old subject."[623] *American Pastoral*, *I Married a Communist*, and *The Human Stain* were the result, all books that deal with America not from the very personal perspective that defined Roth's earlier books, but from a more broadly historical one, and one that could only come with the passing of time in his own life: "I wouldn't know what to write [about Iraq and Afghanistan, or 9/11]. It does take me 20 years to figure it out."[624] Indeed, he tried to write a novel about Vietnam in the 1970s, only to abandon it fifty or so pages in. Twenty years later, he started in on the topic anew and completed *American Pastoral*.[625]

Even with a couple dozen books under his belt, Roth still felt like an amateur every time he looked to the next one. "It's a rare writer who is confident at the outset," he said. "You are just the opposite—you are doubt-ridden, steeped in uncertainty and doubt."[626] When feeling out a new book, Roth began writing without exactly knowing where he was going. In those early pages, he was looking for that conflict, "for what's going to resist you."[627] Until he found the tension inherent to all his best characters, the writing served as mere exercise. "I often have to write a hundred pages or more before there's a paragraph that's alive," he said.[628] Reviewing his work early in the cycle, Roth underlined the paragraphs, sentences, or phrases that he wanted to keep in red. Six months of work might get distilled into a single page of quality work from which the novel ultimately grew.

Roth called this part of the process awful. But on its heels came a phase in which he delighted—the months of "freewheeling play," when moving through the plot became a sort of game, a period of pulling literary strings to see what he was capable of. After this, he again encountered difficulties, when he turned on his own ideas and ended up—temporarily—hating the book.[629] He would use the word "crisis" to describe this phase. In the writing of *Zuckerman Unbound*, for example, the crisis mounted as Roth continued to have the book begin with Zuckerman's father already dead. He spent months knowing something was off, but was unable to put his finger on it: "I couldn't give up the premise of my earliest drafts until I saw that the novel's obsessive concern with assassinations, death threats, funerals, and funeral homes was leading up to, rather than away from, the death of Zuckerman's father."[630]

Sometimes the problems and crises didn't work out the way he would have liked them to. When things weren't coming together, Roth was known to set a partly finished novel aside to be finished later. Struggling with *My Life as a Man* in the early 1970s, he put it on the back burner first to write *Our Gang*, then *The Great American Novel*, and finally *The Breast*. He saw each of these books as a step in blasting through a tunnel toward the book he was try-ing to write all along, and only after they were finished did he feel ready to return to *My Life as a Man*.[631]

Roth abandoned some manuscripts completely, like a sequel to *The Breast* that he'd written eighty or so pages of.[632] In other scenarios, abandoned manuscripts served as kindling for another novel that would eventually catch fire. After his first three books, Roth found himself at an uncomfortable crossroads. Unsure what he wanted to do next, he didn't publish a book between 1962 and

1967, a notable drought for a man who commonly put out a book as often as every year.[633] In the end, though, those five years were productive in a different way. Roth wrote two hundred pages of a manuscript he called "Jewboy," about a Jewish kid growing up in Newark. He also abandoned a play in progress called *The Nice Jewish Boy*. He began writing an experimental monologue that contained a few thousand words on adolescent masturbation—the only part upon reflection that seemed worth keeping, although he didn't know for what. And then he wrote a few hundred pages of an autobiographical novel about growing up in New Jersey. In each of these four works, while circling the themes and attitudes that would encapsulate *Portnoy's Complaint*, Roth was "oscillating between the extremes of unmanageable fable or fantasy and familiar surface realism or documentation, and thereby holding at bay what was still trying to become my subject, if only I would let it."[634] As it happened, in an attempt to make his autobiographical novel more exciting, Roth invented some relatives to live upstairs from the central family. He called those relatives the Portnoys. They were a composite of the many Jewish families Roth had known growing up, and they soon took over the project and put forth Alexander Portnoy.[635]

Early in the process, Roth tended not to show his work to others, but when a novel approached completion, he printed four or five copies and distributed them among a few select and trusted readers. He then visited their respective homes and tape-recorded discussions about the novel, solicited their reactions, summaries, and critiques.[636] Roth also relied heavily on the wisdom of his editors. He speaks highly of all his editors over the years. To Veronica Geng, his editor on *The Ghost Writer*, he doled out characteristic praise: "She invariably landed squarely on what was wrong and left me to face it down, if I could."[637] After *The Ghost Writer*, he continued to send his drafts to her, even if she wasn't his editor on the book.

Roth was at his happiest during these later phases of completing a novel, and the moments of sending it off to the publisher were a joy, however fleeting: "When you finish a novel, you feel triumphant, until ten days later, that is, when you have to begin thinking about the undoability of the next novel."[638] The process, at this very point, came full circle and began again, with Philip Roth once more looking for trouble.

A DAY IN THE WRITER'S LIFE . . .

Before retiring from the writing life, Philip Roth settled into the writing studio on the grounds of his eighteenth-century home in rural Connecticut by 9:30 a.m. every day with terrifying consistency. He remained there through the morning and afternoon, standing at a lectern next to two wavy old windows, happy if he produced one page of quality writing over the course of the day. In the late afternoon, Roth liked to take a long walk in the countryside. At night, he listened to music, especially if he was alone. Aside from the infrequent occasions on which he joined friends for dinner, Roth passed the evening with a book, and it wasn't an unusual day that ended without his having seen another soul.

TWO TAKES ON THE DIGITAL AGE

Which explains her objections to having her work so often classified as science fiction. Atwood's best-known novel, *The Handmaid's Tale*, in fact won the Arthur C. Clarke Award in 1987 for
best science-fiction novel published in the United Kingdom, attract-
ing legions of fans of the genre. But Atwood rejects the label precisely because it does not encapsulate that key element in her fiction,
"thinking about the future with tools we already have," as she puts
it.[640] She prefers instead the term "speculative fiction," which dis-
tinguishes her work from novels featuring, say, life-forms that don't
exist. Atwood rejects her work as feminist, another commonly
applied label, for similar reasons: The word intimates a call to
action, or at least a debate in the making, which Atwood insists isn't
present in her novels; she is just telling what she sees in the world
around her, or what that world has proven capable of producing.

The authenticity of Atwood's fiction is achieved through
scrupulous attention to life's details, and she is forever collecting
them. When something strikes her—an interesting thing happens around her, a slogan on a T-shirt, a curious brand name—
she records it on any writing surface available, then sets it to the
side of her desk, to be retrieved at an opportune time.[641] "I'm a
magpie with prose," she says. "I collect little pieces of information,
overheard conversation."[642] Sometimes she has been storing that
information for years. One template for creating her American dys-
topia of the future for *The Handmaid's Tale* came not from recent
history, but from "the heavy-handed theocracy of 17th-century
Puritan New England, with its marked bias against women, which
would need only the opportunity of a period of social chaos to
reassert itself" (in the 1960s, Atwood did postgraduate work studying seventeenth- and eighteenth-century America at Harvard in
Cambridge, Massachusetts, where the novel is set).[643] Before writing that book, Atwood was also collecting newspaper clippings
on certain events—extreme statements being made by American

religious leaders, or the Iranian theocracy of the 1980s[644]—for four years when she finally decided she needed to get them out of her system, and she set aside her other work for this new novel.[645]

Atwood isn't big on formal note-taking—she's tried keeping travel journals, for example, but says she's no good at it.[646] And she doesn't deliberately research a novel before starting it, although once the writing starts, she goes to whatever lengths necessary to acquire the information she needs. Some of her research helps with overarching themes, like when she consulted a friend with a PhD about certain elements of the gothic tradition that factored into *The Year of the Flood*, a novel about a small community of survivors on a postapocalyptic Earth.[647] But again, much of it has simply to do with getting the details right: what the phone booth at a certain corner is like, or the song typically sung during a particular ritual.[648] She spends a lot of time researching names, to ensure that each one carries some kind of meaning appropriate to its character.[649] And she understands her characters thoroughly, envisioning much more about the intricacies of their lives and personalities than ever appears in the book. Her efforts result in passages like the following, from *The Blind Assassin*:

> Laid out in front of me are a cup of tea, an apple cut into quarters, and a pad of paper with blue lines on it, like men's pyjamas once. I've bought a new pen as well, a cheap one, black plastic with a rolling tip. I remember my first fountain pen, how sleek it felt, how blue the ink made my fingers. It was Bakelite, with silver trim. The year was 1929. I was thirteen. Laura borrowed this pen—without asking, as she borrowed everything—then broke it, effortlessly. I forgave her, of course. I always did.[650]

Through the details offered up here, we know this character is old, that her sister played a complicated role in her life, and that she had been privileged enough to own a nice fountain pen at age thirteen.

It is through these details that the reader becomes seduced by the novel, curious to know more about what was obviously a complicated relationship between these two sisters.

But the details can sometimes come back to bite Atwood. If she runs into trouble, it's often because she gets enthralled by the details and descriptions to the detriment of plot. She has in fact abandoned novels that, as she puts it, "have wonderful descriptions of things, but nothing actually occurs."[651]

An unusual childhood fostered Atwood's ability to contemplate life's minutiae. She grew up straddling the rural and urban spheres, spending the warmer half of each year in the remote northern reaches of Quebec, where her father ran an insect research station, and the colder half back in Toronto, usually settling into a different apartment each fall. "I came from a very isolated background. This is probably the key to some of my writing," she says.[652] The isolation not only steered her toward books, but also left her with the ability to be shocked by things in everyday human society that the rest of us have likely become immune to by the time we reach adulthood. She fell under the influence of an older brother with a penchant for storytelling and read avidly. Drawn to fairy tales and romance, she especially loved *Grimms' Fairy Tales*, for their audacity, their well-placed magic, their twisting of our world, and, interestingly, for their complicated and hands-on female characters.[653]

At age sixteen, Atwood seemingly out of nowhere realized she wanted to be a writer, and with the decision made, she never looked back. The origin story is simple: One day while walking home from school, Atwood was struck with an idea. "I wrote a poem in my head and then I wrote it down, and after that writing was the only thing I wanted to do."[654] This also marked the moment that she became more high-minded about her reading, although to this day she still enjoys a good murder mystery in her down time.[655] During the first decade or so of her writing career, certain authors had a clear influence on Atwood's own work. George Orwell helped inspire her taste for dystopias, along with *A Brave New World* and *Darkness at Noon*.[656] She read *1984* as an adolescent, a few years after it came out in 1949, around the same time she discovered Edgar Allan Poe, E. Nesbit, and Andrew Lang's folktales.[657] Sweeping English novels like George Eliot's *Middlemarch* and Emily Brontë's *Wuthering Heights* also had an early impact.

Atwood is steeped in classic literature, but she also appreciates more contemporary media. She sees the Internet not as the writer's enemy, but simply as the next medium of expression in a line of them dating back to handwritten letters and the telegram. Atwood keeps a frequently updated website, created a stand-alone website to experiment with marketing and audience engagement for her novel *The Year of the Flood*, and for a while kept a blog on WordPress (not updated since 2012). "I particularly like Twitter," she says of the platform on which she has almost half a million followers, "because it's short and can be very funny and informative."[658] Atwood has also shown an eagerness to experiment with her fiction online—"I always try everything," she says.[659] She wrote a short story for the digital-only publisher Byliner in 2012, then upon seeing its popularity agreed to continue the story, turning it into a serialized novel on that site. She incorporated feedback from published chapters into the direction of subsequent chapters. And—no surprise—she received much of that feedback via Twitter. She also collaborated with another author, Naomi Alderman, on a zombie novel called *The Happy Zombie Sunrise Home*, distributed on the self-publishing app Wattpad.

Despite embracing the Internet, though, Atwood recognizes the need to manage one's time spent on it. She limits her Twitter time to ten minutes per day,[660] and perhaps even more tellingly, she has two desks in the writing room she keeps in her Toronto home, one with a computer hooked up to the Internet, one with a disconnected machine.[661] She says, "In order to actually finish a novel I have to isolate myself from all distraction because if it's a question of a choice between the work and the distraction I'll take the distraction every time."[662] This kind of discipline—and recognition of its necessity—in part explains why Atwood is usually a fast worker. Early in her career, she ambitiously tried but mostly failed to work through ten pages per day.[663] By the time of a 1990 interview with the *Paris Review*, Atwood had settled into a routine in which one to two thousand words in a day is considered productive, anything less a letdown of sorts.[664]

If Atwood finds herself stuck, she might switch to another form of writing for the moment—a travel piece or some poetry can shake her out of a novel-writing malaise.[665] On a daily basis, she finds that rote chores provide crucial brainstorming time: "I think it induces ideas to do a repetitive activity that is not connected with writing."[666] As a novel progresses, she puts increasingly more time into it: in the beginning maybe only a couple of hours per day, toward the end somewhere between six and eight.[667] Coffee appears to be a critical part of the working day for Atwood, and in her novels, coffee withheld is a sure sign of a society gone off the rails. She doesn't typically work on anything else while writing a novel and likes to have just one project going at a time.

With a book finally behind her, Atwood has no problem taking her time to devise the next one. The inspiration, the moment of conception, usually comes to Atwood not as an expansive theme to be tackled, but as a single image. Or a single image that is soon joined by more images, and out of those images, "a voice starts operating, somebody starts talking, and I want to know more about him, find out about it."[668] Sometimes that voice is presented in the form of a real person, as was the case for *Bodily Harm*: She had some scenes and images in mind for a while, but they didn't coalesce into a novel until she met a woman on a beach in the

Caribbean who told Atwood her life story. Sometimes the image emerges from a negative space: She gets interested in something precisely because she notices that no one else has done it yet.[669] Sometimes the spark is found in one of her poems. "It's almost as if the poems open something, like opening a room or a box or a pathway," she says. "And then the novel can go in and see what else is in there."[670] Over the years and decades, Atwood's subject matter has become broader. In the beginning, she says, "you have to pick subjects that are small enough for you to handle."[671] Early novels like *The Edible Woman* and *Surfacing* focus on the plight of a single protagonist, while later novels tend to feature more comprehensively constructed worlds inhabited by the characters.

With the subject in place, Atwood just starts writing—this moment, she says, is "terrifying every time."[672] She puts a lot of pressure on herself to get a first draft of a novel down, usually doing so quickly, and then taking revisions slowly. Sometimes the story comes out linearly, while other times the scenes present themselves to her erratically. She tends to keep track of the number of pages completed in her journal "as a way of urging myself on."[673] With a draft in place, the novel can change drastically during revisions. The first draft of *Lady Oracle*, for example, was written as an epistolary novel in the second person, addressing a character named Arthur. But as she worked on it, Atwood realized that Arthur would have already known a lot of the things he was being told in the novel. In its final version, the novel is told in the first person, from Arthur's wife's perspective.

When plowing forward on a novel, Atwood uses a combination of handwriting and typing she once dubbed the "rolling barrage," after the World War I battle technique in which soldiers advanced up the battlefield in two lines, one attacking while the other knelt, preparing their arms for the next round.[674] After handwriting twenty or so pages, she starts the process of typing them up—early in her career on a typewriter, these days on a computer—then returns to longhand for the next twenty pages, and so on. For writing longhand, she prefers "an implement that flows": a good pen that moves across the page briskly in order to accommodate her fast pace.[675] For paper, she like margins and thick lines and plenty of space between those lines, which she fills with edits and notes before heading to the keyboard.[676] Atwood types badly using four fingers (which at least is twice as many as David Foster Wallace used) and manages to see this as a benefit.[677] "If I were a good touch typist, I'd miss a lot of things," she says.[678]

Atwood prefers a quiet space offering complete isolation for these sessions. But while she has created this setup for herself at home, her frequent travels have meant that she doesn't always have control over the circumstances under which she writes. Having spent time living in Boston, Vancouver, Montreal, London, Provence, Berlin, and Edinburgh, in addition to her adopted hometown of Toronto, Atwood has become adaptable by necessity.[679] Over the years, her writing schedule has also shifted to accommodate other commitments. As a graduate student at Harvard and odd-job holder up until the age of about twenty-seven, when her second book of poetry won a major Canadian award that helped launch her success, Atwood often wrote at night, staying up late because it was the only time available for writing. She never expected to be able to live solely off her writing, but as she gradually became a full-time writer, her working hours shifted toward the mornings. When her daughter was a child, Atwood tried to write between 10 a.m. and 4 p.m., when the house was otherwise empty.[680] Still, her tendency to procrastinate meant she might spend the entire morning avoiding her work, "then plunge into the manuscript in a frenzy of anxiety around 3:00 when it looked as though I might not get anything done."[681] She's been known to keep going in the evenings if she's on a roll.

While a work is in progress, Atwood doesn't generally share or talk about it. Even Graeme Gibson, her partner of nearly forty years and an unfailing champion of her work, doesn't get to see the novels until they're published. And although Atwood worked briefly as an editor, she doesn't rely on her own editors very heavily. "By the time they get the work, it's been through six drafts usually," she says.[682]

There's no consistent approach to coming up with the titles of her novels. For some, they're there from the beginning, as was the case with *The Edible Woman* and *Lady Oracle*. Others she comes to later on almost by accident. Once, for example, while doing some reading "of a legal nature," she inadvertently came up with the title *Bodily Harm*, after having searched down other paths for some time. And often the title changes as she works—*The Handmaid's Tale* began life as "Offred," the name of the novel's protagonist.[683] She renamed "Notes on the Mesozoic" as *Life before Man*, primarily because the original title seemed incomprehensible to those she floated it to.[684]

Ultimately, Margaret Atwood's novels take anywhere from six months to a few years to complete.[685] *The Edible Woman* and *Surfacing* each took just six months, although she'd been considering them for far longer. After her years of accumulating material, she wrote *The Handmaid's Tale* in a year. *Lady Oracle* took her a little over two years, as did *The Blind Assassin*.[686] When a novel is finished, Atwood tends to not write at all for a while, then write poetry until she's sick of it, then return to fiction.[687] Even after decades as a master at the art of fiction, Atwood insists there's no unerring approach to achieving great writing: "If we knew what worked, we could sell it as an unbeatable program for writing masterpieces."[688] Ultimately, writing is an improvisational act, every time. "I have no routine. I have no foolproof anything. There's nothing foolproof."[689]

A DAY IN THE WRITER'S LIFE . . .

Margaret Atwood insists that there is no tried-and-true approach to her daily writing. But there is a general routine: After waking, she has breakfast and coffee, then before too long approaches the task of writing. Her writing room at home has two desks, a computer on each, only one hooked up to the Internet. She allows herself just ten minutes per day on her favorite of the social media, Twitter. Still, she tends to procrastinate and might do so for hours. At some point, the possibility of failure gets her going, and Atwood gets to work toward her mark of one to two thousand words per day, first writing pages by hand, then transferring them chunks at a time to the computer. She normally works through the afternoon, but if on a roll, Atwood happily continues into the evening.

18

ZADIE SMITH

It sounds almost too simple: The first sentence comes first, and after it, the second. From there, all subsequent sentences tend to follow in order. It can come as a surprise to Zadie Smith, a good number of these sentences in, to discover that she's created a character, and that a plot is under way. Even then, she remains preoccupied with the individual building blocks, a few words strung together with a period at the end. For Smith, everything—plot, characters, structure—is "contained in the sensibility of a sentence."[690] An unexpected one can change the direction of the whole endeavor, and she thus takes them very seriously, gives them the meticulous attention they require if they are to eventually assemble themselves into a coherent whole.

The way Smith sees it, this kind of approach denotes a certain category of writer: the Micro Manager. Authors fall into one of two primary camps, she explained in her 2009 book of essays, *Changing My Mind*.[691] Macro Planners work out the structure of their novels and then write within that structure. Micro Managers, on the other hand, don't rely on an overarching configuration (don't even conceive of one), but rather home in on each sentence, one by one, and each sentence, as they come to it, becomes the only thing that exists. If there is a spectrum starting with Macro Planners on one end and Micro Managers on the other, Smith would be somewhere to the right of the page. Smith's writing is entirely incremental and cumulative. The grand plan is that there is no grand plan; working things out ahead of time ruins everything, "feels disastrous."She prefers the writing of a novel as a process of discovery. "The thinking goes on on the page," not beforehand.[692]

Even when immersed in writing a novel, Smith dislikes conducting research for it because it leads her away from the thinking on the page.[693] Her approach to nonfiction is similar: "I'm not able, not capable of deciding beforehand, my angle or some overarching theory."[694] For both her nonfiction and her novels, Smith has usually accumulated a mere dusting of notes before getting started, just a few points of reference. She of course recognizes the drawbacks to this approach—"after you've read four or five books, and don't seem to have any notes, the column is due on Tuesday"[695]— but prefers it to being confined by them from the outset.

Smith began writing her first novel at the age of twenty—"I was working when everybody else was getting drunk"[696]—and completed the bulk of its 484 pages before graduating from Cambridge University. It's a rare thing, the first novel that makes an author financially secure before the age of twenty-five, but Smith pulled it off with *White Teeth*, a sprawling story about the lives of two friends from World War II in latter-day multicultural London. She was thus able to skip past the early phase of a more typical author's trajectory, with the promising but fruitless years filled with odd jobs and writing in haphazard moments as they become available. "It's the ongoing shock of my life," she says of *White Teeth*'s success. "In one way, I'm incredibly grateful. The money meant—and has meant—that I can write as I like."[697]

The instant success may also have played a role in fostering her meandering writing routine. Smith's daily habits have proven consistent only in their general refusal to adhere to any edicts of consistency. She notes that her writing schedule falls to the whims of her moods. "I find it hard to write when I'm very sad," she says, for example.[698] When she went through a years-long gloomy streak, she didn't write fiction at all. If the writing is going well, she might work like a nine-to-fiver, keeping with it into the early evening. But when she's not quite sure where she's going with a project, or when her mood fails to inspire her, she might manage only an hour or two.[699] Now that she has children, Smith's time for writing has contracted, which surprisingly has been a positive kind of pressure. "An hour for me used to be, 'I think I'll go into the kitchen—oh, an hour's gone by.' And now four hours is all I have a day. And you learn that you can write a novel in that time, if you absolutely do not go on the Internet."[700]

Like many first novels, Smith's first effort poured out quickly. But the pace didn't remain quite so brisk. She published her second and third novels, *The Autograph Man* and *On Beauty*, at roughly three-year intervals, and then spent more than seven years on her 2012 novel, *NW*, and only during the last four months of that time did it really come together. The rest of those seven years were spent "figuring out what I was doing," she says.[701]

Smith also attributes her slow progress in part to her habit of starting every working day by reading what she's already written, editing as she goes, before adding new text to the novel. "It's incredibly laborious," she says, "and toward the end of a long novel it's intolerable actually."[702] The bright side of this approach is that when she reaches the end of the novel, she's done with it: "If you edit as you go along, there are no first, second, third drafts. There is only one draft, and when it's done, it's done."[703] It's an approach that a writer of a century ago wouldn't recognize as physically possible—it's an option only available to the writer in the age of the computer.

When she's writing, Smith prefers a small room with little natural light, the blinds drawn to close out the daylight. Books are strewn across her desk. She generally does her best work in the afternoons.[704] She makes great effort to restrict her access to the Internet during her writing hours. Smith, in fact, does not believe in the redeeming qualities of the Internet as it exists today (Web 2.0, social media, etc.). On a personal level, she finds the Internet dangerously addictive. Smith joined Facebook and quickly quit it, horrified by its ability to eat up her time. "With Facebook hours, afternoons, entire days went by without my noticing," she says of her time on it.[705] Unlike a writer like Margaret Atwood, Smith also dislikes the kind of instantaneous feedback that putting work online elicits. "I think constant feedback is not a very healthy thing for a writer," she says.[706]

Nor does she feel it's healthy on a social level, as she wrote in a 2010 essay for the *New York Review of Books*: "In Facebook, as it is with other online social networks, life is turned into a database, and this is a degradation . . . We know the consequences of this instinctively; we feel them."[707] Smith doesn't qualify as a social butterfly, but she likes people, and she likes to keep her relationships with them in the physical realm, feels they are more properly human there. Eventually, she employed the Internet-blocking programs Freedom and SelfControl to force her off websites and into her Word document. They proved so helpful that she thanked the programs in the acknowledgments of *NW* "for creating the time."

Although Smith doesn't plan her novels out in any detail, she does work from a framework that she likens to scaffolding—a structure used to hold the novel up in the beginning, almost as a gimmick to trick herself into thinking there's a larger order to the project. Her list of potential scaffolding (as yet unused) includes the liner notes to the Beatles' *The White Album*, the speeches of Donald Rumsfeld, and a chapter each on the books of the prophets in the Old Testament.[708] These topics get her started and give her a point of reference until the novel takes on a life of its own. For her novel *On Beauty*, the scaffolding was E. M. Forster's *Howards End*, which gave her a guide for her plot. For *White Teeth*, she knew she wanted to write a book about a man who "gets through the [twentieth] century in a good way . . . The rest of it formed itself around him."[709]

The scaffolding, in the end, serves more as a catalyst than a true backbone for her novels. Of *On Beauty*, she says, "The points where *On Beauty* meets *Howards End* are the least interesting bits of the book for me. It was simply a way of writing inside a certain genre: the literary update."[710] She didn't even reread Forster's novel before starting her own. In retrospect, she often finds that the scaffolding hadn't been necessary at all; it's there to make the initial task less daunting, but not much of a factor once it's under way.

Smith does, however, approach each novel with a new perspective in mind. In order to keep herself engaged, she has to not repeat her own successes. *NW* emerged as a far more experimental novel than her previous one, and that was intentional. "I had to do something which interests me," she says. "I was very bored. I get bored."[711] She's mentioned that her next novel will be in the science-fiction vein.[712]

No matter the novel, the first twenty pages are the most critical to the outcome of the book. While writing them, Smith works out what kind of novel she is in fact writing, and this part is full of false starts and wrong turns. These twenty pages are also the most laborious, and during the precarious time of composing them, more than at any other time, she says, "the whole nature of the thing changes by the choice of a few words."[713] Smith's obsession with getting those first twenty pages right—and they have to be right, if the rest of the novel is to rely on them—can verge on paralyzing: She spent almost two years agonizing over the first twenty pages of *On Beauty*.

When the first twenty pages are finally where she wants them, Smith is off to the races. Even though she's been working on the opening all that time, on a more subconscious level the rest of the novel has been finding its shape. Smith writes quickly from page twenty-one through to the end—after those nearly two years, she finished the rest of *On Beauty* in five months. This is the phase during which a "magical thinking" takes over, and the novel seamlessly becomes the focal point of her existence. During this phase, "you sit down to write at 9 a.m., you blink, the evening news is on and four thousand words are written, more words than you wrote in three long months, a year ago."[714] And then, nearing the end, she revisits those first twenty pages, only to invariably discover that they're almost comical in their intensity, in their leaving nothing to chance or interpretation. "Calmly," she says of reviewing them at this point, "I take off the top, let a little air in."[715]

Along the way, Smith solicits input from editors and early readers. "I love to be edited if the editing is intelligent," she says.[716] During the writing of *White Teeth* toward the end of her university days, she shared her work in progress freely: "I had about five good friends who were essential to the germination and progression of the book."[717] Her husband and fellow writer Nick Laird today serves as a dependable first reader. And then there are her magazine editors. Shortly after *White Teeth* shot her into the upper echelon of English-language writers, Smith began writing essays and short stories for American publications like the *New Yorker* and *Harper's*. Her editors on these projects transformed her writing for the better, encouraging shorter, tighter sentences and forcing her to cut pieces down, sometimes by thousands of words. Smith doesn't believe that a shorter, simpler sentence is always a better one, but coming from the English tradition—in which learning the structure of the essay is a priority, but keeping that structure from becoming unwieldy is not—the tenacity of American editors gave her a new sense of control in her writing.[718]

Smith is acutely receptive to feedback and even coaxes it out of people when it's not forthcoming. When she finished *NW* and set out to get reactions to it, she could tell there was something about the ending that no one was telling her. "There was this horrible radio silence," she says. "I had to get it out of them, mostly from friends, because friends don't want to be mean. But nobody liked it. It wasn't good. I knew it wasn't, but I just had a little hope that maybe I could make it work."[719] After this feedback, she knew she couldn't leave the ending as it was and rewrote the entire last section.

The cumulative effect of Smith's efforts includes, among other traits, splashes of adroit humor. In its brief review of *White Teeth* in 2000, the *New Yorker* made a point of referring to Smith's "deft comic touch," an opinion that was repeated almost universally. But when Smith wrote *White Teeth*, she had no idea there was humor in it. She doesn't intentionally insert comedy into her work, but the comic element is a natural expression of her own tastes. She's noted that the novels she loves always offer "a little laughter in the dark."[720] Those lacking it, like *Wuthering Heights* and the works of Dostoyevsky, she is able to appreciate but not embrace on a more visceral level. This sensibility has seeped into her own work.

Given her allergy to present technologies and the grand realism of her novels, Smith can come across as a writer from another era caught in the present, and that's not always far off. As a young mixed-race girl growing up not exactly poor in a London council estate—her mother Jamaican, her father "a short white guy"[721]—there were novels around the house, but the Smith household wasn't particularly bookish, and Smith looked up to the rarefied literary world from the outside. As a teenager, she discovered Forster and fell into a reverie over his work. As she puts it, his novels provided "the first intimations I ever had of the power and beauty of this funny, artificial little construction, the novel."[722] She also discovered Keats at age fourteen and saw for the first time an example of someone rising through the literary ranks from a background at least somewhat resembling her own.[723]

When she arrived at Cambridge, Smith brought with her a determination to go toe-to-toe with the entrenched academic and literary tradition that came more naturally to many of her peers. Both ambitious and talented, she proved more than capable on both counts—before she wrote *White Teeth* she expected to go into academia. Her need to prove she belonged in the upper echelons of the country's best thinkers took her years to finally work through, staying with her well after college. Reimagining *Howards End* as *On Beauty* was, in part, an effort to prove herself up to the standards of England's lofty literary canon. When *On Beauty* came out in 2005, she said, "Working through my Forster habit has got me to a new place," in which she was finally freed from its constraints.[724]

She never participated in a formal creative writing education; Smith has what she calls a "horror" of creative writing classes. To her, they encourage the wrong kind of perspective, a kind of writing as therapy. "The best, the only real training you can get is from reading other people's books," she says.[725] In college, she read insatiably and considers this to have been her foundational education as a writer. Her literary loves range from Updike to Nabokov to Zora Neale Hurston to Bret Easton Ellis. Kingsley Amis. Dickens. Kafka. David Foster Wallace. Ian McEwan. Forster, of course. The list could easily become unwieldy. She once named Philip Larkin as definitively her favorite writer.[726] George Eliot's *Middlemarch* was an essential early guide.

Smith continues to consider reading integral to her writing process and, in a way, the most enjoyable part of it. "Reading is a magic thing," she says. "But writing, I actually feel, is considerably less magic."[727] She always has the novels of others open on her desk while working on her own, which she uses to tease out a certain tone or voice in her own work. If she feels she's writing with too much sentimentality, for example, Smith will read something spare to snap her out of it. If she's over-agonizing about composing the perfect set of words, she'll pick up Dostoyevsky, the "patron saint of substance over style."[728] While writing *NW*, she spent a lot of time reading existentialist philosophers like Camus and Sartre, in which she found a way to be positive and life affirming without falling into mawkishness.[729] She likens the approach to that of an orchestra member who needs to hear all the other members playing their instruments in order to strike just the right chord herself.[730]

Smith also keeps carefully selected quotes posted around her workspace. This strangely pessimistic line from Thomas Pynchon's *Gravity's Rainbow* was pinned to her door for five years: "We have to find meters whose scales are unknown in the world, draw our own schematics, getting feedback, making connections, reducing the error, trying to learn the real function . . . zeroing in on what incalculable plot?" And she made a screen saver out of the following quote from Derrida: "If a right to a secret is not maintained then we are in a totalitarian space."[731]

Alongside her ongoing links to England's highbrow literary sphere, Smith remains irreducibly tied to her humbler background and writes toward it in a way that has not faded over the years. "It matters to me that [my work] can be read by the people I came from," she says. "I can't get rid of that idea. I can't ever really leave to write some novel that is so dense or so complex or so obscure that I can't have at least a hope that my family might read it."[732] You'd never call Smith an autobiographical writer—her first novel was so notable in part because it wasn't a typical navel-gazing debut—but the milieu of her background is there, and the London of her childhood figures prominently in her novels. All of her novels feature a multiracial cast, and she approaches her characters through the subtleties of their social stations in life. Her ability to depict characters from different classes is on full display (along with her natural comic talent) in *On Beauty*, her novel examining the social complexities in the families of two competing black professors. In this scene, the two men's daughters meet for the first time:

> So it was Zora whom Howard [her father] sent to the door when the bell went; Zora who opened the door to the family Kipps. The penny did not drop immediately. Here was a tall, imperious black man, in his late fifties, with a pug dog's distended eyes. To his right, his taller, equally dignified son; on the other side, his gallingly pretty daughter. Before conversation, Zora waded around in the visual information: the strangely Victorian get-up of the older man—the waistcoat, the pocket-handkerchief—and again that searing glimpse of the girl, the instantaneous recognition (on both sides) of her physical superiority. Now they moved in a triangle behind Zora through the hallway as she babbled about coats and drinks and her own parents, neither of whom, for the moment, could be found. Howard had vanished.
>
> 'God, he was right here. *God*. He's around here some place ... God, where *is* he?'
>
> It was an ailment Zora inherited from her father: when confronted with people she knew to be religious she began to blaspheme wildly.

With work like this, Smith has taken her place in England's literary canon and even moved beyond it. Having done so, she no longer feels the same urgency to be a fiction writer. She's stated that if she stopped writing novels altogether, she'd be content, and after publishing *On Beauty*, she even thought for a while that might be it for her, three novels and done. She loves writing essays as much as writing fiction and finds it far less difficult to boot. And she's fulfilled by teaching; she's been a professor at New York University since 2010, and before that took temporary posts at Harvard and Columbia. She now splits her time between New York City and London, and a similar split—a life of academia and essay writing—would seem to be a very real possibility.

Possible, but perhaps not probable. As long as she keeps finding something new to do with fiction, and as long as she can keep herself off the Internet, she's likely to keep going, sentence by sentence, through to the end of another novel. For Zadie Smith, there is no better part of the writing life than the end of a long project. "To have written is a lovely feeling," she says.[733] Of the very last day of working on a novel, she says, "It's a feeling of happiness that knocks me clean out of adjectives."[734]

A DAY IN THE WRITER'S LIFE . . .

Zadie Smith does not adhere to any particular daily schedule as a writer, and in fact has spent long stretches not writing at all. These days, she writes around her duties as a professor at New York University and a mother to two children (and a dog). She prefers to hunker down in a small room, the blinds drawn to keep out the afternoon light. At the start of a session, Smith opens up the Internet-blocking program, Freedom, and reviews her work from the previous day before adding new pages. If the work is going well, she might work a full day on it. If it's not, an hour or two is all she has in her. Smith enjoys a low-key conversation, a glass of wine, and time spent with her family as the day winds down.

ACKNOWLEDGMENTS

Thank you to Greg Wands, Erum Naqvi, Peter Foges, Tyler Gore, Christopher Carroll, Jordan Ellenberg, and Lee Klein for reading early versions of this book and offering thoughtful critiques that played no small part in helping the project come together. Thanks to my agent, Brandi Bowles, and editor, Katie Salisbury, for championing the book before there was a book to champion. I am grateful to all the literary scholars and biographers who came before me; without their millions of hours of research, this book could not have been written. The *Paris Review*'s Art of Fiction series has been an impossibly rich source of information. I feel lucky to have spent time in the New York Public Library's Berg Collection. A thank-you a long time coming to my grad school writing professor Melissa Monroe; her sound guidance and encouragement came during a time it was much needed. Special thanks to my parents for mostly finding my wayward career choices charming. I am grateful to my dog, Yacha, who served as a constant if unlikely sounding board during all those hours and days of otherwise quiet endeavor. Finally, I reserve the most thanks for Scott Rosenstein, who encouraged this book from the outset, who continues to bravely provide critiques of my work despite the near-certain wrath that follows each time, and who anchors this author's writing life and entire life.

ABOUT THE AUTHOR

©2014 Micilin O'Donaghue

Sarah Stodola grew up in Kentucky and now lives in New York City. Her writing has appeared in the *New York Times, Wall Street Journal, Daily Beast, Awl,* and others. She founded the literary journal *Me Three* and served as an adjunct scholar for *Lapham's Quarterly.* She is currently the editorial director of Strolby.

NOTES

NINE-TO-FIVERS
Chapter 1: Franz Kafka

1. Stach, Reiner. *Kafka: The Decisive Years* (Orlando, FL: Harcourt, 2005), 194–195.
2. Unseld, Joachim. *Franz Kafka: A Writer's Life*, translated by Paul F. Dvorak (Riverside, CA: Ariadne Press, 1994), 15.
3. Stach, *Kafka*, 295.
4. Kafka, Franz. *Letter to My Father*, translated by Howard Colyer (Morrisville, NC: lulu.com, 2008), Kindle edition.
5. Stach, *Kafka*, 23.
6. Kafka, Franz. *The Diaries, 1901–1923*, edited by Max Brod (New York: Schocken Books, 1976), 33.
7. Unseld, *Franz Kafka*, 75.
8. Kafka, Franz. *Letters to Felice*, edited by Erich Heller and Jürgen Born, translated by James Stern and Elisabeth Duckworth (New York: Schocken Books, 1973), 275.
9. Stach, *Kafka*, 463.
10. Ibid., 23.
11. Ibid., 25.
12. Kafka, *Diaries*, 202.
13. Batuman, Elif. "Franz Kafka's Last Trial," *New York Times Magazine*, September 22, 2010, accessed online at http://www.nytimes .com/2010/09/26/magazine/26kafka-t.html?ref=magazine.
14. Unseld, *Franz Kafka*, 74.
15. Stach, *Kafka*, 246.
16. Kafka, *Diaries*, 29.
17. Stach, *Kafka*, 465.
18. Unseld, *Franz Kafka*, 76.
19. Stach, *Kafka*, 79.
20. Ibid., 80.
21. Ibid., 127.

22. Banville, John. "Franz Kafka's Other Trial," *Guardian*, January 14, 2011, accessed online at http://www.theguardian.com/books/2011/jan/15/john -banville-kafka-trial-rereading.

23. Stach, *Kafka*, 40.

24. Ibid., 179.

25. Unseld, *Franz Kafka*, 110.

26. "*Letters to Felice*," Random House, catalog, at http://www.randomhouse .com/acmart/catalog/display.pperl?isbn=9780804150767&view=print.

27. Stach, *Kafka*, 3.

28. Ibid., 77.

29. Kafka, *Diaries*, 30.

30. Batuman, "Franz Kafka's Last Trial."

31. Kafka, *Diaries*, 193.

32. Unseld, *Franz Kafka*, 134–135.

33. Ibid., 29.

34. Kafka, *Diaries*, 393.

Chapter 2: Toni Morrison

35. Dreifus, Claudia. "Chloe Wofford Talks about Toni Morrison," *New York Times Magazine*, September 11, 1994, accessed online at http://www .nytimes.com/1994/09/11/magazine/chloe-wofford-talks-about-toni -morrison.html?pagewanted=all&src=pm.

36. Ibid.

37. Ibid.

38. Ibid.

39. Stepto, Robert. "Intimate Things in Place: A Conversation with Toni Morrison," *Massachusetts Review* 18, no. 3 (Autumn 1977): 473–489, reprinted in *Conversations with Toni Morrison*, edited by Danille Taylor -Guthrie (Jackson: University Press of Mississippi, 1994), 23.

40. Dreifus, "Chloe Wofford Talks about Toni Morrison."

41. Ibid.

42. Washington, Elsie B. "Talk with Toni Morrison," *Essence*, October 1987, reprinted in Taylor-Guthrie, ed., *Conversations with Toni Morrison*, 237.

43. Bollen, Christopher. "Toni Morrison," *Interview Magazine*, May 2012, accessed online at http://www.interviewmagazine.com/culture/toni -morrison.

44. Schappell, Elissa. "Toni Morrison, The Art of Fiction No. 134," *Paris Review*, Fall 1993, accessed online at http://www.theparisreview.org /interviews/1888/the-art-of-fiction-no-134-toni-morrison.

45. Brockes, Emma. "Toni Morrison: 'I Want to Feel What I Feel. Even if It's Not Happiness,'" *Guardian*, April 13, 2012, accessed online at http://www.theguardian.com/books/2012/apr/13/toni-morrison-home-son-love.

46. Dreifus, "Chloe Wofford Talks about Toni Morrison."

47. Schappell, "Toni Morrison, The Art of Fiction No. 134."

48. Ibid.

49. Dowling, Colette. "The Song of Toni Morrison," *New York Times Magazine*, May 20, 1979, reprinted in Taylor-Guthrie, ed., *Conversations with Toni Morrison*, 53.

50. Ruas, Charles. *Conversations with American Writers* in Taylor-Guthrie, ed., *Conversations with Toni Morrison*, 99.

51. Kachka, Boris. "Who Is the Author of Toni Morrison?" *New York Magazine*, April 29, 2012, accessed online at http://nymag.com/news/features/toni-morrison-2012-5/.

52. Brockes, "Toni Morrison."

53. Ibid.

54. Schappell, "Toni Morrison, The Art of Fiction No. 134."

55. Ibid.

56. Watkins, Mel. "Talk with Toni Morrison," *New York Times Book Review*, September 11, 1977, reprinted in Taylor-Guthrie, ed., *Conversations with Toni Morrison*, 44.

57. Bakerman, Jane. "The Seams Can't Show: An Interview with Toni Morrison," *Black American Literature Forum* 12, no. 2 (Summer 1978): 56–60, reprinted in Taylor-Guthrie, ed., *Conversations with Toni Morrison*, 33.

58. Jones, Bessie W., and Audrey L. Vinson. "An Interview with Toni Morrison," in *The World of Toni Morrison* (Dubuque, IA: Kendall/Hunt, 1985), reprinted in Taylor-Guthrie, ed., *Conversations with Toni Morrison*, 179.

59. LeClair, Thomas, "The Language Must Not Sweat: A Conversation with Toni Morrison," *New Republic*, March 21, 1981, reprinted in Taylor-Guthrie, ed., *Conversations with Toni Morrison*, 127.

60. Schappell, "Toni Morrison, The Art of Fiction No. 134."

61. Ibid.

62. Houston, Pam. "A Conversation with Toni Morrison," *O, The Oprah Magazine*, July 2009, accessed online at http://www.oprah.com/omagazine/Toni-Morrison-on-Writing.

63. Morrison, Toni. "Unspeakable Things Unspoken: The Afro-American Presence in American Literature," lecture delivered at the Tanner Lectures on Human Values, University of Michigan, Ann Arbor, October 7, 1988, accessed online at http://tannerlectures.utah.edu/_documents/a-to-z/m/morrison90.pdf, 161–162.

64. Schappell, "Toni Morrison, The Art of Fiction No. 134."

65. Schappell, Elissa. "Toni Morrison, The Art of Fiction No. 134," *Paris Review*, Fall 1993, accessed online at http://www.theparisreview.org /interviews/1888/the-art-of-fiction-no-134-toni-morrison.

66. Morrison, "Unspeakable Things Unspoken," 152.

67. Stepto, "Intimate Things in Place," in Taylor-Guthrie, ed., *Conversations with Toni Morrison*, 15.

68. Schappell, "Toni Morrison, The Art of Fiction No. 134."

69. Ibid.

70. Dreifus, "Chloe Wofford Talks about Toni Morrison."

71. Tate, Claudia. "Toni Morrison," *Black Women Writers at Work* (New York: Continuum, 1983), reprinted in Taylor-Guthrie, ed., *Conversations with Toni Morrison*, 159.

72. Schappell, "Toni Morrison, The Art of Fiction No. 134."

73. Bakerman, "The Seams Can't Show," in Taylor-Guthrie, ed., *Conversations with Toni Morrison*, 34.

74. Ruas, *Conversations with American Writers*, in Taylor-Guthrie, ed., *Conversations with Toni Morrison*, 97.

75. Neustadt, Kathy. "The Visits of the Writers Toni Morrison and Eudora Welty," *Bryn Mawr Alumnae Bulletin*, Spring 1980, reprinted in Taylor -Guthrie, ed., *Conversations with Toni Morrison*, 87.

76. Schappell, "Toni Morrison, The Art of Fiction No. 134."

77. Ibid.

78. Bakerman, "The Seams Can't Show," in Taylor-Guthrie, ed., *Conversations with Toni Morrison*, 34.

79. Bollen, "Toni Morrison."

80. Waterhouse, Gail. "Toni Morrison Discusses Writing Tips at Northeastern," *Huntington News*, January 24, 2013, accessed online at http://huntnewsnu .com/2013/01/toni-morrison-discusses-writing-tips-at-northeastern/.

81. Dreifus, "Chloe Wofford Talks about Toni Morrison."

82. Schappell, "Toni Morrison, The Art of Fiction No. 134."

83. Houston, "A Conversation with Toni Morrison."

PRODUCTIVE PROCRASTINATORS
Chapter 3: David Foster Wallace

84. Max, D. T. *Every Love Story Is a Ghost Story: A Life of David Foster Wallace* (New York: Viking, 2012), 44.

85. Ibid., 141.

86. Ibid., 258.

87. Rose, Charlie. Interview with David Foster Wallace, *Charlie Rose*, PBS, March 27, 1997.

88. Max, *Every Love Story Is a Ghost Story*, 116.

89. David Foster Wallace to Don DeLillo, October 10, 1995, *Letters of Note*, http://www.lettersofnote.com/2012/02/i-dont-enjoy-this-war-one-bit.html.

90. Wallace, David Foster. "The Nature of the Fun," *Both Flesh and Not* (New York: Little, Brown, 2012), 196–197.

91. Rose interview with David Foster Wallace.

92. Author interview with Juliana Harms, August 20, 2013.

93. McGrath, Charles. "Piecing Together Wallace's Posthumous Novel," *New York Times*, April 8, 2011, accessed online at http://www.nytimes.com/2011/04/09/books/david-foster-wallace-and-the-pale-king.html?_r=0.

94. Schmeidel, Stacey. "Brief Interview with a Five Draft Man," *Amherst Magazine*, Spring 1999, accessed online at https://www.amherst.edu/aboutamherst/magazine/extra/node/66410.

95. Max, *Every Love Story Is a Ghost Story*, 43.

96. Ibid., 75.

97. Ibid., 123.

98. Author interview with Juliana Harms.

99. Lipsky, David. "The Lost Years and Last Days of David Foster Wallace," *Rolling Stone*, October 30, 2008.

100. Max, D. T. "The Unfinished: David Foster Wallace's Struggle to Surpass *Infinite Jest*," *New Yorker*, March 9, 2009, accessed online at http://www.newyorker.com/reporting/2009/03/09/090309fa_fact_max.

101. Author interview with Juliana Harms.

102. Max, *Every Love Story Is a Ghost Story*, 283.

103. Eggers, Dave. Interview with David Foster Wallace, *Believer*, November 2003, accessed online at http://www.believermag.com/issues/200311/?read=interview_wallace.

104. Max, *Every Love Story Is a Ghost Story*, 43.

105. Author interview with Juliana Harms.

106. Ibid.

107. Wallace, David Foster. "E Unibus Plurum: Television and U.S. Fiction," *A Supposedly Fun Thing I'll Never Do Again* (Boston: Little, Brown, 1997), 22.

108. Max, *Every Love Story Is a Ghost Story*, 260.

109. Ibid.

110. Scocca, Tom. "'It's Not Very Good for Me When People Treat Me Like a Big Shot': David Foster Wallace on Nonfiction, 1998, Part 5," *Slate*, November 28, 2010, http://www.slate.com/content/slate/blogs/scocca/2010/11/28/it_s_not_very_good_for_me_when_people_treat_me_like_a_big_shot_david_foster_wallace_on_nonfiction_1998_part_5.html.

111. Author interview with Juliana Harms.

112. Kennedy, Hugh, and Geoffrey Polk. "Looking for a Garde of Which to Be Avant: An Interview with David Foster Wallace," *Whiskey Island Magazine*, Spring 1993, accessed online at http://www.thehowlingfantods.com /dfwstuff/Whiskey%20Island%20DFW%20Interview%20Looking%20 for%20a%20Garde%20of%20Which%20to%20be%20Avant.pdf.

113. Moore, Steven. "The First Draft Version of *Infinite Jest*," *Howling Fantods*, http://www.thehowlingfantods.com/ij_first.htm.

114. "Finite Jest: Editors and Writers Remember David Foster Wallace," *Slate*, September 17, 2008, http://www.slate.com/articles/arts/culturebox/2008/09 /finite_jest_2.html.

115. Max, "The Unfinished."

116. Max, *Every Love Story Is a Ghost Story*, 29.

117. Ibid., 154.

118. Williams, John. "God, Mary Karr and Ronald Reagan: D. T. Max on David Foster Wallace," *ArtsBeat* (blog), *New York Times*, September 12, 2012, http://artsbeat.blogs.nytimes.com/2012/09/12/god-mary-karr-and -ronald-reagan-d-t-max-on-david-foster-wallace/?_r=0.

119. Scocca, "'It's Not Very Good.'"

120. Author interview with Juliana Harms.

121. Schmeidel, "Brief Interview with a Five Draft Man."

122. Ibid.

Chapter 4: Richard Price

123. Wroe, Nicholas. "Excavation of the Lower East Side," *Guardian*, August 15, 2008, accessed online at http://www.guardian.co.uk/books/2008/aug/16 /fiction1.

124. Price, Richard. "The Fonzie of Literature," *New York Times Book Review*, October 25, 1981, accessed online at http://www.nytimes.com /books/98/06/07/specials/price-fonzie.html.

125. Ibid.

126. Linville, James. "Richard Price, The Art of Fiction No. 144," *Paris Review*, Spring 1996, accessed online at http://www.theparisreview.org /interviews/1431/the-art-of-fiction-no-144-richard-price.

127. Price, "The Fonzie of Literature."

128. Author interview with Richard Price, July 2, 2013.

129. Buchwald, Laura. "A Conversation with Richard Price," *Bold Type*, http:// www.randomhouse.com/boldtype/0103/price/interview.html.

130. Michod, Alec. Interview with Richard Price, *Believer*, May 2008, accessed online at http://www.believermag.com/issues/200805/?read=interview_price.

131. Ibid.

132. Author interview with Richard Price.

133. Price, "The Fonzie of Literature."

134. Linville, "Richard Price, The Art of Fiction No. 144."

135. Michod interview with Richard Price.

136. Grant, Richard. "Richard Price: True Grit," *Telegraph*, August 9, 2008, accessed online at http://www.telegraph.co.uk/culture /donotmigrate/3558266/Richard-Price-true-grit.html.

137. Linville, "Richard Price, The Art of Fiction No. 144."

138. "One on 1: Author Richard Price on the 'Terror' of Writing," NY1 News, July 21, 2008, accessed online at http://www.ny1.com/content/shows/one _on_1_archives_hp/one_on__1_pfpz/84007/one-on-1--author-richard -price-on-the--terror--of-writing.

139. Author interview with Richard Price.

140. Michod, Alec. Interview with Richard Price, *Believer*, May 2008, accessed online at http://www.believermag.com/ issues/200805/?read=interview_price.

141. Grant, "Richard Price: True Grit."

142. Wroe, "Excavation of the Lower East Side."

143. Linville, "Richard Price, The Art of Fiction No. 144."

144. Author interview with Richard Price.

145. Ibid.

146. Ibid.

147. Michod interview with Richard Price.

148. "One on 1: Richard Price on the 'Terror' of Writing."

149. Buchwald, "A Conversation with Richard Price."

150. Linville, "Richard Price, The Art of Fiction No. 144."

151. Author interview with Richard Price.

152. Grant, "Richard Price: True Grit."

153. Linville, "Richard Price, The Art of Fiction No. 144."

154. Author interview with Richard Price.

155. Linville, "Richard Price, The Art of Fiction No. 144."

156. Author interview with Richard Price.

157. Linville, "Richard Price, The Art of Fiction No. 144."

158. "One on 1: Richard Price on the 'Terror' of Writing."

159. Linville, "Richard Price, The Art of Fiction No. 144."

AUTODIDACTS
Chapter 5: Edith Wharton

160. Lee, Hermione. *Edith Wharton* (New York: Alfred A. Knopf, 2007), 176.

161. Wharton, Edith. *A Backward Glance* (New York: Simon & Schuster, 1998 [1933]), 204.

162. Lee, *Edith Wharton*, 40.

163. Wharton, *A Backward Glance*, 169.

164. Ibid., 121.

165. Ibid., 66–68.

166. Wharton, Edith. *The Writing of Fiction* (New York: Simon & Schuster, 1997 [1925]), 9.

167. Lee, *Edith Wharton*, 23.

168. Haralson, Eric L., ed. *Encyclopedia of American Poetry: The Nineteenth Century* (Chicago: Fitzroy Dearborn, 1998), 457.

169. Lewis, R. W. B. *Edith Wharton: A Biography* (New York: Harper & Row, 1975), 65–66.

170. Lee, *Edith Wharton*, 162.

171. Wharton, *A Backward Glance*, 208–209.

172. Lee, *Edith Wharton*, 726.

173. Wharton, *A Backward Glance*, 204.

174. Lee, *Edith Wharton*, 176.

175. Lewis, *Edith Wharton: A Biography*, 7.

176. Lee, *Edith Wharton*, 176.

177 Lewis, *Edith Wharton: A Biography*, 353–354.

178. Lee, *Edith Wharton*, 599.

179. Ibid., 349.

180. Ibid., 423.

181. Wharton, Edith. *The Letters of Edith Wharton*, edited by R. W. B. Lewis and Nancy Lewis (New York: Collier Books, 1989), 275.

182. Lewis, *Edith Wharton: A Biography*, 503.

183. Lee, *Edith Wharton*, 180.

184. Ibid., 174.

185. Ibid., 180.

186. Wharton, *A Backward Glance*, 6.

187. Ibid., 103.

188. Ibid., 116.

189. Ibid., 296.

190. Lee, *Edith Wharton*, 217.

191. Ibid., 111.

192. Kakutani, Michiko. "Books of the Times; Letters from an Unlikely Literary Friendship," *New York Times*, January 9, 1990, accessed online at http://www.nytimes.com/1990/01/09/books/books-of-the-times-letters-from-an-unlikely-literary-friendship.html.

193. Wharton, *The Writing of Fiction*, 58.

194. Lee, *Edith Wharton*, 153.

195. Lewis, *Edith Wharton: A Biography*, 308.

196. Wharton, *A Backward Glance*, 210.

197. Lee, *Edith Wharton*, 419.

198. Ibid., 147.

199. Ibid., 278–279.

200. Ibid., 178.

201. Ibid., 177.

202. Ibid., 176.

Chapter 6: George Orwell

203. Stansky, Peter. *The Unknown Orwell; Orwell, the Transformation* (Stanford, CA: Stanford University Press, 1994), 228.

204. Ibid., 72–73.

205. Ibid., 273.

206. Orwell, George. *The Complete Works of George Orwell*, edited by Peter Davison, vol. 10, *A Kind of Compulsion, 1903–1936* (London: Secker & Warburg, 1997), 236.

207. George Orwell to Arthur Koestler, April 13, 1946, reprinted in *George Orwell: The Collected Essays, Journalism, and Letters*, edited by Ian Angus and Sonia Orwell, vol. 4, *In Front of Your Nose, 1945–1950* (Boston: David R. Godine, 2000), 146.

208. Orwell, George. *The Complete Works of George Orwell*, edited by Peter Davison, vol. 18, *Smothered Under Journalism, 1946* (London: Secker & Warburg, 1997), 343.

209. Stansky, *The Unknown Orwell*, 263–264.

210. McCrum, Robert. "The Masterpiece That Killed George Orwell," *Guardian*, May 9, 2009, accessed online at http://www.theguardian.com /books/2009/may/10/1984-george-orwell.

211. Stansky, *The Unknown Orwell*, 74, 97.

212. McCrum, "The Masterpiece That Killed George Orwell."

213. Stansky, *The Unknown Orwell*, 180.

214. Ingle, Stephen. *George Orwell: A Political Life* (Manchester, UK: Manchester University Press, 1993), 84.

215. Orwell, George. Preface to the Ukrainian Edition of *Animal Farm*, March 1947, accessed online at http://orwell.ru/library/novels/Animal_Farm /english/epfc_go.

216. Ibid.

217. McCrum, "The Masterpiece That Killed George Orwell."

218. Davison, Peter. *George Orwell: A Literary Life* (New York: St. Martin's Press, 1996), 94.

219. Stansky, *The Unknown Orwell*, 19.

220. Ibid., 230.

221. Owen, Paul. "1984 Thoughtcrime? Does It Matter That George Orwell Pinched the Plot?" *Books Blog, Guardian*, June 8, 2009, http://www.guardian.co.uk/books/booksblog/2009/jun/08/george-orwell-1984-zamyatin-we.

222. McCrum, "The Masterpiece That Killed George Orwell."

223. Stansky, *The Unknown Orwell*, 224.

224. Davison, *George Orwell*, 129.

225. Stansky, *The Unknown Orwell*, 156.

226. Davison, *George Orwell*, 31.

PLOTTING AHEAD

Chapter 7: Virginia Woolf

227. L., Lee, Hermione. *Virginia Woolf* (New York: Alfred A. Knopf, 1998), 390.

228. Virginia Woolf to Violet Dickinson, January 1905, quoted in Lee, *Virginia Woolf*, 217.

229. Woolf, Virginia. *A Writer's Diary* (San Diego, CA: Harcourt, 2003 [1954]), 146.

230. Lee, *Virginia Woolf*, 139.

231. Ibid., 141.

232. Woolf, Leonard. "Virginia Woolf: Writer and Personality," *Listener*, March 4, 1965, reprinted in *Virginia Woolf: Interviews and Recollections*, edited by J. H. Stape (Iowa City: University of Iowa Press, 1995), 149.

233. Woolf, Virginia. Editor's note to *Moments of Being*, edited by Jeanne Schulkind, 2nd ed. (San Diego, CA: Harvest Books, 1985), 25.

234. Bell, Clive. "A Genius Who Worked Magic," *Old Friends: Personal Recollections* (London: Chatto & Windus, 1956), reprinted in Stape, ed., *Virginia Woolf*, 94.

235. Woolf, Virginia. "Old Bloomsbury," in Woolf, *Moments of Being*, 197.

236. Ibid., 198.

237. Woolf, Leonard. *Downhill All the Way: An Autobiography of the Years 1919–1939* (New York: Harcourt, Brace & World, 1967), 52.

238. Vita Sackville-West to Harold Nicholson, February 18, 1941, reprinted in Stape, ed., *Virginia Woolf*, 80.

239. Lehmann, John. "Working with Virginia Woolf," *Listener*, January 13, 1955, reprinted in Stape, ed., *Virginia Woolf*, 124.

240. Woolf, L., *Downhill All the Way*, 52.

241. Woolf, V., *A Writer's Diary*, 84.

242. Woolf, Virginia. *The Diary of Virginia Woolf*, edited by Anne Olivier Bell, vol. 1, *1915–1919* (London: Hogarth Press, 1977), 165.

243. Woolf, V., *A Writer's Diary*, 25, 29, 35.

244. Lee, *Virginia Woolf*, 471.

245. Grant, Duncan. "Virginia Stephen," *Horizon*, June 1941, reprinted in Stape, ed., *Virginia Woolf*, 136.

246. Lee, *Virginia Woolf*, 314.

247. Leonard Woolf to Lytton Strachey, April 1913, quoted in Lee, *Virginia Woolf*, 321.

248. Woolf, L., *Downhill All the Way*, 156.

249. Ibid.

250. Lee, *Virginia Woolf*, 405.

251. Ibid., 427.

252. Woolf, V., *A Writer's Diary*, 27.

253. Ibid., 125.

254. Leonard Woolf to T. S. Eliot, April 30, 1925, quoted in Lee, *Virginia Woolf*, 442.

255. Woolf, V., *A Writer's Diary*, 7.

256. Ibid., 13.

257. Ibid., 61.

258. Ibid., 66.

259. Ibid., 75–76.

260. Ibid., 104.

261. Lee, *Virginia Woolf*, 22–24.

262. Woolf, V., *A Writer's Diary*, 67.

263. Ibid., 120.

264. Bell, "A Genius Who Worked Magic," in Stape, ed., *Virginia Woolf*, 98.

265. Lee, *Virginia Woolf*, 287.

266. Ibid., 515.

Chapter 8: Vladimir Nabokov

267. Boyd, Brian. *Vladimir Nabokov: The Russian Years* (Princeton, NJ: Princeton University Press, 1990), 111.

268. Nabokov, Vladimir. *Strong Opinions* (New York: McGraw-Hill, 1973), 10.

269. Boyd, *Vladimir Nabokov: The Russian Years*, 345.

270. Nabokov, Vladimir. *Vladimir Nabokov: Selected Letters 1940–1977*, edited by Dmitri Nabokov and Matthew J. Bruccoli (San Diego, CA: Harcourt Brace Jovanovich, 1989), 60.

271. Boyd, Brian. *Vladimir Nabokov: The American Years* (Princeton, NJ: Princeton University Press, 1991), 89.

272. Ibid., 92.

273. Field, Andrew. *VN: The Life and Art of Vladimir Nabokov* (New York: Crown, 1986), 123.

274. Boyd, *Vladimir Nabokov: The American Years*, 107.

275. Field, *VN*, 145.

276. Nabokov, *Strong Opinions*, 58.

277. Boyd, *Vladimir Nabokov: The American Years*, 148.

278. Ibid., 226.

279. Field, *VN*, 268.

280. Nabokov, Vladimir. "Inspiration," *Saturday Review*, November 20, 1972, reprinted in Nabokov, *Strong Opinions*, 269.

281. Boyd, *Vladimir Nabokov: The Russian Years*, 171.

282. Nabokov, *Strong Opinions*, 101.

283. Field, *VN*, 175.

284. Boyd, *Vladimir Nabokov: The Russian Years*, 496

285. Boyd, *Vladimir Nabokov: The American Years*, 201.

286. Boyd, *Vladimir Nabokov: The Russian Years*, 289.

287. Nabokov, *Strong Opinions*, 24.

288. Nabokov, Vladimir. *Speak, Memory*, rev. ed. (New York: Vintage International, 1989), 257.

289. Nabokov, *Strong Opinions*, 110.

290. Gold, Herbert. "Vladimir Nabokov, The Art of Fiction No. 40," *Paris Review*, Summer–Fall 1967, accessed online at http://www.theparisreview.org/interviews/4310/the-art-of-fiction-no-40-vladimir-nabokov.

291. Nabokov, *Strong Opinions*, 47.

292. Ibid., 104.

293. Ibid., 268.

294. Boyd, *Vladimir Nabokov: The Russian Years*, 274, 276.

295. Boyd, *Vladimir Nabokov: The American Years*, 169.

296. Boyd, *Vladimir Nabokov: The Russian Years*, 345.

297. Nabokov, *Strong Opinions*, 15.

298. Ibid., 27.

299. Ibid., 3.

300. Nabokov, *Speak, Memory*, 178.

301. Nabokov, *Strong Opinions*, 58.

302. Boyd, *Vladimir Nabokov: The Russian Years*, 440–442.

303. Gold, "Vladimir Nabokov, The Art of Fiction No. 40."

304. Ibid.

305. Vladimir Nabokov to Pyke Johnson Jr., August 16, 1959, reprinted in Nabokov, *Selected Letters*, 297.

306. Nabokov, *Strong Opinions*, 99.

307. Nabokov, *Speak, Memory*, 265.

308. Ibid., 257.

309. Nabokov, *Strong Opinions*, 66.

310. Field, *VN*, 36.

311. Ibid., 64.

312. Ibid., 268.

313. Ibid., 119.

314. Boyd, *Vladimir Nabokov: The American Years*, 211.

315. Nabokov, *Strong Opinions*, 23.

316. Ibid., 93.

WINGING IT

Chapter 9: Salman Rushdie

317. Livings, Jack. "Salman Rushdie, The Art of Fiction No. 186," *Paris Review*, Summer 2005, accessed online at http://www.theparisreview.org /interviews/5531/the-art-of-fiction-no-186-salman-rushdie.

318. Dhillon, Amrit. "'I Am Pessimistic about Changes Occurring in India,'" *India Today*, September 30, 1995, reprinted in *Conversations with Salman Rushdie*, edited by Michael Reder (Jackson: University Press of Mississippi, 2000), 172; Ross, Jean W. "*Contemporary Authors* Interview: Salman Rushdie," *Contemporary Authors*, vol. 111 (Detroit: Gale, 1984), reprinted in Reder, ed., *Conversations with Salman Rushdie*, 4.

319. Ross, "*Contemporary Authors* Interview: Salman Rushdie," in Reder, ed., *Conversations with Salman Rushdie*, 1.

320. Ibid., 4.

321. Rushdie, Salman. *Joseph Anton* (New York: Random House, 2012), 227.

322. Livings, "Salman Rushdie, The Art of Fiction No. 186."

323. Stufflebeam, Shawn. "Interview with Salman Rushdie," About.com, March 3, 2009, http://contemporarylit.about.com/od/authorinterviews/a /rushdieInterview.htm.

324. Ibid.

325. Crichton, Sarah, and Laura Shapiro. "An Exclusive Talk with Salman Rushdie," *Newsweek*, February 12, 1990, reprinted in Reder, ed., *Conversations with Salman Rushdie*, 127.

326. Ross, "*Contemporary Authors* Interview: Salman Rushdie," in Reder, ed., *Conversations with Salman Rushdie*, 4.

327. Durix, Jean-Pierre. "Salman Rushdie," *Kunapipi* 4, no. 2 (1982), reprinted in Reder, ed., *Conversations with Salman Rushdie*, 8.

328. Rushdie, *Joseph Anton*, 57–58.

329. Durix, "Salman Rushdie," in Reder, ed., *Conversations with Salman Rushdie*, 9.

330. Livings, "Salman Rushdie, The Art of Fiction No. 186."

331. Rushdie, *Joseph Anton*, 153.

332. Rushdie, Salman. "Inspiration Is Nonsense," interview by Max Miller, Big Think, November 29, 2010, http://bigthink.com/videos/inspiration-is-nonsense.

333. Rushdie, Salman. "Heavy Threads," *New Yorker*, November 7, 1994.

334. Hamilton, Ian. "The First Life of Salman Rushdie," *New Yorker*, December 25, 1995.

335. Rushdie, *Joseph Anton*, 3.

336. Ibid., 102.

337. Ibid., 91.

338. Max, D. T. "The Concrete beneath His Feet," *New York Times Magazine*, September 17, 2000, accessed online at http://partners.nytimes.com/library/magazine/home/20000917mag-max.html.

339. Holson, Laura M. "From Exile to Everywhere," *New York Times*, March 23, 2012, accessed online at http://www.nytimes.com/2012/03/25/fashion/salman-rushdie-out-of-exile-is-a-fixture-on-the-social-scene.html.

340. Livings, "Salman Rushdie, The Art of Fiction No. 186."

341. Grass, Gunter. "Fictions Are Lies That Tell the Truth: Salman Rushdie and Gunter Grass in Conversation," *Listener*, June 27, 1985, reprinted in Reder, ed., *Conversations with Salman Rushdie*, 75.

342. Brooks, David. "Salman Rushdie," *Helix*, 1984, reprinted in Reder, ed., *Conversations with Salman Rushdie*, 69.

343. "Cronenberg Meets Rushdie," *Shift*, June–July 1995, online at http://www.davidcronenberg.de/cr_rushd.htm.

344. Ibid.

345. Trubek, Anne. "Why Authors Tweet," *New York Times*, January 6, 2012, accessed online at http://www.nytimes.com/2012/01/08/books/review/why-authors-tweet.html?pagewanted=all&_r=0.

346. Randol, Shaun. "The Art of Bravery: An Interview with Salman Rushdie," *Los Angeles Review of Books*, April 25, 2013, accessed online at http://lareviewofbooks.org/article.php?id=1611&fulltext=1.

347. Livings, "Salman Rushdie, The Art of Fiction No. 186."

348. Rushdie, *Joseph Anton*, 27, 31.

349. Ibid., 27.

350. Ibid., 342.

351. Pattanayak, Chandrabhanu. "Interview with Salman Rushdie," *Literary Criterion* 18, no. 3 (1983), reprinted in Reder, ed., *Conversations with Salman Rushdie*, 17.

352. Ball, John Clement. "An Interview with Salman Rushdie," *Toronto South Asian Review* 10, no. 1 (Summer 1991), reprinted in Reder, ed., *Conversations with Salman Rushdie*, 106.

353. Rushdie, Salman. "Out of Kansas," *New Yorker*, May 11, 1992.

354. Livings, "Salman Rushdie, The Art of Fiction No. 186."

355. Rushdie, *Joseph Anton*, 495.

356. Livings, "Salman Rushdie, The Art of Fiction No. 186."

357. Stufflebeam, "Interview with Salman Rushdie."

358. "Homeless Is Where the Art Is," *Bookseller*, July 15, 1994, reprinted in Reder, ed., *Conversations with Salman Rushdie*, 164.

359. Rushdie, "Inspiration Is Nonsense."

360. Livings, "Salman Rushdie, The Art of Fiction No. 186."

361. Ibid.

362. Durix, "Salman Rushdie," in Reder, ed., *Conversations with Salman Rushdie*, 9.

363. Livings, "Salman Rushdie, The Art of Fiction No. 186."

364. Chaudhuri, Una. "Imaginative Maps: Excerpts from a Conversation with Salman Rushdie," *Turnstile* 2, no. 1 (1990): 36–47, accessed online at http://www.subir.com/rushdie/uc_maps.html.

365. Chaudhuri, "Imaginative Maps."

366. Rushdie, *Joseph Anton*, 169.

367. Livings, "Salman Rushdie, The Art of Fiction No. 186."

368. Chaudhuri, "Imaginative Maps."

369. Livings, "Salman Rushdie, The Art of Fiction No. 186."

Chapter 10: Joan Didion

370. Didion, Joan. "Why I Write," *New York Times Book Review*, December 5, 1976, accessed online at http://query.nytimes.com/mem/archive/pdf?res=F10917FA345816768FDDAC0894DA415B868BF1D3.

371. Didion, "Why I Write."

372. Didion, Joan. Preface to *Slouching towards Bethlehem* (New York: Farrar, Straus & Giroux, 1990), xvi.

373. Didion, Joan. *The Year of Magical Thinking* (New York: Knopf, 2006), 23.

374. Davidson, Sara. "A Visit with Joan Didion," *New York Times Book Review*, April 3, 1977, accessed online at http://www.saradavidson.com/NytDidion.html.

375. Als, Hilton. "Joan Didion, The Art of Fiction No. 1," *Paris Review*, Spring 2006, accessed online at http://www.theparisreview.org/interviews/5601/the-art-of-nonfiction-no-1-joan-didion.

376. Ibid.

377. Davidson, "A Visit with Joan Didion."

378. Als, "Joan Didion, The Art of Fiction No. 1."

379. Kuehl, Linda. "Joan Didion, The Art of Fiction No. 71," *Paris Review*, Fall–Winter 1978, accessed online at http://www.theparisreview.org /interviews/3439/the-art-of-fiction-no-71-joan-didion.

380. Davidson, "A Visit with Joan Didion."

381. Ibid.

382. Kuehl, "Joan Didion, The Art of Fiction No. 71."

383. Davidson, "A Visit with Joan Didion."

384. Kuehl, "Joan Didion, The Art of Fiction No. 71."

385. Davidson, "A Visit with Joan Didion."

386. Academy of Achievement. Interview with Joan Didion, June 3 2006, http://www.achievement.org/autodoc/page/did0int-1.

387. Ibid.

388. Didion, *The Year of Magical Thinking*, 36, 47.

389. Didion, *Slouching towards Bethlehem*, 232.

390. Garis, Leslie. "Didion and Dunne: The Rewards of a Literary Marriage," *New York Times Book Review*, February 8, 1987, accessed online at http:// www.nytimes.com/books/97/03/02/reviews/dunne-didion.html.

391. Riley, John. "Writers Joan Didion and John Gregory Dunne Play It as It Lays in Malibu," *People*, July 26, 1976, accessed online at http://www .people.com/people/archive/article/0,,20066717,00.html.

392. Als, "Joan Didion, The Art of Fiction No. 1."

393. Brockes, Emma. "Q: How Were You Able to Keep Writing after the Death of Your Husband? A: There Was Nothing Else to Do. I Had to Write My Way Out of It," *Guardian*, December 15, 2005, accessed online at http:// www.guardian.co.uk/film/2005/dec/16/biography.features.

394. Davidson, "A Visit with Joan Didion."

395. Kuehl, "Joan Didion, The Art of Fiction No. 71."

396. Riley, "Writers Joan Didion and John Gregory Dunne Play It as It Lays."

397. Davidson, "A Visit with Joan Didion."

398. Als, "Joan Didion, The Art of Fiction No. 1."

399. Didion, *The Year of Magical Thinking*, 112.

THE AUTHOR AS PROTAGONIST
Chapter 11: Jack Kerouac

400. McNally, Dennis. *Desolate Angel: Jack Kerouac, the Beat Generation, and America* (Cambridge, MA: Da Capo Press, 2003 [1979]), 35.

401. Ibid., 22.

402. Kerouac, Jack. *Jack Kerouac: Selected Letters, 1940–1956*, edited by Ann Charters (New York: Viking, 1995), 31.

403. McNally, *Desolate Angel*, 24–25.

404. Charters, Ann. *Kerouac: A Biography* (New York: St. Martin's Press, 1994), 30, 32.

405. McNally, *Desolate Angel*, 44.

406. Berrigan, Ted. "Jack Kerouac, The Art of Fiction No. 41," *Paris Review*, Summer 1968, accessed online at http://www.theparisreview.org /interviews/4260/the-art-of-fiction-no-41-jack-kerouac.

407. McNally, *Desolate Angel*, 62–63.

408. Charters, *Kerouac*, 53.

409. Ibid., 62.

410. Kerouac, *Jack Kerouac: Selected Letters, 1940–1956*, 115.

411. Charters, *Kerouac*, 68.

412. Berrigan, "Jack Kerouac, The Art of Fiction No. 41."

413. Staton, Scott. "Neal Cassady: American Muse, Holy Fool," *Page-Turner* (blog), *New Yorker*, December 12, 2012, http://www.newyorker.com/online /blogs/books/2012/12/neal-cassady-american-muse-holy-fool.html.

414. Charters, *Kerouac*, 127.

415. Ibid., 55.

416. Kerouac, Jack. *Jack Kerouac: Selected Letters, 1957–1969*, edited by Ann Charters (New York: Viking, 1999), 242.

417. Ibid., 242.

418. Charters, *Kerouac*, 159.

419. Kerouac, *Jack Kerouac: Selected Letters, 1940–1956*, 107.

420. Kerouac, Jack. "On the Road Again," *New Yorker*, June 22, 1998, accessed online at http://www.newyorker.com/arcive/1998/06/22/1998_06_22 _046_TNY_LIBRY_000015809.

421. Jack Kerouac Papers, Henry W. and Albert A. Berg Collection of English and American Literature, New York Public Library.

422. Ibid.

423. Berrigan, "Jack Kerouac, The Art of Fiction No. 41."

424. Ibid.

425. Charters, *Kerouac*, 139–140.

426. Pertinax [Mary Sampas], *Lowell Sun*, September 20, 1962, reprinted in *Empty Phantoms: Interviews and Encounters with Jack Kerouac*, edited by Paul Maher Jr. (New York: Thunder's Mouth Press, 2005), 207.

427. Kerouac, "On the Road Again."

428. Jack Kerouac Papers, Berg Collection.

429. Ibid.

430. Johnson, Joyce. *Minor Characters* (New York: Penguin, 1999 [1983]), 131.

431. Charters, *Kerouac*, 291.

432. Kerouac, *Jack Kerouac: Selected Letters, 1957–1969*, xxiv.

433. Gifford, Barry, and Lawrence Lee. *Jack's Book: An Oral Biography of Jack Kerouac* (New York: Penguin, 1994 [1978]), 45–46.

434. Press release for *Visions of Gerard* from Farrar, Straus & Cudahy, 1963, reprinted in Maher, ed., *Empty Phantoms*, 222.

435. Jack Kerouac to Gary Snyder, June 24, 1957, reprinted in Kerouac, *Jack Kerouac: Selected Letters, 1957–1969*, 43–46.

436. Press release for *Visions of Gerard* in Maher, ed., *Empty Phantoms*, 222.

437. Berrigan, "Jack Kerouac, The Art of Fiction No. 41."

438. Kerouac, "On the Road Again."

439. Kerouac, *Jack Kerouac: Selected Letters, 1957–1969*, 15.

440. Shattuck, Kathryn. "Kerouac's 'Road' Scroll Is Going to Auction," *New York Times*, March 22, 2001, accessed online at http://www.nytimes.com/2001/03/22/books/kerouac-s-road-scroll-is-going-to-auction.html?pagewanted=all&src=pm.

441. Jack Kerouac to Malcolm Cowley, July 21, 1957, reprinted in Kerouac, *Jack Kerouac: Selected Letters, 1957–1969*, 52.

442. Duncan, Val. "Kerouac Revisited," *Long Island Newsday*, July 18, 1964, reprinted in Maher, ed., *Empty Phantoms*, 254.

443. Charters, *Kerouac*, 288.

Chapter 12: Ernest Hemingway

444. Mellow, James R. *Hemingway: A Life without Consequences* (Cambridge, MA: Da Capo Press, 1992), 13.

445. Plimpton, George. "Ernest Hemingway, The Art of Fiction No. 21," *Paris Review*, Spring 1958, accessed online at http://www.theparisreview.org/interviews/4825/the-art-of-fiction-no-21-ernest-hemingway.

446. Mellow, *Hemingway*, 304.

447. Reynolds, Michael. *Hemingway: The Paris Years* (New York: W. W. Norton, 1999), 5.

448. Bernheim, Kurt. "*McCall's* Visits Ernest Hemingway," *McCall's*, May 1956, reprinted in *Conversations with Ernest Hemingway*, edited by Matthew J. Bruccoli (Jackson: University Press of Mississippi, 1986), 107.

449. Hemingway, Ernest. *A Moveable Feast* (New York: Scribner, 2003 [1964]), 25.

450. Mellow, *Hemingway*, 159.

451. Ibid., 250.

452. Ibid., 332.

453. Plimpton, "Ernest Hemingway, The Art of Fiction No. 21."

454. Mellow, *Hemingway*, 107.

455. Stafford, Edward. "An Afternoon with Hemingway," *Writer's Digest*, December 1964, accessed online at http://www.writersdigest.com/writing -articles/by-writing-genre/literary-fiction-by-writing-genre/an_interview _with_hemingway.

456. Mellow, *Hemingway*, 302.

457. Ibid., 364.

458. Plimpton, "Ernest Hemingway, The Art of Fiction No. 21."

459. Mellow, *Hemingway*, 303.

460. Hotchner, A. E. "Hemingway Talks to American Youth," *New York Herald Tribune*, October 18, 1959, reprinted in Bruccoli, ed., *Conversations with Ernest Hemingway*, 148–149.

461. Goodman, Jack, et al. "Hemingway Tells of Early Career; States That He 'Won't Quit Now.'" *Daily Princetonian*, April 14, 1955, reprinted in Bruccoli, ed., *Conversations with Ernest Hemingway*, 101.

462. Reynolds, *Hemingway*, 267.

463. Hotchner, "Hemingway Talks to American Youth," in Bruccoli, ed., *Conversations with Ernest Hemingway*, 149.

464. Plimpton, "Ernest Hemingway, The Art of Fiction No. 21."

465. Ibid.

466. Ibid.

467. Ibid.

468. Breit, Harvey. "Talk with Ernest Hemingway," *New York Times Book Review*, September 7, 1952, reprinted in Bruccoli, ed., *Conversations with Ernest Hemingway*, 69.

469. Ross, Lillian. *Portrait of Hemingway* (New York: Modern Library, 1999), 29.

470. Mellow, *Hemingway*, 385.

471. Gill, Brendan. "Indestructible," *New Yorker*, January 4, 1947.

472. Plimpton, "Ernest Hemingway, The Art of Fiction No. 21."

473. Hotchner, "Hemingway Talks to American Youth," in Bruccoli, ed., *Conversations with Ernest Hemingway*, 146.

SLOW AND STEADY

Chapter 13: James Joyce

474. Menand, Louis. "Silence, Exile, Punning," *New Yorker*, July 2, 2012, accessed online at http://www.newyorker.com/arts/critics /atlarge/2012/07/02/120702crat_atlarge_menand.

475. Parrinder, Patrick. *James Joyce* (Cambridge: Cambridge University Press, 1984), 200.

476. Ellmann, Richard. *James Joyce*, rev. ed. (Oxford: Oxford University Press, 1982 [1959]), 598.

477. Beja, Morris. *James Joyce: A Literary Life* (Columbus: Ohio State University Press, 1992), 77.

478. Ellmann, *James Joyce*, 308–309.

479. Beja, *James Joyce: A Literary Life*, 51.

480. Ellmann, *James Joyce*, 270, 273.

481. Power, Arthur. *Conversations with James Joyce*, edited by Clive Hart (Dublin: Lilliput Press, 1999 [1974]), 40.

482. Joyce, Stanislaus. *My Brother's Keeper: James Joyce's Early Years* (New York: Viking, 1958), 85.

483. Ibid., 95.

484. Beja, *James Joyce: A Literary Life*, 66.

485. Ellmann, *James Joyce*, 354.

486. Ibid., 59.

487. Joyce, *My Brother's Keeper*, 125.

488. Beja, *James Joyce: A Literary Life*, 30.

489. Ellmann, *James Joyce*, 144.

490. Menand, "Silence, Exile, Punning."

491. *James Joyce*, directed by Chris Warren (A&E Television Networks, 2004), available online at http://www.biography.com/people/james-joyce-9358676.

492. Beja, *James Joyce: A Literary Life*, 67.

493. Butler, Sarah Funke. "Document: Happy Birthday, James Joyce," *The Daily* (blog), *Paris Review*, February 2, 2012, http://www.theparisreview.org /blog/2012/02/02/document-happy-birthday-james-joyce/.

494. Notebook II.i.1, Joyce Papers 2002, c. 1903–1928, National Library of Ireland, accessed online at http://catalogue.nli.ie/Record/vtls000357760 /HierarchyTree#page/12/mode/1up.

495. Butler, "Document: Happy Birthday, James Joyce."

496. Joyce, *My Brother's Keeper*, 118.

497. Butler, "Document: Happy Birthday, James Joyce."

498. Ellmann, *James Joyce*, 28.

499. Beja, *James Joyce: A Literary Life*, 36.

500. Ellmann, *James Joyce*, 475.

501. Joyce, *My Brother's Keeper*, 106.

502. Ellmann, *James Joyce*, 438.

503. Power, *Conversations with James Joyce*, 40.

504. Beja, *James Joyce: A Literary Life*, 80.

505. Ellmann, *James Joyce*, 590.

506. Ibid.

507. McCourt, John. *The Years of Bloom: James Joyce in Trieste, 1904–1920* (Madison: University of Wisconsin Press, 2000), 172.

508. Power, *Conversations with James Joyce*, 51.

509. Menand, "Silence, Exile, Punning."

510. Power, *Conversations with James Joyce*, 105.

Chapter 14: Junot Díaz

511. Díaz, Junot. "Becoming a Writer," *O, The Oprah Magazine*, November 2009, accessed online at http://www.oprah.com/spirit/Junot-Diaz-Talks -About-What-Made-Him-Become-a-Writer.

512. Ibid.

513. Anderson, Sam. "Junot Díaz Hates Writing Short Stories," *New York Times*, September 27, 2012, accessed online at http://www.nytimes. com/2012/09/30/magazine/junot-diaz-hates-writing-short-stories.html.

514. Danticat, Edwidge. "Junot Díaz," *BOMB*, Fall 2007, accessed online at http://bombmagazine.org/article/2948/junot-d-az.

515. Anderson, "Junot Díaz Hates Writing Short Stories."

516. Williamson, Eugenia. "Whether in Boston or New York, Writing Is a Slow Process for Junot Diaz," *Boston Globe*, September 21, 2013, accessed online at http://www.bostonglobe.com/arts/books/2013/09/21/pulitzer -winner-and-macarthur-grant-winner-junot-diaz-shares-his-writing-habits /mWPOYUbdxsMadFMVgqpPaL/story.html.

517. Ibid.

518. Morton, Paul. "A Brief Wondrous Interview with Junot Díaz," *Millions*, October 22, 2012, http://www.themillions.com/2012/10/a-brief-wondrous -interview-with-junot-diaz.html.

519. "Writers' Confessions—Junot Díaz Discusses the Writing Process," YouTube video, 3:55, from interview with Junot Díaz at the International Festival of Authors, Toronto, in 2008, posted by "Writers' Confessions," September 9, 2010, https://www.youtube.com/watch?v=WE8bO8HeuOY.

520. Danticat, "Junot Díaz."

521. Fassler, Joe. "'The Baseline Is, You Suck': Junot Diaz on Men Who Write about Women," *Atlantic*, September 12, 2012, accessed online at http:// www.theatlantic.com/entertainment/archive/2012/09/the-baseline-is-you -suck-junot-Díaz-on-men-who-write-about-women/262163/.

522. Ibid.

523. Anderson, "Junot Díaz Hates Writing Short Stories."

524. Alter, Alexandra. "How to Write a Great Novel," *Wall Street Journal*, November 13, 2009, accessed online at http://online.wsj.com/news/articles /SB10001424052748703740004574513463106012106.

525. Marriott, Edward. "The Return of the Young Master," *Guardian*, February 9, 2008, accessed online at http://www.theguardian.com/books/2008 /feb/10/culture.fiction.

526. Williams, Paige. "Junot Díaz on Imagination, Language, Success, the Role of the Teacher, the Health of American Literature and *Star Wars* as a Narrative Teaching Tool," *Nieman Storyboard*, October 12, 2012, http:// www.niemanstoryboard.org/2012/10/12/junot-diaz-on-imagination -language-success-the-role-of-the-teacher-the-health-of-american-literature -and-star-wars-as-a-narrative-teaching-tool/.

527. Charney, Noah. "Junot Díaz: How I Write," *Daily Beast*, August 21 2013, http://www.thedailybeast.com/articles/2013/08/21/junot-d-az-how-i-write. html.

528. Williams, "Junot Díaz on Imagination"

529. Charney, "Junot Díaz: How I Write."

530. McCauley, Mary Carole. "Junot Diaz: This Is Why Men Cheat," *Baltimore Sun*, November 10, 2012, accessed online at http://articles.baltimoresun. com/2012-11-10/entertainment/bs-ae-book-diaz-20121110_1_yunior -wondrous-life-oscar-wao.

531. Zuarino, John. "An Interview with Junot Diaz," *Bookslut*, September 2007, http://www.bookslut.com/features/2007_09_011634.php.

532. O'Rourke, Meghan. "Questions for Junot Díaz," *Slate*, April 8, 2008, http://www.slate.com/articles/news_and_politics/recycled/2008/04 /questions_for_junot_daz.html.

533. Zuarino, "An Interview with Junot Diaz."

534. Williams, "Junot Díaz on Imagination"

535. Morton, "A Brief Wondrous Interview with Junot Díaz."

536. Josi, Hannah. "Junot Díaz Speaks on Campus about Influences, Activism, Heritage," *Columbia Daily Spectator*, April 8, 2014, accessed online at http:// www.columbiaspectator.com/arts-and-entertainment/2014/04/08/junot -d%C3%ADaz-speaks-campus-about-influences-activism-heritage.

537. Díaz, Junot. "Advice for Young Writers on Creating a Strong Voice," *Huffington Post*, November 5, 2011, http://www.huffingtonpost .com/2011/11/05/junot-diaz-creating-a-str_n_1077760.html.

538. Danticat, "Junot Díaz."

539. Ibid.

540. Ibid.

541. Zuarino, "An Interview with Junot Diaz."

542. Leyshon, Cressida. "This Week in Fiction: Questions for Junot Díaz," *Page-Turner* (blog), *New Yorker*, March 15, 2010, http://www.newyorker .com/online/blogs/books/2010/03/this-week-in-fiction-talking-with-junot -diaz.html.

543. Kiper, Dmitry. "Junot Diaz on Heartbreak, Love and His Latest Book, 'This Is How You Lose Her,'" NBC New York, December 23, 2012, accessed online at http://www.nbcnewyork.com/the-scene/events/Junot -Diaz-Talks-about-His-New-Book-Heartbreak-Poetry-and-The-Craft-of -Writing-169354486.html.

544. Danticat, "Junot Díaz."

545. "Toni Morrison and Junot Díaz," YouTube video, 1:22:20, Live from the New York Public Library, posted by "jbegley9," December 13, 2013, https:// www.youtube.com/watch?v=J5kytPjYjSQ.

546. Barnet, Anna. "Words on a Page: An Interview with Junot Diaz," *Harvard Advocate*, Spring 2009, accessed online at http://www.theharvardadvocate .com/content/words-page-interview-junot-diaz.

547. Díaz, Junot. "MFA vs. POC," *Page-Turner* (blog), *New Yorker*, April 30, 2014, http://www.newyorker.com/online/blogs/books/2014/04/mfa-vs-poc.html.

548. Charney, "Junot Díaz: How I Write."

549. Williams, "Junot Díaz on Imagination"

550. Marriott, "The Return of the Young Master."

551. Charney, "Junot Díaz: How I Write."

552. Alter, "How to Write a Great Novel."

553. Anderson, "Junot Díaz Hates Writing Short Stories."

554. Williamson, "Whether in Boston or New York."

555. Anderson, "Junot Díaz Hates Writing Short Stories."

556. Brand, Madeleine, and A. Martínez. "Junot Diaz Reflects on Love in His Latest Book," *Brand & Martínez*, 89.3 KPCC, September 13, 2012, available online at http://www.scpr.org/programs/brand-martinez/2012/09/13/28399 /junot-diaz-love-immigrant-this-is-how-you-lose-her/.

557. Williamson, "Whether in Boston or New York."

THE SOCIAL BUTTERFLY AND THE LONE WOLF

Chapter 15: F. Scott Fitzgerald

558. Fitzgerald, F. Scott. *The Crack-up*, edited by Edmund Wilson (New York: NDP, 2009), 89.

559. Ibid.

560. Ibid.

561. Fitzgerald, F. Scott. *A Life in Letters*, edited by Matthew J. Bruccoli (New York: Simon & Schuster, 1994), 277.

562. Ibid., 272.

563. Bruccoli, Matthew J. *Some Sort of Epic Grandeur: The Life of F. Scott Fitzgerald* (New York: Harcourt Brace Jovanovich, 1981), 101.

564. Bruccoli, *Some Sort of Epic Grandeur*, 194."

565. Bruccoli, *Some Sort of Epic Grandeur*, 154.

566. Fitzgerald, F. Scott. "One Hundred False Starts," *Saturday Evening Post*, March 4, 1933.

567. Bruccoli, *Some Sort of Epic Grandeur*, 174.

568. Ibid., 192.

569. Ibid., 28.

570. Ibid., 19.

571. Ibid., 20.

572. Ibid., 73.

573. Fitzgerald, *The Crack-up*, 79.

574. Bruccoli, *Some Sort of Epic Grandeur*, 49.

575. Ibid., 111.

576. Fitzgerald, *A Life in Letters*, 111.

577. Ibid., 263.

578. Ibid., 81.

579. Ibid., 87–88.

580. Ibid., 89.

581. Bruccoli, *Some Sort of Epic Grandeur*, 335.

582. F. Scott Fitzgerald's Ledger, 1919–1938, Matthew J. and Arlyn Bruccoli Collection of F. Scott Fitzgerald, Irvin Department of Rare Books and Special Collections, Ernest F. Hollings Special Collections Library, University of South Carolina, accessed online at http://library.sc.edu/digital/collections/Fitzgerald_Ledger_-_USC_Transcription_2013.pdf.

583. Fitzgerald, *A Life in Letters*, 30.

584. Meyers, Jeffrey. *Scott Fitzgerald: A Biography* (New York: HarperCollins, 1994), 58.

585. Bruccoli, *Some Sort of Epic Grandeur*, 127.

586. Fitzgerald, "One Hundred False Starts."

587. Meyers, *Scott Fitzgerald*, 126.

588. Bruccoli, *Some Sort of Epic Grandeur*, 184.

589. Ibid., 59.

590. Ibid., 183.

591. Meyers, *Scott Fitzgerald*, 78–79.

592. Fitzgerald, *A Life in Letters*, 31.

593. Bruccoli, *Some Sort of Epic Grandeur*, 185.

594. Ibid., 217–218.

595. Ibid., 209.

596. Ibid., 112.

Chapter 16: Philip Roth

597. Lee, Hermione. "Philip Roth, The Art of Fiction No. 84," *Paris Review*, Fall 1984, accessed online at http://www.theparisreview.org/interviews/2957/the -art-of-fiction-no-84-philip-roth.

598. Roth, Philip. *The Facts: A Novelist's Autobiography* (New York: Farrar, Straus & Giroux, 1988), 133.

599. Atlas, James. "A Visit with Philip Roth," *New York Times Book Review*, September 2, 1979, reprinted in *Conversations with Philip Roth*, edited by George J. Searles (Jackson: University Press of Mississippi, 1992), 110.

600. Roth, Philip. *Reading Myself and Others* (New York: Farrar, Straus & Giroux, 1975), 100.

601. Dalley, Jan. "At Home with Philip Roth," *Slate*, June 26, 2011, http:// www.slate.com/articles/life/ft/2011/06/at_home_with_philip_roth.html; Chambers, Andrea. "Philip Roth," *People*, December 19, 1983, accessed online at http://www.people.com/people/article/0,,20086626,00.html.

602. Pierpont, Claudia Roth. "The Book of Laughter: Philip Roth and His Friends," *New Yorker*, October 7, 2013, accessed online at http://www .newyorker.com/magazine/2013/10/07/the-book-of-laughter.

603. *Philip Roth: Unmasked*, directed by William Karel and Livia Manera (Cinétévé and American Masters, 2013), available online at http://www.pbs .org/wnet/americanmasters/episodes/philip-roth/philip-roth-unmasked/2467/.

604. Brown, Tina. "Philip Roth Unbound: Interview Transcript," *Daily Beast*, October 30, 2009, http://www.thedailybeast.com/articles/2009/10/30 /philip-roth-unbound-interview-transcript.html.

605. Lee, "Philip Roth, The Art of Fiction No. 84."

606. Karel and Manera, dir., *Philip Roth: Unmasked*.

607. Pierpont, "The Book of Laughter."

608. Brown, "Philip Roth Unbound."

609. Lee, "Philip Roth, The Art of Fiction No. 84."

610. Roth, *The Facts*, 40.

611. Ibid., 60.

612. Ibid., 59.

613. Pierpont, "The Book of Laughter."

614. Karel and Manera, dir., *Philip Roth: Unmasked*.

615. Roth, *The Facts*, 157.

616. Roth, *Reading Myself and Others*, 21.

617. Dalley, "At Home with Philip Roth."

618. Savigneau, Josyane. "Philip Roth: 'I Don't Wish to Be a Slave Any Longer to the Stringent Exigencies of Literature,'" *Le Monde*, February 14, 2013, accessed online at http://www.lemonde.fr/livres/article/2013/02/14/philip -roth-i-don-t-wish-to-be-a-slave-any-longer-to-the-stringent-exigencies-of -literature_1831662_3260.html.

619. Roth, *Reading Myself and Others*, xii.

620. Davidson, Sara. "Talk with Philip Roth," *New York Times Book Review*, September 18, 1977, accessed online at http://www.nytimes.com /books/98/10/11/specials/roth-talkwith.html.

621. Roth, *Reading Myself and Others*, 218.

622. Bloom, Claire. *Leaving a Doll's House* (Boston: Little, Brown, 1996), 168–169.

623. Brown, "Philip Roth Unbound."

624. Dalley, "At Home with Philip Roth."

625. Pierpont, "The Book of Laughter."

626. Savigneau, "Philip Roth."

627. Lee, "Philip Roth, The Art of Fiction No. 84."

628. Ibid.

629. Ibid.

630. Ibid.

631. Ibid.

632. Davidson, "Talk with Philip Roth."

633. Lee, "Philip Roth, The Art of Fiction No. 84."

634. Roth, *Reading Myself and Others*, 33–37.

635. Ibid., 37–38.

636. Karel and Manera, dir., *Philip Roth: Unmasked*.

637. Pierpont, "The Book of Laughter."

638. Savigneau, "Philip Roth."

TWO TAKES ON THE DIGITAL AGE

Chapter 17: Margaret Atwood

639. Atwood, Margaret. "Haunted by *The Handmaid's Tale*," *Guardian*, January 20, 2012, accessed online at http://www.theguardian.com/books/2012 /jan/20/handmaids-tale-margaret-atwood.

640. Rose, Charlie. Interview with Margaret Atwood, *Charlie Rose*, PBS, October 8, 2013, accessed online at http://www.hulu.com/watch/543990.

641. Hammond, Karla. "Defying Distinctions," *Concerning Poetry*, 1979, reprinted in *Margaret Atwood: Conversations*, edited by Earl G. Ingersoll (Princeton, NJ: Ontario Review Press, 1990), 105.

642. Ibid.

643. Atwood, "Haunted by *The Handmaid's Tale*."

644. "Reader's Companion to *The Handmaid's Tale* by Margaret Atwood," *Book Group Corner*, Doubleday, 1998, accessed online at http://www .randomhouse.com/resources/bookgroup/handmaidstale_bgc.html.

645. Malcolm, Andrew H. "Margaret Atwood Reflects on a Hit," *New York Times*, April 14, 1990, accessed online at http://www.nytimes.com/1990/04/14/movies/margaret-atwood-reflects-on-a-hit.html.

646. Hancock, Geoff. "Tightrope-Walking over Niagara Falls," *Canadian Writers at Work* (Toronto: Oxford University Press, 1987), reprinted in Ingersoll, ed., *Margaret Atwood: Conversations*, 214.

647. Lee, Felicia R. "Back to the Scary Future and the Best-Seller List," *New York Times*, September 21, 2009, accessed online at http://www.nytimes.com/2009/09/22/books/22atwood.html.

648. Lyons, Bonnie. "Using Other People's Dreadful Childhoods," *Shenandoah* 3, no. 2 (1987), reprinted in Ingersoll, ed., *Margaret Atwood: Conversations*, 230–231.

649. Hancock, "Tightrope-Walking over Niagara Falls," in Ingersoll, ed., *Margaret Atwood: Conversations*, 212.

650. Atwood, Margaret. *The Blind Assassin* (New York: Anchor Books, 2000), 42.

651. Hancock, "Tightrope-Walking over Niagara Falls," in Ingersoll, ed., *Margaret Atwood: Conversations*, 203.

652. Twigg, Alan. "Just Looking at Things That Are There," *Strong Voices: Conversations with Fifty Canadian Authors* (Madeira Park, BC: Harbour Publishing, 1988), reprinted in Ingersoll, ed., *Margaret Atwood: Conversations*, 121.

653. Lyons, "Using Other People's Dreadful Childhoods," in Ingersoll, ed., *Margaret Atwood: Conversations*, 224.

654. Atwood, Margaret. *Negotiating with the Dead: A Writer on Writing* (New York: Anchor Books, 2003), 14.

655. Malcolm, "Margaret Atwood Reflects on a Hit."

656. "Margaret Atwood," Big Think, n.d., http://bigthink.com/users/margaretatwood.

657. Atwood, *Negotiating with the Dead*, 11.

658. Rothman, Lily. "Margaret Atwood on Serial Fiction and the Future of the Book," *Time*, October 8, 2012, accessed online at http://entertainment.time.com/2012/10/08/margaret-atwood-on-serial-fiction-and-the-future-of-the-book/.

659. Ibid.

660. Hoby, Hermione. "Margaret Atwood: Interview," *Telegraph*, August 18, 2013, accessed online at http://www.telegraph.co.uk/culture/books/10246937/Margaret-Atwood-interview.html.

661. Charney, Noah. "How I Write: Margaret Atwood," *Daily Beast*, October 10, 2013, http://www.thedailybeast.com/articles/2013/10/10/how-i-write-margaret-atwood.html.

662. Gibson, Graeme. "Dissecting the Way a Writer Works," *Eleven Canadian Novelists* (Toronto: Anansi, 1973), reprinted in Ingersoll, ed., *Margaret Atwood: Conversations*, 4.

663. Ibid.

664. Charney, "How I Write: Margaret Atwood."

665. Mendez-Egle, Beatrice. "Witness Is What You Must Bear," *Margaret Atwood: Reflection and Reality* (Edinburg, TX: Pan American University, 1987), reprinted in Ingersoll, ed., *Margaret Atwood: Conversations*, 164–165.

666. Rose interview with Margaret Atwood.

667. Hammond, "Defying Distinctions," in Ingersoll, ed., *Margaret Atwood: Conversations*, 106.

668. Mendez-Egle, "Witness Is What You Must Bear," in Ingersoll, ed., *Margaret Atwood: Conversations*, 164.

669. Ingersoll, Earl G. "Waltzing Again," *Ontario Review* 32 (Spring–Summer 1990), reprinted in Ingersoll, ed., *Margaret Atwood: Conversations*, 236.

670. Morris, Mary. "Margaret Atwood, The Art of Fiction No. 121," *Paris Review*, Winter 1990, accessed online at http://www.theparisreview.org/interviews/2262/the-art-of-fiction-no-121-margaret-atwood.

671. Ibid.

672. Ibid.

673. Atwood, "Haunted by *The Handmaid's Tale*."

674. "Margaret Atwood," Big Think.

675. Charney, "How I Write: Margaret Atwood."

676. Morris, "Margaret Atwood, The Art of Fiction No. 121."

677. Atwood, *Negotiating with the Dead*, 21.

678. Hammond, "Defying Distinctions," in Ingersoll, ed., *Margaret Atwood: Conversations*, 106.

679. "Reader's Companion to *The Handmaid's Tale* by Margaret Atwood."

680. Morris, "Margaret Atwood, The Art of Fiction No. 121."

681. Oates, Joyce Carol. "Dancing on the Edge of the Precipice," *Ontario Review* 9 (Fall–Winter 1978–1979), reprinted in Ingersoll, ed., *Margaret Atwood: Conversations*, 79.

682. Hancock, "Tightrope-Walking over Niagara Falls," in Ingersoll, ed., *Margaret Atwood: Conversations*, 195.

683. Morris, "Margaret Atwood, The Art of Fiction No. 121."

684. Twigg, "Just Looking at Things That Are There," in Ingersoll, ed., *Margaret Atwood: Conversations*, 122–123.

685. Mendez-Egle, "Witness Is What You Must Bear," in Ingersoll, ed., *Margaret Atwood: Conversations*, 170.

686. Sandler, Linda. "A Question of Metamorphosis," *Malahat Review* 41 (1977), reprinted in Ingersoll, ed., *Margaret Atwood: Conversations*, 46.

687. Mendez-Egle, "Witness Is What You Must Bear," in Ingersoll, ed., *Margaret Atwood: Conversations*, 170.

688. Hancock, "Tightrope-Walking over Niagara Falls," in Ingersoll, ed., *Margaret Atwood: Conversations*, 207.

689. Hoby, "Margaret Atwood: Interview."

Chapter 18: Zadie Smith

690. Smith, Zadie. *Changing My Mind: Occasional Essays* (New York: Penguin Press, 2009), 101.

691. Ibid., 99–100.

692. Sieff, Gemma. "New Books: A Conversation with Zadie Smith," *Harper's Blog, Harper's Magazine*, February 23, 2011, http://harpers.org /blog/2011/02/new-books-a-conversation-with-zadie-smith/.

693. Leistman, Victoria. "Zadie Smith Discusses Work, Writing Process," *Tufts Daily*, March 28, 2012, accessed online at http://www.tuftsdaily.com/news /view.php/790866/Zadie-Smith-discusses-work-writing-proce.

694. Sieff, "New Books."

695. Ibid.

696. McBee, Thomas Page. "The *Rumpus* Interview with Zadie Smith," *Rumpus*, January 1, 2013, ttp://therumpus.net/2013/01/the-rumpus-interview-with -zadie-smith/.

697. Bollen, Christopher. "Zadie Smith," *Interview Magazine*, September 2012, accessed online at http://www.interviewmagazine.com/culture/zadie -smith/#_.

698. Sieff, "New Books."

699. "A Conversation with Zadie Smith," *Bold Type*, https://www.randomhouse .com/boldtype/0700/smith/interview.html.

700. Sieff, "New Books."

701. Leistman, "Zadie Smith Discusses Work, Writing Process."

702. Traps, Yevgeniya. "Zadie Smith on 'Little Sparks of Something Like Actual Life' and Her Latest, 'NW,'" *Capital New York*, October 2, 2012, http:// www.capitalnewyork.com/article/culture/2012/10/6537714/zadie-smith -little-sparks-something-actual-life-and-her-latest-nw.

703. Smith, *Changing My Mind*, 107.

704. "A Conversation with Zadie Smith," *Bold Type*.

705. Smith, Zadie. "Generation Why?" *New York Review of Books*, November 25, 2010, accessed online at http://www.nybooks.com/articles/archives/2010 /nov/25/generation-why/.

706. McBee, "The *Rumpus* Interview with Zadie Smith."

707. Smith, "Generation Why."

708. Smith, *Changing My Mind*, 105.

709. "An Interview with Zadie Smith," PBS, http://www.pbs.org/wgbh /masterpiece/teeth/ei_smith_int.html.

710. "A Conversation with Zadie Smith about *On Beauty*," *Bold Type*, reproduced at http://www.bookbrowse.com/author_interviews/full/index .cfm/author_number/344/zadie-smith.

711. Bollen, "Zadie Smith."

712. Godwin, Richard. "The World According to Zadie Smith," *London Evening Standard*, June 28, 2013, accessed online at http://www.standard.co.uk /lifestyle/esmagazine/the-world-according-to-zadie-smith-8677420.html.

713. Smith, *Changing My Mind*, 100.

714. Ibid., 104.

715. Ibid., 106.

716. "A Conversation with Zadie Smith," *Bold Type*.

717. Ibid.

718. Sieff, "New Books."

719. Bollen, "Zadie Smith."

720. "A Conversation with Zadie Smith about *On Beauty*," *Bold Type*.

721. Bollen, "Zadie Smith."

722. "A Conversation with Zadie Smith about *On Beauty*," *Bold Type*.

723. Smith, *Changing My Mind*, 103.

724. "A Conversation with Zadie Smith about *On Beauty*," *Bold Type*.

725. "A Conversation with Zadie Smith," *Bold Type*.

726. "An Interview with Zadie Smith," PBS.

727. McBee, "The *Rumpus* Interview with Zadie Smith."

728. Smith, *Changing My Mind*, 103.

729. Bollen, "Zadie Smith."

730. Smith, *Changing My Mind*, 103.

731. Ibid., 102.

732. Sieff, "New Books."

733. Leistman, "Zadie Smith Discusses Work, Writing Process."

734. Smith, *Changing My Mind*, 107.

3350

Rene
Rydell
605-310-4629

Routing # :

RDR Credit
S.F Fed
Act 13 0000 14 33 795
Rout 29 14 79 974

046 69 63202
5126 44 9769
email